BLETCHLEY PARK AND D-DAY

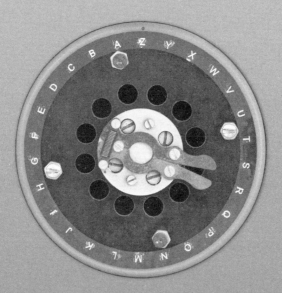

BLETCHLEY PARK AND D-DAY

DAVID KENYON

The Untold Story of How the Battle for Normandy Was Won

YALE UNIVERSITY PRESS
NEW HAVEN AND LONDON

For information about this and other Yale University Press publications, please contact:
U.S. Office: sales.press@yale.edu   yalebooks.com
Europe Office: sales@yaleup.co.uk   yalebooks.co.uk

Set in Minion Pro Regular by IDSUK (DataConnection) Ltd
Printed in Great Britain by TJ International Ltd, Padstow, Cornwall

Library of Congress Control Number: 2019938490

ISBN 978-0-300-24357-4

A catalogue record for this book is available from the British Library.

10 9 8 7 6 5 4 3 2 1

The king hath note of all that they intend,
By interception which they dream not of.

Shakespeare, *Henry V*, Act II, Scene 2

CONTENTS

CONTENTS

FOREWORD

ROBERT HANNIGAN

Former Director of the Government Communications Headquarters
(GCHQ) Cheltenham and Trustee of Bletchley Park

The enduring memory of D-Day is one of extraordinary human courage, ambition and sacrifice. The scale of the invasion on 6 June 1944, when more than 130,000 US, British, Canadian and other Allied troops crossed the English Channel, preceded by 23,000 airborne soldiers, is staggering; it remains the largest amphibious assault in history. The names of the Normandy beaches – Omaha, Utah, Juno, Gold, Sword – onto which young soldiers threw themselves under heavy fire have passed into the language as examples of extreme bravery. The events of Operation OVERLORD and its subsidiary plans have rightly been chronicled in some fine histories and immortalised in films over the past seventy-five years.

But the ultimate success of the invasion force, and the 2 million Allied personnel who fought their way across Europe in the following months, tends to obscure just how risky the operation was and how precarious its early days and weeks. So uncertain were the first twenty-four hours that General Eisenhower, as Supreme Allied Commander, famously drafted a statement accepting full personal responsibility for its failure, which had been based on 'the best information available'. The key part of that information, alongside everything from weather forecasting to estimates of the topography of the landing beaches, was intelligence. Examining the role of that intelligence and its importance to the Allied victory has been the subject of a number of studies, often focusing on the gripping stories of deception operations by secret agents to convince German commanders that the attack would take place elsewhere, or dummy landing craft designed to fool German reconnaissance flights. But until now there has been no single account which tells the story of the central role played by Bletchley Park and evaluates its importance.

Since the veil was lifted in the early 1970s on the codebreaking work of the Government Code and Cipher School (GC&CS) at Bletchley Park, historians have tended to focus on three areas. There are detailed technical accounts of mathematical and cryptanalytic achievements and how machines like Enigma were broken; biographies of extraordinary and sometimes eccentric individuals whose contributions were seminal, notably Alan Turing; and popular accounts of the unusual daily life of staff at Bletchley Park. What has sometimes been missing, particularly in relation to D-Day, is an evaluation of what the intelligence that was produced actually achieved and whether it made a significant difference. Codebreaking was not an end in itself, intellectually challenging as it was, and unless it could be used by the right people in a timely way it was of little value.

Addressing these questions, David Kenyon's book breaks new ground in a number of areas. In addition to a highly readable account of how Bletchley Park came to be, and an admirably comprehensible description of the codebreaking process, he focuses in a new way on the intelligence production factory which Bletchley Park had become by 1944. It was no longer a small-scale and eclectic operation, but, from the large network of Y stations intercepting traffic, passing it through Bletchley and its subsidiaries to commanders in the field, it had become a slick and agile industrial producer of intelligence. Just as importantly, Bletchley was by now assimilating intelligence from sources way beyond intercepted messages, a point brought out in depth here for the first time.

This account therefore shows GC&CS at the very height of its powers and reach. It was grappling with all the problems which those of us who worked in its successor organisation, GCHQ, will recognise: constantly keeping up with new technology or cryptological advances by the enemy; disseminating intelligence to the right commanders in a timely way that made it predictive, rather than purely academic; and prioritising from a vast volume of traffic to find intelligence that would be game-changing.

As this book reminds us, Bletchley Park could only decrypt a very small percentage of the messages intercepted. Choosing which traffic to select was therefore critical. Much of the focus in popular accounts of the codebreakers has been on Enigma – and this was certainly of vital importance throughout, especially in winning the Battle of the Atlantic, without which an invasion across the English Channel would have been unthinkable. However, this study rightly emphasises the importance of other achievements: the cracking of the Lorenz machine which allowed access to the messages of the German High Command, and the American breaking of Japanese diplomatic ciphers, shared with Bletchley, which enabled the Allies to read detailed Japanese accounts of German plans in Europe.

The result, as this book shows, was that GC&CS was producing an unparalleled insight into German thinking, strategy and detailed orders of battle. This was of enormous practical importance for Allied commanders: they had never been better informed about the enemy's strength or its plans. This picture was not complete or perfect – intelligence rarely is – but it gave assurance to commanders about the threats they were facing and the risks they were taking. From Hitler's and Rommel's personal thinking, to battle orders of local commanders and whether the clever Allied deception operations were working, there was little that GC&CS could not shed some light upon.

Pace was a constant challenge for GC&CS, particularly as the Normandy invasion itself got underway. David Kenyon describes the gripping drama of the first day and his account is infused with stories of individuals which bring the history to life. For students of intelligence, his insights into the human management challenges of the SIGINT factory that GC&CS had become are particularly valuable.

As the official research historian at Bletchley Park, Kenyon could be forgiven for eulogising its achievements. But he never overstates its value and subjects some previous claims to scrutiny. He examines perceived failures, for example the suggestion that Allied intelligence missed the scale of German forces defending Omaha beach. His conclusions about the importance of ULTRA material in very significantly reducing the risks of the invasion for the Allies are all the more powerful as a result.

The final D-Day tribute should always go to those who died, some 10,000 Allied soldiers on the first day alone. Key staff at Bletchley appreciated, as the days unfolded, the scale of suffering of those fighting in France, in contrast to their own work in the safety of Bletchley, however exhausting it might be. That those Allied casualties were significantly lower than the figures estimated by Eisenhower's planners, and that their sacrifice led to victory, is where Bletchley Park can rightly claim to have played a major role. David Kenyon has done us a great service in uncovering and describing how this happened.

ILLUSTRATIONS AND MAPS

ILLUSTRATIONS

IN PLATE SECTION

1. Gerd von Rundstedt meets Erwin Rommel in Paris, December 1943. Bundesarchiv, Bild 101I-718-0149-18A / Photographer: Jesse.
2. General Ōshima touring the Atlantic Wall with other Japanese and German officials, September 1943. Bundesarchiv, Bild 101I-262-1544-13 / Photographer: Werner.
3. Eric Jones, head of Hut 3, 1957. © National Portrait Gallery, London.
4. Brigadier John Tiltman, head of Military Section at Bletchley Park. Courtesy of the George C. Marshall Foundation, Lexington, Virginia.
5. William 'Bill' Tutte, member of Bletchley Park Research Section. Courtesy of Richard Youlden.
6. A 'Morrison Wall' at Bletchley Park. Crown Copyright. Reproduced by kind permission, Director GCHQ.
7. A Robinson machine in the Newmanry at Bletchley Park. Crown Copyright. Reproduced by kind permission, Director GCHQ.
8. Bombe machines in 'Greece' bay at Eastcote Outstation. Crown Copyright. Reproduced by kind permission, Director GCHQ.

IN TEXT

MAPS

ABBREVIATIONS, CODENAMES AND TECHNICAL TERMS

3A	Air Section within Hut 3 at Bletchley Park
3G	Research Section within Hut 3 at Bletchley Park
3L	Liaison Section within Hut 3 at Bletchley Park, responsible for links to external customers
3M	Military Section within Hut 3 at Bletchley Park
3N	Naval Section within Hut 3 at Bletchley Park
6IS	No. 6 Intelligence School, based at Beaumanor
Abwehr	*Amt Auslandsnachrichten und Abwehr* – the German military intelligence service
ANCXF	Allied Naval Commander Expeditionary Force – the commander of the naval elements of the invasion force, post held on D-Day by Admiral Ramsay
Ast	*Abwehrstellung* – a regional office of the *Abwehr* in Germany or occupied countries

BEETLE	Bletchley Park codename for Enigma key used by Luftwaffe Command on the Eastern Front
BODYGUARD	The overall Allied codename for deception operations prior to the invasion
Bombe	The key-finding machine devised by Alan Turing and Gordon Welchman, fundamental to the successful decryption of Enigma messages
BP	Common wartime nickname for Bletchley Park
BREAM	Bletchley codename for the Lorenz teleprinter link between Berlin and *O.B. Südwest* (q.v.) in Rome
C	The head of the Secret Intelligence Service (SIS/MI6), post occupied by Hugh Sinclair and Stewart Menzies during the Second World War
CIS	Combined Intelligence Section – joint group of British army and naval intelligence
Colossus	Codename for the key-finding machine developed to assist in decrypting German teleprinter traffic (see FISH)
COMINT	See SIGINT
CORAL	Allied codename for cipher used by Japanese naval attaches
COSSAC	Chief of Staff to Supreme Allied Commander – organisation led by Lt Gen. F.E. Morgan, tasked with planning the Allied invasion during 1943

Crib	A portion of the plaintext (q.v.) of an encrypted message which could be guessed, and used to assist in the decryption process
CX/MSS	File prefix allocated to high-level (q.v.) intercepts (see also ULTRA)
DAFFODIL	Bletchley codename for Enigma key used by *Luftgau XI (Westfront)* (q.v.)
D-Day	6 June 1944, the day on which the invasion of Normandy began. The 'D' has no significance other than as the initial letter of 'Day' (similarly 'H-Hour', etc.). Dates before and after the invasion were expressed in days, for example 'D-20' or 'D+10' – twenty days before or ten days after the invasion, respectively
Depth	In codebreaking several messages composed using the same cipher key
D/F	Direction finding – identification of the location of enemy wireless transmitters by use of bearings taken at intercept stations
DOLPHIN	Bletchley codename for Enigma key used by *Kriegsmarine* (q.v.) surface vessels and by U-boats in 'home waters'
DTN	Defence Teleprinter Network – a military cable network which connected Bletchley Park with its outstations and customers via telephone and teleprinter
E-boat	Allied designation for German fast attack craft
Enigma	A family of rotor-based electro-mechanical encryption machines used by Axis forces

FALCON	Bletchley codename for Enigma key used by the German military administrative districts (*Wehrkreis*)
FHO	*Fremde Heere Ost* – the German intelligence organisation tasked with the study of Allied armies in the eastern (Soviet) theatre
FHW	*Fremde Heere West* – the German intelligence organisation tasked with the study of Allied armies in the western theatre
FISH	Codename given at Bletchley to German teleprinter traffic encrypted using the Lorenz SZ40/42 cipher machines
Flivo	*Fliegerverbindungsoffizier* – air liaison officer
FORTITUDE	Allied codename for the deception operations mounted prior to D-Day in 1944
FUSAG	First US Army Group – the title given to the fictional force created as part of the Operation FORTITUDE deception operation
GADFLY	Bletchley codename for Enigma key used by *X. Fliegerkorps* in the Mediterranean
GAF	German Air Force (Luftwaffe)
GANNET	Bletchley codename for Enigma key used by German High Command in Norway
GC&CS	Government Code and Cipher School – the codebreaking organisation at Bletchley Park during the Second World War
GCHQ	Cover name applied to GC&CS, latterly adopted post-war as the formal name of the organisation
Gold	Codename for British invasion beach on D-Day

GPO	General Post Office
GRAMPUS	Bletchley codename for the Enigma key used in the Black Sea
GRILSE	Bletchley codename for the Lorenz teleprinter link between Berlin and *Heeresgruppe B* (Army Group B) in France (grilse is a type of young salmon)
GURNARD	Bletchley codename for the Lorenz teleprinter link between Berlin and *O.B. Südost* (q.v.) in Greece
Heer	German army
High-level	machine-enciphered
Hollerith machine	A device for processing data via punched cards, used as part of the decryption process
HUMINT	Human intelligence – information gained by human agents behind enemy lines, either members of the Allied secret services or local inhabitants and members of resistance organisations, or by interrogation of prisoners of war
Hut 3	German Army and Air Force Enigma Reporting Section responsible for processing and distributing decrypted German army and air force Enigma traffic
Hut 6	German Army and Air Force Enigma Processing and Decryption Section responsible for breaking army and air force Enigma messages
Hut 8	German Naval Enigma Processing and Decryption Section responsible for breaking naval Enigma messages

IMINT	Imagery intelligence – aerial photography of enemy forces and installations
Indoctrinated recipient	An individual who had been let in on the secret of Bletchley Park
ISK	Illicit Signals Knox – section at Bletchley Park dealing with high-level (q.v.) communications using the *Abwehr* (q.v.) variants of Enigma
ISOS	Illicit Signals Oliver Strachey – section at Bletchley Park dealing with lower-level hand ciphers used by German intelligence agents
JADE	Allied codename for a Japanese diplomatic cipher system used particularly by Japanese attachés
JELLYFISH	Bletchley codename for the Lorenz teleprinter link between Berlin and *O.B. West* (q.v.) in Paris
JMA	Allied codename for code used by Japanese military attachés
Juno	Codename for Canadian invasion beach on D-Day
Key	The specific settings for a particular encryption machine
KO	*Kriegsorganisation* – *Abwehr* (q.v.) outstations in neutral countries
Kriegsmarine	German navy
Lorenz SZ40/42	Cipher machine used by German forces to encrypt wireless teleprinter traffic (see FISH)
Luftgau	Luftwaffe regional command
Luftwaffe	German air force

MAGIC	Allied codename for traffic intercepted using the Japanese PURPLE cipher
Martian	Codename applied to reports from the Combined Intelligence Section (q.v.) concerning German defences in France
MI14	Department of Military Intelligence at the War Office tasked with investigation of the German armed forces
MULLET	Bletchley codename for the Lorenz teleprinter link between Berlin and Norway
NEPTUNE	Allied codename for the naval part of the OVERLORD invasion operation
Newmanry	Machine Section – named after Max Newman, responsible for machine breaking of German Lorenz-enciphered teleprinter traffic
NUTHATCH	Bletchley codename for Enigma key connecting Berlin with Belgrade
O.B. Südost	*Oberbefehlshaber Südost* – the German commander-in-chief in Greece, a position held on D-Day by *Generalfeldmarschall* Maximilian von Weichs
O.B. Südwest	*Oberbefehlshaber Südwest* – the German commander-in-chief in Italy, a position held on D-Day by *Generalfeldmarschall* Albert Kesselring
O.B. West	*Oberbefehlshaber West* – the German commander-in-chief in France and the Low Countries, a position held on D-Day by *Generalfeldmarschall* Gerd von Rundstedt

OIC	Operational Intelligence Centre – the planning headquarters of the Royal Navy at the Admiralty in London
OKH	*Oberkommando des Heeres* – the Army High Command of Nazi Germany
OKM	*Oberkommando der Marine* – the Naval High Command of Nazi Germany
OKW	*Oberkommando der Wehrmacht* – the High Command of the armed forces of Nazi Germany
Omaha	Codename for US invasion beach on D-Day
OCELOT	Bletchley codename for Enigma key used by army–air liaison officers (known as a *Flivo* (q.v.) key after the *Fliegerverbindungsoffizier*, air liaison officer)
ORANGE	Bletchley codename for Enigma key used by Waffen SS
OVERLORD	Codename for the allied invasion of Europe in 1944
Plaintext	The original text of a message prior to its encryption; or equally, the same text after decryption by the recipient
PORPOISE	Bletchley codename for Enigma key used by German Mediterranean shore installations
PURPLE	Allied codename for a Japanese diplomatic cipher system used particularly by the Japanese ambassador in Berlin
QUINCE	Bletchley codename for Enigma key used by the Waffen SS
RED	Bletchley codename for Enigma key used by the German air force

RSS	Initially the Radio Security Section (later the Radio Security Service) – body tasked with the interception of *Abwehr* wireless traffic
SCU	Special Communications Unit – unit attached to a field headquarters tasked with the reception of ULTRA messages from Bletchley Park
SD	*Sicherheitsdienst* – the security branch of the SS
SHAEF	Supreme Headquarters Allied Expeditionary Force – the headquarters led by Gen. Eisenhower responsible for planning and carrying out the invasion of north-west Europe in 1944
SHARK	Bletchley codename for the German U-boat four-rotor Enigma key *Triton*, introduced in 1942
SIGINT	Signals intelligence – interception of enemy transmissions; in the context of the Second World War, this mostly meant 'wireless' or radio transmissions. Not all SIGINT takes the form of messages: some transmissions originate from pieces of equipment, such as radar sets. Modern intelligence experts therefore distinguish between SIGINT in all its forms and the more specific 'communications intelligence' or COMINT, which is the interception of enemy messages
SIS	Secret Intelligence Service (MI6), based at Broadway Buildings, London
SIXTA	Formerly 'No. 6 Intelligence School' – the body responsible for traffic analysis (see T/A) at Bletchley Park in 1944

Slip	Sequences of bumps, representing letters, on teleprinter tape
SLU	Special Liaison Unit – unit attached to a field headquarters responsible for presentation of ULTRA messages to indoctrinated (q.v.) commanders
SNOWDROP	Bletchley codename for Enigma key used by *Luftgau V* (q.v.)
STICKLEBACK	Bletchley codename for the Lorenz teleprinter link between Berlin and *Heeresgruppe Süd* (Army Group South) in Ukraine
SWG	Special Wireless Group
T/A	Traffic analysis – intelligence recovered from intercepted traffic without breaking the encrypted message text; analysis of frequencies, call-signs, etc.
Testery	Fish Section – named after Ralph Tester, responsible for hand breaking of German Lorenz-enciphered teleprinter traffic
TICOM	Target Intelligence Committee – organisation responsible for collecting German communications and SIGINT equipment, as well as information about codes and ciphers, in Germany in 1945
TUNNY	Bletchley codename for intercepted teleprinter traffic encrypted using the Lorenz cipher machine. The name was also applied to an analogue of the Lorenz machine used by Bletchley Park in the decryption process
TURBOT	Bletchley codename for the Lorenz teleprinter link between Berlin and Denmark

TYPEX	British rotor-based cipher machine, used for encryption of Allied messages, and as an analogue for Enigma during the decryption process
ULTRA	Codename applied to intelligence derived from high-level (q.v.) SIGINT at Bletchley Park, also used as a security classification
USAAF	United States Army Air Forces
Utah	Codename for US invasion beach on D-Day
VHF	very high frequency (radio)
VULTURE	Bletchley codename for an OKH (q.v.) key used on the Eastern Front
WAAF	Women's Auxiliary Air Force
WHITING	Bletchley codename for the Lorenz teleprinter link between Berlin and *Heeresgruppe Nord* (Army Group North) in Ukraine
W.O.	War Office
WRNS (Wrens)	Women's Royal Naval Service – Wren female naval personnel were responsible for a variety of tasks at Bletchley
W/T	Wireless telegraphy
XX	'Double Cross' – the deception operation carried out in 1944 via turned German spies in the UK
Y stations	Wireless intercept stations located around the UK and overseas, responsible for the interception of enemy messages

A NOTE ON MILITARY UNITS AND RANKS

Wherever possible in this account, German military units and formations have been given in their original form, rather than being translated (except when they occur in direct quotations of wartime documents).

For clarity, and in keeping with UK military historical practice, Axis formations are rendered in *italics* thus: *Heeresgruppe B, 6. Armee, XLVII. Panzer-Korps, 3. SS-Panzer-Division, Grenadier-Regiment 920*.

Where unit types are not readily understandable, translations are provided (e.g. *Fallschirmjäger* – 'paratrooper').

GERMAN ARMED FORCES RANKS AND THEIR APPROXIMATE EQUIVALENTS IN ENGLISH

Generalfeldmarschall	Field marshal (commanding an army group)
Generaloberst	General (commanding an army)
General der Infanterie/ Kavallerie/Artillerie	Lieutenant general (commanding a corps)
Generalleutnant	Major general (commanding a division)
Generalmajor	Brigadier general (commanding a brigade)
Oberst	Colonel (commanding a regiment)

Oberstleutnant	Lieutenant colonel (commanding a battalion)
Major	Major (battalion second in command)
Vizeadmiral	Vice admiral (naval equivalent to *Generalleutnant*)
Kapitänleutnant	Lieutenant (navy) (commander of smaller naval vessels)

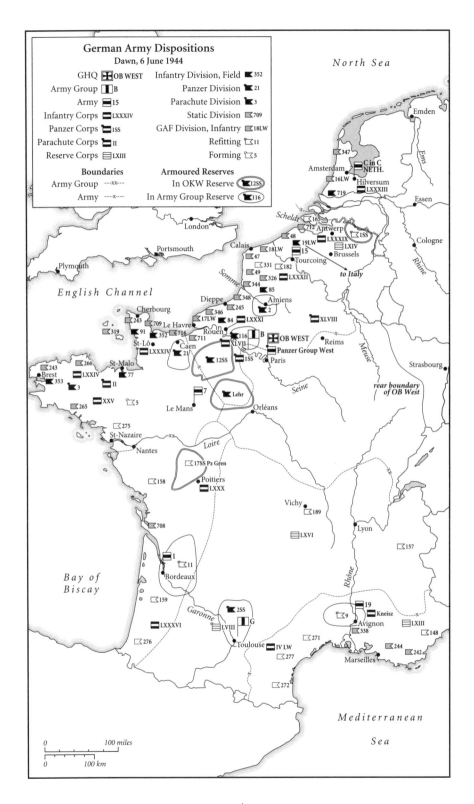

German Army Dispositions
Dawn, 6 June 1944

GHQ	⊞ OB WEST	
Army Group	▮ B	
Army	▬ 15	
Infantry Corps	☐ LXXXIV	
Panzer Corps	☐ ISS	
Parachute Corps	☐ II	
Reserve Corps	☐ LXIII	

Infantry Division, Field	◼ 352
Panzer Division	◤ 21
Parachute Division	◤ 3
Static Division	◼ 709
GAF Division, Infantry	◼ 18LW
Refitting	◿ 11
Forming	◿ 5

Boundaries
Army Group ---xx---
Army ---x---

Armoured Reserves
In OKW Reserve ⬭ 12SS
In Army Group Reserve ⬭ 116

North Sea

Emden

⬓ 347

C in C NETH.

Amsterdam
◼ 16LW
Hilversum
☐ LXXXIII
◼ 719

Essen

Scheldt ◿ 165

◿ 712 Antwerp
⬭ 1SS

London

◿ 48
◼ 19LW
☐ LXXXIX
Cologne
☐ LXIV

Portsmouth

Calais
◼ 18LW
◼ 15
Tourcoing
Brussels

Rhine

◿ 47
◿ 331
◼ 182
to Italy

◿ 49
◼ 326
☐ LXXXII

Plymouth

English Channel

◼ 344
◼ 85

◼ 348
Dieppe
Amiens
◼ 2

◼ 346
◼ 245
☐ XLVIII

Cherbourg
◼ 243
◼ 709 Le Havre
◼ 17LW
◼ 84
☐ LXXXI

◼ 319
◼ 91
◼ 352 ◿ 716 Rouen
◼ 116 ▮ B ⊞ OB WEST
St-Lô
◼ 711
☐ XLVII **Panzer Group West**
Caen
☐ LXXXIV ◤ 21
Reims

◤ 12SS ☐ ISS
Paris

Meuse

Strasbourg

St-Malo
◼ 266
◼ 243
◼ 77
☐ LXXIV
Brest
◼ 353 ◤ 3
☐ II
◤ 7
◤ Lehr
Seine

◼ 265
◼ XXV ◿ 5
Le Mans
Orléans

rear boundary of OB West

◿ 275
St-Nazaire
Loire

Nantes
◿ 17SS Pz Gren

◿ 158
Poitiers
☐ LXXX

Vichy
◿ 189

◼ LXVI
Lyon

◿ 708

◿ 157

◼ 1
◿ 11
Bordeaux

Bay of Biscay

◿ 159

Garonne

◼ 19
◿ 9 ◼ Kneisz
Avignon
☐ LXIII

◤ 2SS
☐ LVIII ▮ G
◼ 338
◿ 148

◼ LXXXVI
Toulouse
◿ 271
◿ 244 ◿ 242

◿ 276
IV LW
◿ 277
Marseilles

◿ 272

Mediterranean Sea

0	100 miles
0	100 km

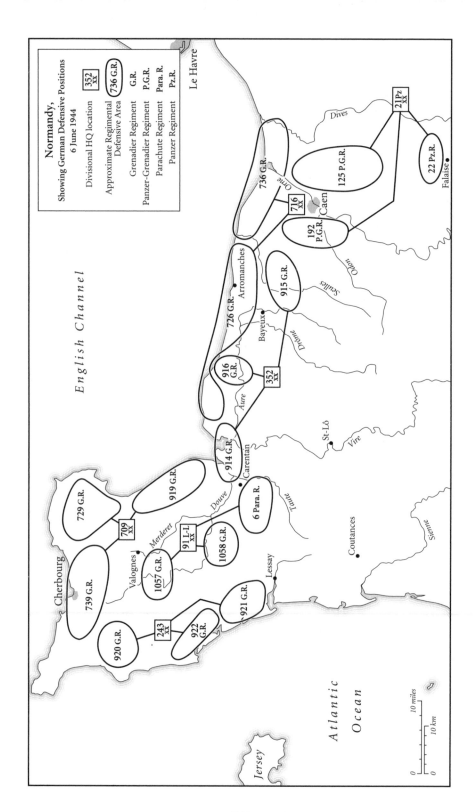

Normandy,

Showing German Defensive Positions
6 June 1944

352̄ XX Divisional HQ location

736 G.R. Approximate Regimental
Defensive Area

G.R. Grenadier Regiment
P.G.R. Panzer-Grenadier Regiment
Para. R. Parachute Regiment
Pz.R. Panzer Regiment

Le Havre

English Channel

Dives

21 Pz XX

22 Pz.R.

Falaise

125 P.G.R.

736 G.R.

Orne

716 XX

Caen

192 P.G.R.

Odon

Arromanches

915 G.R.

726 G.R.

Seulles

Bayeux

Drôme

916 G.R.

352 XX

Aure

914 G.R.

Carentan

St-Lô

Vire

919 G.R.

729 G.R.

Douve

6 Para. R.

Taute

709 XX

Merderet

91 L-L XX

1058 G.R.

Coutances

Cherbourg

739 G.R.

Valognes

1057 G.R.

Lessay

Sienne

920 G.R.

243 XX

922 G.R.

921 G.R.

*Atlantic
Ocean*

Jersey

10 miles

10 km

0

0

xxx

OVERTURE TO OVERLORD

A rromanches, 1 June 1944. *General der Artillerie* Erich Marcks stood on the high bluff above the Normandy beach resort studying the grey English Channel. As commander of the German *LXXXIV. Armeekorps*, he had responsibility for defending this section of coast. A slim man, with a sharp nose and chin, his round, gold-rimmed glasses lent him the appearance more of a history professor than a soldier. And yet Marcks knew a great deal about soldiering. Having joined the old Imperial Army in 1910, he had served throughout both the Great War and the present conflict. Though suspected of being luke-warm towards National Socialism, his military prowess had brought him high rank, and he sported the ribbons of an Iron Cross First Class (awarded in 1915) and a more recent Knight's Cross.

After the French campaign of 1940, he had moved east – first to help plan the invasion of the Soviet Union, and then to command a division on the Eastern Front. Two of his three sons had been killed in Russia, and he himself had lost a leg in 1942 in Ukraine.

Now he was back in Normandy. His mind was not on the leaden waves, but on what lay beyond, across the Channel. According to German intelligence, the Allies had nearly 80 divisions in England preparing for the invasion. At a rough guess, that was over a million men. It was also

1

estimated that there were enough landing craft to transport a quarter of those soldiers in a single operation – twenty divisions in one fell swoop.

What did he have? Just three divisions to defend the 50 miles (80km) of coast for which he was responsible. And not for him the young, milk-fed farm boys of the US Army, their pockets full of chewing gum and chocolate . . . Half of his force comprised 'static' units – men of thirty or forty years of age, many (like himself) saddled with wounds from Russia or suffering from medical conditions. And then there were the teenagers, who knew a lot about National Socialism but precious little about fighting. Some weren't even German! Two of his battalions consisted of former PoWs, Poles or anti-communist Ukrainians and others recruited from the occupied territories in the east. Their weapons were old, including antiquated captured French equipment; in his only panzer division, many of the tanks were French and dated back to 1940, or else artillery pieces hastily mounted on outdated chassis.

To cap it all, the defences were incomplete. Despite the huge invest-ment of concrete and steel in the Führer's 'Atlantic Wall', most of it had gone on the more strategically obvious invasion beaches of the Pas-de-Calais. The beaches of Normandy had only belatedly received serious attention when Rommel arrived in late 1943. Many of Marcks' men were still shielded only by earthen trenches and sandbags – and he himself had bitter experience from 1915 of what it was like to withstand a bombardment with only soil for protection.

But, supposedly, there was little to worry about. Von Rundstedt, the commander in the west, had first declared the invasion imminent at the end of March. But April and May had passed without incident. Readiness had waned – how could you be in a constant state of alertness for weeks on end? And, anyway, all the predictions were that the weather in early June would be atrocious.

So unlikely did the Top Brass consider an imminent Allied invasion to be that Marcks and all his senior commanders were due to go to Rennes on 5 June for a staff training wargame. For the exercise Marcks had been picked to command the Allied landing forces – could it be an ironic dig at his suspected lack of enthusiasm for Nazism? In any case, Hitler had confidently predicted only days before that if an invasion did occur in Normandy, it would only be a feint, before the main event at Calais.

But Marcks was not so sure. As he surveyed the Channel, he turned to his aide, an army captain:

> If I know the British, they will go to church next Sunday for one last time, and sail on Monday. Army Group B says they're not going to come yet, and when they do come it'll be at Calais. So I think we'll be welcoming them on Monday *right here*.

In the event, Marcks was wrong: bad weather caused the Allied invasion – codenamed OVERLORD – to be postponed for twenty-four hours. But it came on Tuesday, 6 June, Marcks' fifty-third birthday. He just had time to raise a glass in celebration on the evening of the 5th before heading for Rennes. By then, the first Allied parachute and glider troops were in the air over the Channel.

Within a week Marcks was dead, the 50 miles of coast for which he had been responsible were in Allied hands, and the chances of the Germans pushing the invaders back into the sea were fading fast.

In fact, the 80 Allied divisions that German intelligence and senior commanders had warned Marcks about were a fiction, cooked up by Allied intelligence to mask their actual intentions. The Germans knew next to nothing about the real invasion to come. In contrast to these fairy tales, the Allied commanders knew exactly what threat they were facing across the Channel, and they knew how to defeat it. That knowledge had started to be assembled years before – much of it at Bletchley Park.

*

All military operations, from the earliest times, have required a secret intelligence effort. It is necessary to know who and where your enemy is, and what he intends. This information should also be obtained without the knowledge of the enemy, since if he realises that his plans are compromised, he will inevitably alter them. This was as true for Shakespeare's Henry V as it was for Wellington at Waterloo, or for Eisenhower or Montgomery on D-Day.

The Allied invasion of Europe on 6 June 1944 and the fighting in Normandy that followed undoubtedly constitute the most famous campaign of the Second World War. Almost from the moment they were undertaken, these battles have been the subject of innumerable books, films and television programmes. They have also provided the backdrop for huge amounts of fiction, both on paper and on the screen. It would be fair to say that the military operations have been covered and re-covered in so many works that it would take a lifetime to digest them all. Yet the intelligence operations that actually underpinned the campaign have been curiously overlooked – either taken for granted in accounts of the campaign, or mentioned only on the rare occasions when the flow of intelligence fell short of what was expected by battlefield commanders (or indeed post-war critics).

The range of intelligence sources available to Allied commanders during the Second World War was broad indeed. They extended from basic reconnaissance and patrols on the front lines of the battlefield, to information gained by human agents behind enemy lines, whether members of the Allied secret services or local inhabitants and members of Resistance organisations. Information could also be gained through the interrogation of prisoners of war. These various sources are often grouped under the title of 'human intelligence', abbreviated nowadays as HUMINT. Supplementary information could be obtained from aerial photography of enemy forces and installations – 'imagery intelligence' or IMINT. And then there was 'signals intelligence' or SIGINT. This involves the interception of enemy transmissions: in the Second World War that mostly meant 'wireless' or radio transmissions. Not all SIGINT takes the form of messages; some transmissions originate from pieces of equipment, such as radar sets. This was known at Bletchley Park as 'noise'. Modern intelligence experts therefore distinguish between SIGINT in all its forms and the more specific 'communications intelligence' or COMINT, which involves the interception of enemy messages. It was SIGINT and in particular its subset COMINT that occupied the staff of the Government Code and Cipher School (GC&CS) – or, as they are more commonly known, the codebreakers of Bletchley Park.

The intelligence effort required for military operations is also proportional to the size of the operation in question. The briefing for a section attack may require just a few words; but as the scale of the intended battle increases, so too does the size and complexity of the intelligence requirement. The Normandy invasion was one of the largest amphibious operations ever undertaken, and the accompanying intelligence effort was equally unprecedented in scope. Such was the power of signals intelligence, and so far-reaching were its effects, that, while SIGINT formed only part of the intelligence picture, that part was a very large one. And an examination of this field of activity offers a substantial insight into the intelligence effort as a whole during the campaign. There were very few areas of enemy activity that did not require communication in some form; thus, the interception and analysis of that communication could shed light on almost all aspects of German operations. Seldom have commanders known more about their opponents in advance of a battle than the Allies did on 6 June 1944. Much of that knowledge was acquired at Bletchley Park.

The intelligence behind the Normandy invasion has also historically perhaps been a victim of its own success. There is little doubt that by 6 June 1944, the Allies had achieved what one expert has described as 'information dominance' over the Axis forces in France and the Low Countries.[1] Allied intelligence knew nearly everything there was to know about the Germans at all levels – tactical, operational, strategic and administrative. Their positions, numbers, equipment and level of morale were known, and their defensive plans were well understood. By contrast, the Germans knew little about the Allies. While the overall strategic intention – an invasion of Europe sometime in 1944 – was a relatively simple conclusion to reach, the exact timing and location remained a mystery, and significant errors in their estimates of the Allied order of battle led the Germans to predict operations that were actually beyond the capacity of the Allies to achieve. This was due partly to Allied air superiority (which made it very difficult for German reconnaissance aircraft to penetrate UK air space) and partly to systemic failings in the German intelligence apparatus. Deliberate deception operations – the well-known and colourful story of Operation FORTITUDE, with its inflatable dummy tanks and Spitfires, and 'Double Cross' turned German agents – also clouded the picture, although not quite as much as some sources would suggest. The impact of this intelligence imbalance on the Normandy campaign was enormous. Not only were the Germans kept guessing about how and when an attack would come, but also, once the Allies were ashore, German counterattacks were more often than not detected in advance and halted in their tracks before they could build momentum. The result was ultimately a crushing defeat for the Germans, although the invading armies still had a stiff two-month fight on their hands.

In part, the lack of investigation of the intelligence story and the focus on its few failures are a product of the declassification process. Some intelligence-related stories publicly broke shortly after the conflict ended, mostly related to Allied deception operations rather than intelligence gathering, and featured in such films as *I Was Monty's Double* (1958) with John Mills, or *The Man Who Never Was* (1956), concerning the invasion of Sicily in 1943. These films placed intelligence-related stories in the public eye but left out huge parts of the supporting story (which was still classified) and made bold claims for the effectiveness of the deception operations based almost entirely on the accounts of those who were involved. This has led to a distorted and partial picture of Allied intelligence efforts during the war. Only relatively recently has sufficient information become publicly available to place these more dramatic episodes in their proper historical context, to allow analysis of the intelligence effort as a whole, and to judge its successes and failures.

Neither do we have a fully complete picture of Bletchley Park and GC&CS. This is partly a consequence of the secrecy of the project, which was broken only by the publication of Frederick Winterbotham's *The Ultra Secret* in 1974 and the number of accounts that followed. Nevertheless, much of the historical documentation relating to what went on at Bletchley remained classified at the time and hence unavailable. Personal recollections and a focus on 'process' – the activities carried on at Bletchley Park and the intricacies of various codebreaking methodologies – have since dominated, at the expense of properly assessing 'effect': the impact of the resulting intelligence on the conduct of the war. It may seem an obvious point, but the significance of any cryptanalytic achievement is properly measured not by the complexity of the code or cipher attacked, nor by the intellectual feats involved, but by the intelligence value of the resulting decrypted messages: Colossus, the electronic machine used in 'key finding' and which helped break the Germans' Lorenz cipher, would have been entirely redundant if it had transpired that the Germans were encrypting their laundry lists. Similarly, the many popular accounts of Bletchley life written by veterans, telling of what they thought of the food, or their recollections of playing rounders, putting on plays and doing crossword puzzles, have helped cement a particular and, as we shall see, quite limited view of the place in the public's mind – as a slightly cosy collection of brilliant minds deliberately kept aloof from war's reality so that they could objectively intercept and distribute information. And because such reminiscences took time to become publicly available many of the accounts are from the younger, more junior members of the organisation, who rightly have been subsequently congratulated and informed that the work they performed was of vital importance, but at the time had no idea what exactly they were doing and were certainly not party to the application of the finished intelligence. As a result, their memoirs do little to inform the overall assessment of the value of GC&CS as an intelligence organisation.

There are two honourable exceptions to this. Ralph Bennett and Harry Hinsley worked at Bletchley Park during the war, and both wrote accounts in the 1970s benefiting from this inside knowledge which tackled head-on the question of exactly what intelligence was being produced by GC&CS and what use was being made of it by Allied commanders. Bennett and Hinsley are central figures to the way Bletchley intelligence has been understood, and there is more about them and their interpretations in the Note on Sources. But, needless to say, much more information has come to light since their accounts were published, and this book draws upon the full panoply of unclassified documents, recent scholarship and the archives of Bletchley Park itself.

It does so to offer what may seem to be partial view of one aspect of the intelligence effort during the Normandy campaign. It is beyond the scope of this book to deal in any great detail with sources of information other than SIGINT – air photography, for example, or beach reconnaissance parties, or the work of the French Resistance. So too the story of the air intelligence effort against the Luftwaffe, which is included only when it had a specific bearing on activity on the ground war and the Germans' land-based preparations to deal with invasion.[2] But such was the scope of SIGINT in the campaign that analysis of this aspect – not only the intelligence that was supplied, but more importantly its usefulness – will fill in a large part of the hitherto untold intelligence story. Placing the work of Bletchley Park and its outstations, and of SIGINT operations more widely, in the context of the overall intelligence effort also means that the part played by Bletchley Park can be fairly judged and a fresh picture of the work there can emerge. In doing so, we shall see the influence that other intelligence sources had in aiding and supporting Bletchley's work, and the ways in which an organisation hitherto largely understood as standing apart was in fact adept at integrating information from other sources into its operations. Looking again at the land (and sea) battle, and the intelligence behind it, will demonstrate both the complexity and the supreme importance of the work of the codebreakers of Bletchley Park in the successful invasion of Normandy, and in ultimate victory in the Second World War.

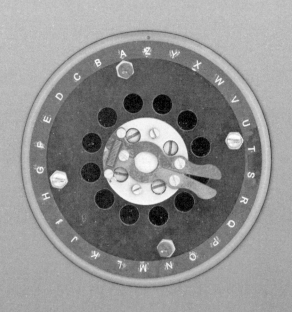

PART I

BLETCHLEY PARK IN 1944

CHAPTER ONE

THE INTELLIGENCE FACTORY

For many British people in August 1939, war with Germany seemed inescapable. Haunted by the horrors of the First World War, the UK government had already set about issuing all 38 million people in the country with gas masks. Government departments were also making preparations to evacuate the vital functions of state from the capital in an attempt to avoid the inevitable bombing, which was expected to begin the moment war was declared.

One such group, consisting of just over 100 people, left London and made its way in secret to Bletchley in Buckinghamshire, 50 miles north of the capital. This group was formed of members of the Government Code and Cipher School, who, since the end of the First World War, had been quietly working on reading the communications of Britain's potential enemies – including Germany, Italy and Japan – and trying to devise ways of breaking their codes and ciphers. Their new home for the duration of the war would be a Victorian country house next to the main west coast railway line: Bletchley Park.

Among them was one John Tiltman. Born in London of Scottish parents, by 1939 Tiltman had been a soldier for five years and a codebreaker for nearly twenty. He began his military career in the First World War as an officer in the King's Own Scottish Borderers, and he served on the Western Front for nearly three years. However, his active service was cut short when he was seriously wounded in May 1917, during the Battle of Arras. Of the thirteen officers in Tiltman's battalion who went into battle that day only two survived, and both were wounded; for his bravery, Tiltman was awarded the Military Cross.

Tiltman recovered but continued to be troubled by his wounds for the rest of his life; he always preferred to work standing up, as sitting down was uncomfortable. In 1919, he was sent to Siberia with the British forces assisting in the Russian civil war, but his still-troublesome injuries forced him to return to the UK. In 1920, he embarked on the army's Russian language course at King's College London.

Newly qualified as an interpreter, he was seconded (as a civilian) to the Government Code and Cipher School to work on a backlog of Russian diplomatic messages. This two-week assignment as a translator would turn into a sixty-year career in codes and ciphers, during which time he became one of Britain's most prolific and versatile codebreakers.

Tiltman's military rank was reinstated in 1939 and he was promoted to lieutenant colonel. He arrived at Bletchley Park with the first batch of codebreakers in August 1939, and remained there for the rest of the war. By D-Day, he had been promoted to brigadier, thereby gaining the affectionate nickname used by those who worked with him – 'the Brig'.

The range of problems tackled by Tiltman and his team in Military Section (and later Research Section) was remarkably broad, encompassing both hand and machine ciphers from around the world. However, his own personal feats of codebreaking would be crucial to OVERLORD. Not only was he able to break several Japanese diplomatic ciphers which provided vital information on German defences, but he also made the first crucial breakthroughs in solving the German Lorenz machine cipher (codenamed by Bletchley 'TUNNY'). Reading those messages would be essential to Allied success in 1944.

In the meantime, Tiltman witnessed the growth of GC&CS from the small group that arrived in 1939 to a vast intelligence factory of over 7,000 people by D-Day. We begin this story at the start of that process.

*

Before examining the role of Bletchley Park in the Normandy battles – the incoming intercepts and outgoing intelligence that formed the daily work – it is important to understand the nature of the organisation itself. Bletchley Park as an institution expanded dramatically in the course of the war, and the way it performed its work evolved with equal rapidity over the same period. What the organisation looked like in the summer of 1944, and how it came to be organised in the way that it was, had an impact on the intelligence products that were being produced by Bletchley and the way they subsequently influenced the battlefield.

ORIGINS AND EARLY DAYS

The Government Code and Cipher School was formed in 1919 from the various British army and navy cryptological organisations that had existed during the First World War. It was initially funded and controlled by the Admiralty, but in 1922 responsibility passed to the Foreign Office. The chief of the Secret Intelligence Service ('C') was given the additional role of director of GC&CS. From 1923, this post was held by Admiral Hugh Sinclair, who had previously been director of Naval Intelligence at the Admiralty. The ostensible function of the GC&CS was to 'advise as to the security of codes and ciphers used by all Government departments and to assist in their provision'. However, a secret directive also tasked the organisation with studying 'the methods of cipher communication used by foreign powers'.[1] In the inter-war period, this work focused largely on the interception and cryptanalysis of diplomatic rather than military communications, and of cable as well as wireless traffic.

For the first twenty years of its existence, GC&CS was based in London, and for much of that time at the Secret Intelligence Service (SIS) headquarters at Broadway Buildings, 54–55 Broadway, opposite St James's

Park tube station. A consensus developed in the 1930s that, if there were to be another war, then the effect of aerial bombing of cities would be devastating; as Stanley Baldwin put it in 1932, 'The bomber will always get through.' Plans were thus drawn up for the relocation of vital government functions out of central London in the event of war. Later, reinforced underground accommodation was built for those crucial organs of state that, so it was felt, could not realistically be moved.[2] SIS was involved in this process and in 1938 Admiral Sinclair ('C') identified Bletchley Park as a suitable 'War Station' for his organisation.

The owners of the mansion and estate, the Leon family, had sold the property to a local developer, Hubert Faulkner, and Sinclair was able to purchase from him a portion of the site, including the mansion. After a short preparatory visit during the Munich crisis in September and October 1938, GC&CS and various other parts of SIS moved to Bletchley Park in September 1939. Space constraints and the failure, at least initially, of the predicted catastrophic air attacks to materialise resulted in the relocation back to London of the non-codebreaking parts of SIS; but GC&CS remained based at Bletchley Park for the next seven years, until 1946.

ORDINARY PEOPLE, EXTRAORDINARY WORK

Prior to the Second World War, GC&CS was a very small organisation. Its early history and development were described in 1944 in a typescript written by its deputy director and de facto head, Alastair Denniston.[3] The organisation created after the First World War consisted of fewer than 100 members of staff. In particular, its executive functions were performed by twenty-five 'pensionable officers': one head, six senior assistants and eighteen junior assistants. Initially, all these were veterans of the First World War; but latterly senior and junior assistant officers had been recruited direct from university (almost universally from Oxford or Cambridge). By the early 1930s, their numbers had expanded to fifteen of each grade. These staff were supported by a team of twenty-eight clerks, typists and 'sorters and slipreaders'.[4]

In 1937, as the threat of war grew ever greater, Admiral Sinclair gave instructions for GC&CS to be expanded. Denniston described the new staff:

Through the Chief Clerk's Department we obtained Treasury sanction for 56 seniors, men or women, with the right background and training (salary £600 a year) and 30 girls with a graduate's knowledge of at least two of the languages required (£3 a week).[5]

These staff would be identified and given brief training, ready to take up their posts in the event of hostilities. Many of the most famous codebreakers employed at Bletchley Park were recruited during this process, including Alan Turing and Gordon Welchman.

The urgent requirement for additional accommodation also led to the construction of a series of temporary buildings during 1939 and 1940. Although in fact quite large (Hut 8, for example, is over 120 feet long), the description of these buildings as 'huts' has led to a perception that their inhabitants worked in some kind of primitive 'cottage industry' organisation, relying as much on informality and genius as on organisation or military discipline. It is questionable whether this rather homely concept of Bletchley Park, so beloved of fiction writers and television dramas, ever really existed. What is certain is that it no longer existed in 1944. By D-Day, Bletchley was an intelligence factory, with ancillary operations conducted all around the UK, in British possessions overseas and in the United States. It is actually quite difficult to arrive at a final figure for the number employed: not all who worked for GC&CS were based at Bletchley Park, and large numbers of personnel who worked within SIGINT (such as wireless intercept operators at Y stations around the country) were not formally part of GC&CS. But, according to one official count, on 4 June 1944 there were 7,825 people working at Bletchley Park and its outstations, principally sites housing the 'bombe' machines (see below), which assisted in breaking Enigma ciphers. Alastair Denniston recorded that, in September 1939, GC&CS consisted of '137 persons,' excluding the 'Construction Section' (responsible for producing British codes), which moved soon after to Mansfield College, Oxford.[6] Thus, by summer 1944, for every one person in the organisation at the outbreak of war there were now approximately fifty-seven – an astonishing growth, by any standards. Of the 7,825 staff, some 5,835 (almost 75 per cent) were women, and 4,454 (57 per cent) were uniformed members of one of the armed services. The remainder were civilians, mostly in the pay of the Foreign Office. The total number would rise by a further thousand in the latter half of 1944 to peak at 8,995 in January 1945. This figure declined slightly as the war drew to a close.[7]

By the end of the war, service personnel formed the majority of employees at Bletchley. This was a result of the increasing difficulty in obtaining civilian labour. Also, as GC&CS moved from its pre-war diplomatic and commercial function to an explicitly military focus, recruitment from the services became, as Frank Birch, the head of Naval Section at Bletchley put it, 'more easily justifiable'.[8] It should also be noted that, from 1942, single women were liable to be conscripted alongside their male colleagues, and so larger numbers of female service personnel became available. The division of labour across the three armed services was spelled out explicitly:

> It was under these circumstances that G.C. & C.S. policy became defined into asking the Admiralty to assume responsibility for manning the bombes (and later other cryptanalytical machinery), the army to undertake the main Traffic Analysis task for high echelon Army and G.A.F. [German air force – Luftwaffe] and provide a military guard, pioneers and transport drivers, and the R.A.F. to man the telecommunications and provide the mechanics for servicing the cryptanalytical machinery.[9]

Thus, in crude terms, the navy broke codes; the RAF handled communications and maintenance; and the army and the Foreign Office did everything else. There was also a clear gender divide within the organisation: women were generally allocated 'operator' tasks, particularly using the various mechanical aids to cryptanalysis and communications; but they were not expected to be able to maintain or repair the machines – that was a task for male mechanics. Nor, broadly, were they expected to hold management roles. The only exceptions were the senior officers of each of the women's services; but again their function was specifically to manage the women within each service under their jurisdiction – a personnel function rather than an operational one. Of the three services, the army was the least divided in terms of gender roles, there being no specific male or female tasks allocated.

For most of the staff at Bletchley Park, men and women, life was tedious rather than stimulating. The cryptanalytical achievements of the senior codebreakers had been converted into a series of relatively simple linked tasks, each of which was performed by a different group. This 'production-line' approach meant that many staff had little idea of how their particular task fitted into the process as a whole; however, the system resulted in a highly efficient machine that was capable of processing vast quantities of data on a daily basis.

The Hollerith operation in Block C stands as an example of this. In this section, punched-card sorting machines (known as 'Hollerith machines' after their nineteenth-century inventor) were used to perform various analytical processes on the cipher text of intercepted messages, looking for letter patterns and sequences that might assist with code-breaking. Peggy Munn operated Hollerith machines in Block C with little or no idea of the real purpose of her task:

The supervisor would give me a pack of telegrams, or what looked like telegrams; pieces of paper with white printed bands of blocks of 5 letters or numbers and a space between each block stuck on. There was nothing German, Russian or anything foreign. None of it made sense; I didn't ask questions, I just did it!

When I moved I became a machine operator and had three machines to do, all with cards and each machine did something different. There was a 'thing' that slid in at the side and the boss always had to put the 'shoelaces' in it himself, we never had to do it. It did things with the cards, they went into various slots. I had to take one lot out of one of these slots and put them into the next machine. That machine did the same sort of fiddling and the cards came out into bunches and I then had to take one of those and put it in the end machine ...

The job was boring and hard work. I don't think anybody liked it. There was always so much to do and there wasn't any job satisfaction. I used to think, what am I doing? I don't know how is it affecting the war? But I mustn't grumble because the ATS [Auxiliary Territorial Service] girls were on the search lights out in the fields getting wet and the soldiers, sailors and airmen were fighting and doing all sorts of horrible things.[10]

The scale of this operation was staggering. Ronald Whelan, who worked in the Hollerith section with Peggy, estimated that the section 'did things' to over 2 million punched cards per week, consuming six tons of cards every seven days.[11] This was only one small part of the overall Bletchley operation. Thus the image of the site in 1944 is not one of individual genius (although that was still present), but of vast industrialised processing of data, and clerical effort.

The size and structure of the organisation in the later years of the war also meant that the standard of education was lower than in the pre-war GC&CS, which had been staffed by highly intelligent Oxbridge graduates; now typically a good secondary schooling was considered adequate. Also, whereas in its early days the organisation had been relatively collegiate and had paid little heed to rank, later on the site came to be run on much more hierarchical and disciplined quasi-military (or factory) lines. The popular image of Bletchley Park as a place of relaxed but intense intellectual effort, staffed by a group of gifted creative individuals who worked without distinction of rank, may occasionally have applied early in the war, when the codebreaking techniques were being evolved. But by 1944, for the mass of the rank-and-file of the 'intelligence factory', life was a lot less stimulating. As historian Christopher Grey describes it:

Whilst I have stressed that generalisations are difficult, as a generalisation the work at BP was not glamorous, it was not inspiring and, whilst underpinned by genius, did not in the main require genius even in its cryptanalytic sections. Making BP work required an intensive, and not always successful managerial effort in the face of work which was frequently mundane, physically and mentally tiring, and sometimes appeared, to those who did not know its true purpose, to be almost meaningless.[12]

This is not to suggest that the work of Bletchley Park was not vitally important, or that it is of little significant historical interest. But for those involved in it (as with most war work) life was tiring, difficult and often very boring. The staff were sustained by an awareness of their involvement in a vast communal effort, and by the camaraderie that results from shared hardship.

HUTS AND BLOCKS

The rapid and organic development of GC&CS also led to a complex organisational structure that is not easy to comprehend – a result of the interplay between several (at times) conflicting organisational influences. Before the war, the emphasis of GC&CS's work was largely on foreign diplomatic traffic, and there was a natural division of the work into country and regional sections. There was little explicitly military work. Denniston observed that in the early days of the 1920s there was 'no service traffic ever worth circulating'.[13] However, during the 1930s more material of military and air interest was intercepted, and the three services started to take a closer interest in CG&CS. The first was the War Office. It sent the brilliant codebreaker John Tiltman to Broadway Buildings in the mid-1930s, who as we saw would go on to establish Military Section, which transferred to Bletchley Park in 1939. Similarly, the Air Ministry established an Air Section there in 1936. The Admiralty did not see a need to maintain a presence in GC&CS during peacetime, but arranged for a Naval Section to be immediately created in the event of war (as indeed happened in 1939).[14]

However, the development of complex machine ciphers cut across service boundaries. A prime example is the Enigma cipher, which was adopted progressively during the 1930s by all three German armed services, and later on by the police, the SS and the railways. A strict air/sea/land segregation was therefore no longer useful in the effort to crack the codes. To further complicate the picture, similar cipher systems were used by various different nations: for example, Enigma was used at different times by Spain, Germany, Italy, Hungary and Switzerland. A German memorandum from 1935 records the sale of machines to sixteen different countries, ranging from Chile and Argentina to Afghanistan. It also, incidentally, lists the two machines that were purchased for analysis in 1927 by GC&CS itself.[15] The upshot was that a hybrid organisational structure grew up at Bletchley: some departments were based around a particular crypto-system (Enigma, Lorenz and so on); others were based around ciphers used for particular functions (such as the Meteorological Section); and, at the same time, the original service sections continued to operate – although they often now focused on lower-level 'hand' codes and ciphers (i.e. non-machine-based 'pencil-and-paper' ciphers), rather than 'high-level' machine-generated traffic. The organisation of GC&CS in 1941 was described by Harry Hinsley as

by Whitehall standards poorly organised. This was partly because the growth in its size and the complexity of its activities had outstripped the experience of those who administered it.

It was, he went on,

a loose collection of groups, rather than forming a single, tidy organisation. New sections had to be improvised into existence in response to the needs and opportunities thrown up since the outbreak of war.[16]

Major reforms in 1942 improved the situation, but in 1944 the structure of GC&CS remained a work in progress. In the early days, many of the sections were also housed in the newly built huts. These varied in size and ran from Hut 1 to Hut 25. However, some numbers were left out (such as thirteen, presumably on account of superstition), while other numbers proliferated (for example, as well as Hut 15, there were 15A, 15B and 15C). In addition, there were chauffeurs' huts, stores huts, Home Guard huts and so on.[17]

A number of key functions at Bletchley Park came to be known by their hut number. Four huts in particular are central to our story. When Enigma traffic was first tackled by GC&CS, it became apparent that the German army (*Heer*) and air force (Luftwaffe) were using an operating procedure for their Enigma-encrypted traffic that differed from that of the German navy (*Kriegsmarine*). Indeed, while air force traffic was first deciphered successfully in early 1940, naval traffic remained largely impenetrable until 1941.

Enigma traffic was divided between two teams: Hut 6 dealt with the decryption of army and air force material, while Hut 8 concerned itself with naval intercepts. The deciphered product from these huts was then passed to either the German Army and Air Force Enigma Reporting Section in Hut 3 or (in the case of naval traffic) to the pre-existing German Naval Section in Hut 4. Huts 3 and 4 were responsible for translating the material and determining which messages should be sent out to the Admiralty or government ministries. They also maintained indexes and catalogues of the information contained in the messages. The work of Hut 3, in particular, played a crucial part in the D-Day story and will be examined in more detail later.

In 1941, it became apparent to Bletchley's management that the existing system of huts was not adequate to cope with the long-term requirements of the growing GC&CS organisation, and from May 1941 a series of low (one- or two-storey) brick-built blocks was constructed. These were much larger than the huts and were designed to be, if not actually bomb proof, then at least splinter proof, with thick concrete roofs. In total, eight 'blocks' were built, lettered A to H. The first of these, Block A, was occupied by Naval and Air Sections in August 1942 when they moved from Hut 4 and from parts of the mansion that they had occupied since September 1939. In due course, Naval Section expanded to fill the whole of Block A as well as the adjacent Block B; it squeezed out Air Section, which moved to Block F in August 1943. Block C was built to accommodate the Hollerith punched-card operations (see above).

Block D was completed in January 1943, and lies at the heart of Bletchley Park's involvement in the Normandy campaign. It was the largest block yet built, providing over 40,000 square feet of work space. Constructed to a standard Ministry of Works design, the block consisted of a long west–east corridor with thirteen wings or 'spurs' extending north and south. It was built on a gentle slope, and thus the central corridor descended from west to east via a series of steps (some veterans mistakenly recalled it as being partially underground). It was into this block that the occupants of Huts 6 and 8 (the Enigma decryption teams) and Hut 3 (the Army and Air Force Enigma Reporting Section) moved in February 1943. Thus, the whole of the air/land Enigma operation ended up in one large hub. However, the teams clung to the colloquial titles they had adopted from their previous locations: thus, for example, Hut 6 remained 'Hut 6', even though it was now located in Block D. It was the same for Huts 3 and 8. All further references in this book to these 'huts' are actually to the functional organisations housed in Block D, not to the physical buildings. The Enigma sections were also joined in Block D by SIXTA, the Traffic Analysis Section. It had started life under the misleading title of 'No. 6 Intelligence School' at Beaumanor, near Loughborough, before moving to Bletchley Park in early 1942. It provided vital support to Huts 3, 6 and 8 by analysing and categorising incoming traffic.

A further system of departmental naming was adopted at Bletchley Park. This involved using the name of the head of section as short-hand. Four such sections are relevant to the D-Day story. Two of these dealt with the decryption of traffic from the German military intelligence service

(*Abwehr*), which proved vital to Allied understanding of German planning and strategic intention, as well as to the Allied deception effort. These sections were: 'Illicit Signals Oliver Strachey' (ISOS), which dealt with lower-level hand ciphers used by German intelligence agents; and 'Illicit Signals Knox' (ISK), which dealt with high-level communications using the *Abwehr* variants of Enigma. The latter section was named after codebreaker Dilly Knox, who had developed a methodology for breaking this traffic, but who would not live to see the Normandy invasion itself, succumbing to lymphoma in February 1943. By the time of D-Day, these two sections were located in Block G, on the north side of the Bletchley Park site.

The two other sections relevant to our story were the FISH Subsection (also known as the 'Testery', after its head, Major Ralph Tester), which was responsible for the pencil-and-paper or 'hand' methods used in the decryption of German Lorenz-encrypted teleprinter traffic; and the Statistical Section (or 'Newmanry', after its head, Max Newman), which was responsible for the electro-mechanical machines used in the attack on Lorenz, including the famous Heath Robinson and Colossus machines. In June 1944, these two sections were located in Blocks F and H. The exact role of these various departments in supporting the invasion is explored in later chapters.

Y STATIONS AND OUTSTATIONS

As mentioned above, not all the activities of GC&CS were carried on at Bletchley Park, and not all SIGINT work was done by GC&CS.

The first links in the chain were the so-called 'Y stations' – installations where wireless operators sat at banks of receivers, scanning the airwaves for enemy traffic. There were many stations engaged in different aspects of the work: listening to enemy high-frequency Morse traffic; listening to very high-frequency (VHF) voice chatter from enemy aircraft over the UK and ships at sea; and direction finding (D/F) and interception of electronic signals of other kinds, such as radars or navigational guidance beams for bombers ('noise').

The Y stations most relevant to our story were those that intercepted high-level Enigma and Lorenz traffic (dubbed FISH at Bletchley). They were divided up among the various armed services and distributed around the country. The army maintained stations at Beaumanor, Harpenden, Bishop's Waltham and Forest Moor (near Harrogate). The RAF operated stations at Chicksands (near Bletchley) and Wick.[18] The principal naval stations were at Scarborough and Flowerdown (near Winchester), with Scarborough focusing on German traffic.[19] Stations were also run by the Foreign Office (and staffed by the Metropolitan Police and the General Post Office (GPO)) at Denmark Hill and Whitchurch, listening to *Abwehr* traffic. In total, the army, Foreign Office and RAF operated 549 receiving sets in the UK targeting Enigma traffic, with the navy providing another 120. In addition, there were interception stations overseas, in the Middle East and in North America. There was also a large Y operation in the Far East dedicated to Japanese traffic.

That there were over 600 sets employed gives a sense of the scale of the operation, but the service was still stretched; the available human interceptors had to be carefully managed and have their efforts prioritised each day according to the different networks and frequencies. They had to first find messages that could be cryptographically useful for breaking that day's traffic, and, second, pick up messages of intelligence value. This process naturally required a high level of coordination between the cryptanalytical and intelligence teams at Bletchley and the managers of the Y stations. Significant effort was required to juggle the competing daily demands of the codebreakers for fresh material to feed each of their specialisms. This process was managed for army and air traffic in Hut 6 by a section known as 'Control', which kept in constant touch with the Y stations by telephone and teleprinter, providing feedback on what to listen for next. Derek Taunt, a Cambridge mathematics student, joined this team in August 1941. He later recalled the close relationship with the Y operators:

We developed a heathy respect for the intercepting operators whose task it was to record with great accuracy messages in Morse code comprising up to fifty groups of five apparently random letters. There was no redundancy to spare, as with clear text. Some operators became so skilful that they could recognise their opposite numbers by their style of Morse transmission, just as one may recognise the hand-writing of a friend or (perhaps a more apt comparison) the touch of a well-known pianist.[20]

Raw intercepts of messages were passed to Bletchley from the Y stations either electronically, via teleprinter, or physically, by despatch riders. These went through a 'registration' process, which included preparing back-up copies of the messages and providing each with a serial number, which would allow it to be managed through the multiple processes of decryption and interpretation that would follow. Copies were then passed to SIXTA for analysis of what would nowadays be called 'meta-data' (call-signs, frequencies, locations of transmitters, etc.) and to the codebreaking teams themselves. In the case of Enigma traffic, part of the decryption process also took place away from Bletchley Park.

Messages were encrypted by the enemy using a series of settings for the sender's particular Enigma machine; these were known as the 'key'. These key settings were typically changed daily, and a number might be in use at any one time. (The process is examined in more detail later.) A crucial part of identifying these daily keys was carried out using 'bombe' machines – electro-mechanical devices, each about the size of a large wardrobe. In June 1944, over 160 such machines were in operation in the UK, but only a few were at Bletchley Park itself; the remainder were housed at four 'outstations' – two smaller local sites in the nearby villages of Gayhurst and Adstock, and two large purpose-built sites in north London, at Stanmore and Eastcote.[21] The US Navy had also constructed its own bombes, and ninety of these machines were in operation in Washington DC, and linked direct to Bletchley.[22] Messages themselves were not sent to outstations; instead, so-called 'menus' based on informa-tion contained in the message were dispatched, and information about possible keys was returned, typically by telephone. Again, the volume of work facing Bletchley and the limited number of machines meant that a control room had to be established to manage the flow of work out to these sites.

Once this process had yielded the keys, each day's traffic using a particular key could be decrypted, almost as a matter of routine, by teams of operators in Huts 6 and 8. This work was done using versions of the British Typex cipher machine, which had been adapted to mimic the functioning of an Enigma. Such a machine, programmed with the same settings as the original German machine, would produce 'plaintext' from the enciphered intercepted message. This text would then be passed to either Hut 3 or to Naval Section for the subsequent processes of translation, elucidation of abbreviations, acronyms and technical language, indexing and ultimately dissemination to Bletchley Park's 'customers' in government ministries and overseas commands.

Other sites that were to play a vital role in the D-Day story included the stations used to pick up 'non-Morse' transmissions (sometimes referred to as 'No-Mo'), which were the encrypted teleprinter transmissions of the German Lorenz network (FISH). Initially, these signals were intercepted by the Foreign Office station at Denmark Hill, but later a purpose-built facility was created at Knockholt in Kent, which was fully operational by early 1943.[23] The weakness of the German signals and the distance at which they needed to be intercepted created a significant technical challenge, requiring arrays of aerials, in some cases up to 300 metres across; nevertheless, the challenge was overcome, and Knockholt would eventually employ approximately 600 staff of its own.[24] Interception of this traffic was also carried out at Sandridge and Smallford, near St Albans, at facilities operated by the GPO.

Overall responsibility for the interception of Lorenz traffic was given to Harold Kenworthy, a former First World War signals officer who had worked on radio interception in the 1920s and 1930s for the Metropolitan Police. At the outbreak of war, he had been transferred to GC&CS. Kenworthy found that the weakness of the signals prevented them from being fed straight into a teleprint machine (and thus allowing the cipher text to be recovered directly); but he was able to capture the traffic using a simpler device known as an 'undulator'. This consisted of a receiver and pen, which traced the raw signal onto paper tape. Teleprinter messages were transmitted as a series of on/off signals representing a dot or a space in 'Baudot' teleprinter code (see below). The pen traced when the signal was 'on' or 'off', producing a line with sequences of square bumps representing the letters. A skilled operator could then read these 'slips' (as they were known) and restore them to alphanumerical form.[25]

One of the particular problems with this traffic was that the decryption processes required an absolutely accurate copy of the message. To achieve this, Knockholt would often double or triple the number of wireless sets intercepting a particular signal. Several copies of the text would then be sent in parallel to Bletchley Park, over different teleprinter lines; at all stages, checking and rechecking of the text took place to ensure accuracy. Various mechanical devices were created to assist in this process, but ultimately it fell to the staff involved to carry out lengthy (and no doubt tedious) checking routines on messages that could be tens of thousands of characters in length.[26]

THE EARLY DAYS OF BLETCHLEY'S COMMUNICATIONS

The huge volume of data flowing in and out of Bletchley Park – whether intercepted signals, bombe 'menus' or decrypted messages and reports – required a large and sophisticated communications operation. Fortunately, this had been appreciated at the very outset. Bletchley was on the west coast main railway line and was adjacent to the A5 trunk road. Also, its position on the 'Varsity' railway line from Oxford to Cambridge was convenient for Denniston's 'men and women of a professor type' to come and go from their former homes and colleges.

However, the easy rail links to Oxford and Cambridge were not the only – or indeed the primary – reason for Admiral Sinclair's decision to move to Bletchley. A more compelling reason was the proximity of the main trunk telephone lines from London to the north of England

(London–Birmingham–Liverpool and London–Derby). Ever since the turn of the century, a 'repeater' station (to boost the signals carried by these lines) had existed at Fenny Stratford, a village less than a mile from Bletchley. It was thus a relatively simple affair to create the necessary additional connections to Bletchley Park.

In 1938, the government undertook a review of all communications circuits for the three armed services within the UK. This was of especial concern to the RAF, which had developed a nationwide defence network of radar installations, Observer Corps locations and other defence infrastructure, all of which needed to be able to intercommunicate quickly in the event of attack. In response, the GPO inaugurated the Defence Telecommunications Control organisation, with regional branches around the country. As well as telephones for voice communication, there was substantial demand from the services for telegraph facilities. To cope with this, the GPO proposed the creation of a network independent of the existing civilian services, with voice-frequency equipment installed at the various service establishments. The result was the Defence Teleprinter Network (DTN) installed by Standard and the GPO.

The initial aim was that the DTN should have equivalent capacity to the civil network, but in fact by 1944 it had trebled in size. The backbone of the network consisted of five large switching centres discreetly located around the country. Smaller switchboards and teleprinter terminals (such as at Bletchley Park) were spread around the British Isles at military and government establishments. At its peak, the DTN comprised over 12,000 individual telegraph circuits and 10,000 teleprinters and associated equipment. Many circuits terminated in large teleprinter rooms with anything up to 200 machines.

Leaving aside the actual cable connections, Bletchley Park also required a large body of communications personnel. At the beginning of the war, all GC&CS communications within the UK were the responsibility of the Landline Communications Section of SIS. Bletchley Park was duly incorporated into this network and connected to the DTN. A direct teleprinter connection was also established with the nearby DTN centre at RAF

Stanbridge (Leighton Buzzard). Although many RAF personnel were drafted in as operators, the communications operation as a whole remained under civilian SIS management until 1942.

When GC&CS first moved to Bletchley Park, the entire communications operation – both incoming and outgoing – was contained within the existing mansion and its outbuildings. Telephone and teleprinter facilities were installed initially in the billiard room and the ballroom.[27] In addition to these central facilities, Hut 4 maintained its own teleprinter room through which it could receive traffic from the Y stations at Cheadle and Scarborough and communicate directly with the Admiralty in London, and in particular the Operational Intelligence Centre in the Citadel.[28] Hut 3 also had its own teleprinter facilities installed in May 1941; it had its own signals officer too, responsible for messages out to government departments and commanders in the field, and, by February 1942, sixteen Women's Auxiliary Air Force (WAAF) teleprinter operators were working in the hut.[29]

From early 1941, it was clear that the existing communications facilities were being overwhelmed, and arrangements were made for purpose-built accommodation for the communications sections. Two parallel projects were undertaken. The first involved the construction of Hut 14, which was completed and in operation, along with teleprinter machines, by the end of 1941. The second was the construction of a more permanent reinforced Teleprinter Building. This block was maintained by the GPO staff on site.

As originally constructed, the Teleprinter Building was completely windowless. The idea was to offer protection for the valuable machinery in the event of an air raid; but it made life inside rather unpleasant. A GPO engineer who worked there recalled that staff were given half an hour of sun-ray treatment in one of the huts prior to starting a shift because for the rest of the day they would be working without natural light. The expanding GC&CS operation rapidly outgrew the building, so an additional structure was erected to the north of the main Teleprinter Building. This was begun in mid-1942 and it gained a second storey between November 1943 and February 1944.[30]

THE HEART OF THE OPERATION

In April 1942, responsibility for communications at GC&CS passed to a new Communications Section. This section expanded rapidly: by 1943 it had 710 personnel, and the numbers peaked at the end of 1944, with 1,425 – around 15 per cent of the total staff of GC&CS, a reflection of the vital importance of communications to the overall functioning of the organisation.[31] The majority of the personnel were WAAF and civilian (Foreign Office) signals clerks and cipher machine operators.

In April 1943, communications functions also moved into a new Block E. This was a large, cruciform building positioned at the centre of the site, between Blocks A and B, with the Teleprinter Building to the south and Block D to the north. Its central location reflected its role as the heart of the GC&CS operation. All incoming and outgoing communications passed through, or were managed by, Block E. Incoming intercepts from Y stations around the UK and overseas arrived in the building, were logged and then distributed to the appropriate cryptological or intelligence sections. The incoming traffic was handled by teleprinter operators in the adjacent Teleprinter Building and its annex, while outgoing signals were the province of Block E. Much of the outgoing material was processed through the Cipher Office, where the crucial process of re-encrypting signals that were to be sent by non-secure wireless links to commands overseas was carried out. This was done using Typex machines, as well as a number of other mechanical ciphers operated by female civilian and RAF personnel. Up to sixty-four Typex machines were in use in the Cipher Office in March 1943.[32]

The various departments in Block E were connected by a vacuum tube system, by which documentation could be moved quickly around the building. This system also linked up with Blocks A and B, as well as to Block D to the north (via a small tunnel under the road).[33] One RAF veteran of Block E, teleprinter operator Joyce Roberts, recalled some light-hearted moments for the Wrens (Women's Royal Naval Service) in Block A:

But it wasn't all serious, the persons putting the green sheets [signal traffic] together and sending them to us were somewhere else in Bletchley Park but they must have been near the small lake. This is because the messages came to us in tubes worked by a pneumatic vacuum pump. When the season was right they would collect *frogs* from the lake and put them in the tubes with the message and they would pop out in front of us when we received the message. This happened a lot and relieved the monotony from time to time.[34]

For all the occasional frivolity, Block E had a reputation as one of the unhappiest parts of the park. Much of the work at Bletchley was tedious, but in Block E this was exacerbated by noisy machines, lack of natural light and poor ventilation. Surviving documents from 1943 chronicle how the conditions in the Cipher Office in Block E came under scrutiny. It was noticed that sickness rates and resignations there were running at around twice the average for the rest of Bletchley. Mr White, who was in charge of this section, provided a list of the medical reasons for the discharge of twenty-three women between January and November 1943: 'lassitude and general debility', 'gastritis', 'anxiety state', 'nervous debility', 'nervous breakdown' and 'psychoneurosis'. Proffered solutions included improving the ventilation of the building and introducing broadcast 'music while you work'. Unfortunately, the two were found to be incompatible: opening the windows allowed the music to carry to Naval Section next door, resulting in complaints from the head, Frank Birch, that it was disturbing both him and his team.

Ultimately, management's attitude to Block E's work stress was summarised by Bletchley Park's senior medical officer, Captain Melrose, in a letter to Commander Bradshaw, the head of administration:

With reference to the high incidence of sickness in Mr White's Section. I do not agree that poor ventilation is the reason for this but that the cause is due to the morale of this section. I have checked over the 'types of sickness' and the majority appear to be of the trivial 'nervous disability' type. Resignations appear to be fairly frequent from this section and this alone suggests poor morale. I suggest these girls be talked to by Mr White and reminded that they are doing war work and must be willing to put up with some discomfort. Certificates excusing night work must be absolutely ignored. It is no greater hardship working at night than during the day.[35]

It would appear that the view was that sickness rates were down to 'morale' and that junior staff in particular should simply accept their working conditions and get on with it. At a time when the lives of many, both servicemen and civilians, were at much greater risk at sea, on the battlefield and in the Blitz, there was little sympathy for those who found life in leafy Buckinghamshire too hard.

Alongside Block E and the Teleprinter Building, several sections at Bletchley retained their own communications arrangements. Huts 3 and 6, for instance, maintained their independent facilities even after February 1943, when they moved to Block D. This building was constructed with purpose-built teleprinter rooms at the southern ends of Spur H (serving Hut 3) and Spur K (serving Hut 6). The teleprinter room for Hut 6 was probably concerned with incoming traffic from Y stations, while that serving Hut 3 would have been used for communicating finished intelligence to government ministries and other intelligence customers. Although today both of these spaces have windows, originally they were both windowless, like the Teleprinter Building.[36]

COMMUNICATING WITH COMMANDERS IN THE FIELD

While many of Bletchley Park's intelligence consumers could be reached directly by teleprinter, wireless connections with customers overseas were also required. By the time of OVERLORD, a tried and tested system had been developed. Bletchley Park was able to communicate directly with senior commanders through a system of Special Communications Units (SCUs) and Special Liaison Units (SLUs) attached to their headquarters. The former dealt with the technicalities of maintaining wireless communication, while the latter were responsible for managing the intelligence itself in the form of ULTRA messages – Bletchley's codename for high-level SIGINT. (The role of these units both before and after the Normandy invasion is discussed in a later chapter.)

Prior to the outbreak of war, Admiral Sinclair had determined that SIS's communications needed to be improved. In April 1938, he recruited Richard Gambier-Parry, a wireless expert from the radio manufacturing company Philco. Gambier-Parry was an old Etonian who had served as an infantry officer in the Great War. He was placed in charge of a newly created Communications Section for SIS (also known as Section VIII). It had a number of tasks, but principal among them was communication by covert wireless with SIS personnel and stations overseas. This organisation moved to Bletchley Park in 1939; but in February 1940 it relocated to its own site at Whaddon Hall, 6 miles west of Bletchley.[37] When, in 1941, Bletchley Park started to provide ULTRA direct to headquarters overseas (at that time limited to Cairo and the Western Desert in Egypt), Whaddon Hall was the obvious location from which to send the material. To this end, a unit known as the Special Operations Group was created at the highest point in Whaddon, a spot known as Windy Ridge. Huts were erected behind Whaddon church, one containing the teleprinters that connected the unit with Bletchley and the other containing the wireless equipment. Staff also took over the village hall. On any one shift, around twenty operators, drawn from all three services, were on duty to send out messages. These were typically received from Bletchley already enciphered (using either Typex or highly secure one-time-pad ciphers).[38] The direct link between Bletchley Park, Whaddon and commanders in the field enabled the very efficient dissemination of potentially time-sensitive intelligence. The speed of this intelligence cycle was at times an important factor in the usefulness of the work done by Bletchley Park.

Although this system was logical and effective, it was not particularly popular – at least initially. In the early days of the war in 1939 and 1940, the various service intelligence departments had argued strongly that the job of GC&CS was to provide *them* with SIGINT; and *they* would then decide on its importance and on how it was to be disseminated to their operational units. They strongly resisted the idea that Bletchley was competent effectively to cut them out of the loop. Yet, at the same time, the idea that incoming intelligence could be separated along service lines proved unworkable. For example, was material recovered from the German Luftwaffe networks always the province of Air Intelligence, even if much of it described German army activity? Frank Birch summarised the arguments:

> By November 1940 it had been realised that intelligence derived from German traffic including Enigma, would be required in the Middle East, and, as Italian intelligence summaries were already being sent from G.C. & C.S. it seemed logical that German Special Intelligence should follow suit ... To this the Air Ministry objected: selection of material to be sent should be made, not in Hut 3, but in Air Ministry, and transmission should be over Air Ministry channels – an arrangement that would inevitably involve delay and might well jeopardise security ... In the end – but it had taken four months – Y Board approval to direct transmission from Hut 3 was obtained in March [1941].[39]

Fortunately, by the time of OVERLORD the argument had been won by GC&CS and material could be sent out direct without delay. Combined with the efficient system for getting intercepted material into Bletchley, this communications loop – and its ability to cope with high volumes of material – was fundamental to the success of Bletchley Park.

A SPECIAL INTELLIGENCE RELATIONSHIP

The opening of Block E coincided with a very significant period in the history of British SIGINT. Prior to 1943, the number of external recipients of ULTRA was relatively limited: chiefly government departments and services commands in the UK, and British commanders in the Mediterranean and, in particular, Egypt. However, May 1943 marked the conclusion of an intelligence-sharing agreement negotiated between the US War Department and GC&CS. This, alongside the previous deals signed with the US Navy, firmly cemented the special intelligence relationship between the UK and the US. By the summer of 1944, a highly integrated arrangement for intelligence sharing, and indeed military command, had evolved – and would directly impact on the D-Day campaign.

The developments in SIGINT to get to that point had been considerable. On the outbreak of war in Europe in 1939, both the US and the UK had separate areas of intelligence interest. While the British were obviously concerned with German signals traffic, that was not true of the US, whose strategic concerns lay in the Pacific and whose focus was on Japanese codes. Inevitably, however, as the US became more involved in supplying the UK with munitions and food across the Atlantic during 1940 and 1941, it became further drawn into the conflict, despite its ostensible neutrality. First tentative feelers were extended by both sides in the summer of 1940, though accompanied by a strong element of mutual suspicion: the British were concerned that lax US security might compromise their secrets, in particular progress concerning Enigma, while the Americans were suspicious that the British might use shared information to attack the US's own codes, and thus spy on their future ally. There was also significant friction between rival intelligence agencies in the US. William Friedman, assistant head of the US Army Signal Intelligence Service (confusingly, also known as SIS), was keen to start sharing information with the British in the autumn of 1940, but he was opposed by Commander Laurance Safford, head of the US Navy's SIGINT operation, OP-20-G.[40]

Despite these mutual reservations, a formal intelligence-sharing deal was agreed between senior British and US representatives in Washington DC in December 1940. President Roosevelt overruled the objections of the US Navy and agreed that the US and UK would 'exchange complete technical information re Japanese, German and Italian codes and cipher systems' – though this excluded the exchange of any actual intercepts.[41] This agreement would lead two months later to the so-called 'Sinkov Mission' of February 1941. On 17 January 1941, four US cryptanalysts – Captain Abraham Sinkov and Lieutenant Leo Rosen from the US Army War Department, and Lieutenant Prescott Currier and Ensign Robert Weeks of the US Navy – boarded the British battleship *King George V* and sailed to the UK to be inducted into UK signals intelligence activity. The party arrived at Bletchley Park on the night of 8 February 1941, to be greeted by Alastair Denniston, the head of GC&CS, his deputy Edward Travis, John Tiltman and several glasses of sherry.[42] The team went on to be shown all aspects of Bletchley Park work, but were sworn to strict secrecy and asked to share their findings only with their immediate superiors in their home departments. Prescott Currier later recalled the visit:

> I was struck by the real friendly feeling of complete cooperation which belies some things which have been said about this little trip of ours by others who have written about it since then. We went every-where, including Hut 6. We watched operation of the bombe. We were told in great detail the solution of the Enigma, who worked on it, how the bombe worked, what they had to do in order to get a readable text. Bob Weeks and I were not Enigma mathematicians or cryptanalysts but Abe and Leo Rosen were and it was left to them to do whatever would be done in taking the necessary notes and records that we would take back with us.[43]

In all, the US team stayed for two months in the UK. They visited not only Bletchley Park, but also the Y stations at Scarborough and Flowerdown, as well as other British military facilities.[44]

The information gained by the American visitors served only to increase demands from the US for more details. Although nominally neutral, the US Navy was increasingly involved in supporting Atlantic convoys, and was already potentially at risk from U-boats. Laurance Safford at OP-20-G was very suspicious of the British, whom he felt were not keeping their part of the deal, having been provided by the Americans with information about Japanese codes. GC&CS was reluctant to release more information than absolutely necessary.[45] In the end, Alastair Denniston travelled to the US in August 1941. In his own words, 'Perhaps the most important purpose of the visit is to clear up the position concerning E [Enigma] traffic' (decryptions of which were not being shared).[46] There he had meetings which (temporarily) allayed Safford's concerns.

The situation changed abruptly in the winter of 1941–42 with the formal entry of the US into the war against Germany after the December 1941 attack on Pearl Harbor. John Tiltman paid a visit to the US in April 1942, and advised GC&CS that Bletchley Park needed to be more forthcoming in providing the Americans with information.[47] Subsequently, on 1 July 1942, a further two Americans – Lieutenants Robert Ely and Joseph Eachus – from the US Navy OP-20-G arrived at Bletchley Park to learn more about British operations, and in particular to be briefed on the British bombe machine programme for Enigma key finding. The US Navy men no doubt eased relations with their British counterparts by drawing on American supply stores to make generous gifts of provisions. Joe Eachus later recalled that he would take cups of sugar with him whenever he went to meet UK colleagues, meaning he was always a welcome visitor.[48] Indeed, Eachus was eventually to meet and marry Barbara Abernethy, who had served sherry to the Sinkov party in Denniston's office in 1941.

In October 1942, Edward Travis and Frank Birch from Bletchley Park travelled to Washington and negotiated what would become known as the Travis–Wenger Agreement or the Holden Agreement, after US Navy Director of Naval Communications Captain C.F. Holden, who was the principal US signatory to the document. The agreement covered not only German naval Enigma but also other Axis codes and ciphers. Substantial parts of the agreement also related to Japanese codebreaking, and in addition the US expressed interest in Italian traffic. A very successful relationship developed between Bletchley Park and the US

Navy as a result of the Holden Agreement. Alan Turing travelled to Dayton, Ohio, in December 1942 as part of this knowledge-sharing effort to hold consultations with National Cash Registers (NCR) over its designs for the US Navy bombes, and the first machines were completed by May 1943.[49]

The Holden Agreement was, however, an agreement only between GC&CS and the US Navy; it did not include the US Army or the War Department. Bletchley Park saw no reason to cooperate more widely with US forces if it didn't have to, and in the US too the army and navy were not particularly fond of inter-service intelligence sharing. While the need for US Navy access to German SIGINT in the Atlantic had been apparent from mid-1940 (and German U-boat messages were in many cases audible in North America), for the US Army the need was less clear. GC&CS had stalled requests from the US Army Signals Intelligence Service for Enigma information on the basis that US ground troops were not involved against the Germans in the European theatre of war – and in any case had no intercept capability. This argument was significantly undermined once US troops landed in Algeria as part of Operation TORCH in November 1942.[50]

Further negotiations ensued which resulted in a second intelligence-sharing agreement, this time between GC&CS (represented by Travis) and the US War Department (represented by General Strong, the assistant chief of staff for intelligence). This Travis–Strong Agreement was endorsed by the US secretary of war on 15 June 1943.[51] Under the terms of the agreement, US personnel would be integrated into all aspects of the work at GC&CS and into the ULTRA dissemination systems.

As a result, a number of US personnel were posted to the various 'huts' at Bletchley Park, the first being dispatched to the UK in August 1943, officially under the command of Colonel George A. Bicher. Block E became a physical embodiment of the transatlantic relationship solidified with the Travis–Strong Agreement with the installation of 'Mr White's Secret Wing' in the western part of the building. This space housed the various machines required to maintain a constant twenty-four-hour secure link with the US Navy and War Department intelligence services in New York and Washington DC. These direct links to the US were maintained after 1945 when GC&CS became GCHQ, and they remain strong to this day. In the summer of 1943, Bletchley Park also commenced the first direct sharing of ULTRA intelligence with a US field commander: Lieutenant General George S. Patton, commanding the Seventh United States Army for the invasion of Sicily, beginning in July of that year. As we shall see, he was the first of many US commanders to be served with intelligence directly by Bletchley Park.

In line with the Travis–Strong Agreement, three US formations were established in the UK as part of GC&CS operations. On 28 January 1944, Colonel Bicher wrote to Travis, as head of GC&CS, arguing that the US should be given its own distinct set of bombe machines rather than simply working alongside British personnel.[52] This request was granted, and on 1 February 1944 the American 6812th Signal Security Detachment was set up to run UK bombes at Eastcote.[53] The US personnel were trained in the course of 1944 and eventually moved to their own designated bay within the outstation. Unlike the Wren bombe operators, they did not live on site at Eastcote, but were accommodated in their own camp in Ruislip Woods.

Later, on 29 March 1944, the 6813th Signal Security Detachment was formed, consisting of eighty-five US officers and men, in the Manor House at Little Brickhill, a few miles south-east of Bletchley. Of these, twenty staff remained at Little Brickhill, running the administration for the unit, while the remaining sixty-five were assigned to various departments within GC&CS, including SIXTA for traffic analysis, Hut 6 for cryptanalysis of the Enigma machine, Block F for cryptanalysis of FISH traffic and Hut 3 for evaluation and exploitation of German traffic.[54]

The third US formation to join the UK SIGINT effort was the 6811th Signal Security Detachment, which manned an intercept Y station at Hall Place, an Elizabethan manor house in Bexley, Kent. One member of the US team there, Private Hervie Haufler, went on to describe his experiences. In common with many employees of the Allied SIGINT operation, he was not allowed to know whether his work was actually making any difference:

> In military intelligence, you're informed about only that small part of the whole that you 'need to know' in order to do the job. My need to know back then was very slim. We passed messages on to the British at Station X [Bletchley Park] without ever knowing whether they were being broken. There were times, such as the terrible surprise attack of the German army on our Allied troops in the Battle of the Bulge, when we believed in despair that they were not being deciphered, that they were just piling up in a warehouse someplace in hopes that a code breakthrough would come. Else, how could Hitler have so fooled our commanders? We GIs at Hall Place had to sustain our faith that somehow what we were doing was making a positive contribution.[55]

The life of Hervie and his colleagues was enlivened, however, by the fact that Bexley was directly under the flightpath of German V weapons heading for London – the V1 'flying bomb' (a pilotless aircraft with a large explosive warhead) and the V2 (an early long-range rocket). Several near misses were experienced, and there was harrowing off-duty work looking for survivors at the impact sites:

> Two of our guys received Purple Hearts because of injuries they suffered in the bombings. All this was scary but also balm to our egos: sure, we were rear-echelon troops, but we weren't completely immune to the bloodletting.[56]

In total, fewer than 250 US personnel were recorded as working within GC&CS at the end of 1944 – less than 3 per cent of the total workforce.[57] However, the numbers were less important than what these men (and one woman) represented: they were a physical symbol of the integration of the SIGINT effort between the two allies against the Germans. Such integration was vital. Towards the end of the war, the US Navy provided approximately one-third of the bombe capacity exploited by Bletchley Park – roughly 100 of the 300 machines built – and these machines were dominant in the analysis and breaking of traffic that used a more complex four-rotor Enigma machine (the 'M4'). This debt was owed to OP-20-G, and the irony of the situation (given the troubled beginnings of the relationship) has been summarised by the historian Stephen Budiansky:

> Denying they needed assistance, the British had at last permitted the US Navy to share in the operational exploitation of the German Enigma traffic, and in a little over a year found that they would have been in desperate straits – not only with regard to naval traffic, but to Army and Air Force as well – were it not for their partnership with the US Navy. The British got exactly what they insisted they did not want, and ended up not being able to live without it.[58]

The integration of the US–UK SIGINT effort was a feature of the planning for OVERLORD across the board. Once the two powers had agreed on the principle of the invasion and a combined headquarters had been established, intelligence sharing became the norm. Indeed, Bletchley Park would go on to supply ULTRA direct to both British and American headquarters without distinction. This was a significant element in the success of the intelligence effort, and stands in stark contrast to the fragmentation of Germany's SIGINT operations – and indeed its wider intelligence effort.

*

This chapter may have offered a rather downbeat impression of Bletchley Park, with factory-like drudgery and a huge workforce slaving away in Kafkaesque ignorance of their purpose or part in the overall plan. It is certainly at odds with the popular, rather romantic view of Bletchley as a place of intellectual freedom, liberal values and games of rounders.

However, the picture painted here is not intended to denigrate or undermine GC&CS as an institution, but rather to demonstrate that the make-do-and-mend organisation of 1939–42 (which shapes much of the popular image) had, by 1944, been replaced by a very large and highly efficient intelligence-producing machine. OVERLORD was an operation on an unprecedented scale – the biggest seaborne landing yet attempted. All of its individual components were correspondingly large: from the tens of thousands of tons of concrete poured into the floating Mulberry harbours, to the thousands of landing craft and millions of artillery shells, bombs, grenades and boots required for the operation. A project of such magnitude required intelligence on a similar scale, and only a factory could produce that. The innovations of the previous four years – not only in codebreaking, but also in communications, data handling and personnel management – had produced an organisation that by summer 1944 could absorb the torrent of SIGINT data that flowed into it from multiple sources and process it into an equally impressive outgoing flood of useful intelligence. The following chapters examine that torrent of incoming material in more detail, before turning to Bletchley Park's outputs from it, and ultimately their impact on the campaign.

CHAPTER TWO

INCOMING INTERCEPTS AND CODEBREAKING

In May 1941, William 'Bill' Tutte arrived at Bletchley Park as a newly trained Foreign Office temporary assistant clerk. Tutte had graduated from Cambridge University in 1938 with an MA in natural sciences, but had continued at Trinity College doing mathematical research. In January 1941, he had been approached by his college tutor about a possible government post. This led to his being sent on a cryptography course in London, where he learned 'how to deal with cryptograms of the First World War'.[1]

On arrival at Bletchley a few months later, he was assigned to the Research Section, located in the guest bedroom wing on the first floor of the mansion.[2] This was a small group under the control of the codebreaking genius John Tiltman. The section itself was run by Captain Gerry Morgan, who had been told to pick '3 or 4 of the best students'[3] from the London cryptography course. Aside from Tutte, other members of the team included Morgan's brother Stanley and Norman Sainsbury, 'Assistant Keeper (Second Class)' in the department of oriental books and manuscripts at the British Museum. The Research Section investigated Japanese, Vichy French, Finnish, Hungarian, Polish, Czech and even Irish ciphers; however, Bill Tutte was initially concerned with the

Italian Hagelin machine ciphers, which had been partially broken, though a routine breaking method had yet to be devised.

After some success in devising a breaking procedure for Hagelin messages, Tutte was put onto 'a new German cipher called "Tunny"'.[4] This was the output of the Lorenz teleprinter cipher machine (code-named FISH), used for communication between Germany's most senior commanders. John Tiltman had made a vital breakthrough in late August 1941, but progress had then stalled. In October, Bill Tutte was approached by Captain Morgan almost as a last resort. Tutte recalled something he had learned on the London cryptology course: underlying patterns can often be detected by writing out a sequence in a grid. After a few failed attempts, Tutte put the letters of the cipher key in a particular pattern and 'marvelled at the many repetitions down the columns from row to row'. He had stumbled across one of the elements of the Lorenz machine cipher.

After that, the rest of the Research Section were drafted in to work out the remaining elements. Tutte was later to acknowledge modestly that he 'had a stroke of undeserved luck'[5] in spotting the patterns in the cipher. But what he did was to achieve the crucial breakthrough into one of the most secure ciphers yet invented.

This breakthrough allowed Research Section to work out how the cipher machine operated. It would take until spring 1942 to complete the task, but, thanks to the insights of Tiltman and Tutte, an almost complete understanding of Lorenz was achieved.

It would still be a long haul before Lorenz-encrypted traffic could be read routinely; but by spring 1944 decrypts were being produced on a regular basis. The consequences for OVERLORD were profound – FISH was a vital source of intelligence both before and after D-Day. But the German Lorenz-encrypted teleprinter network was not the only infor-mation source handled by Bletchley. The most famous of these German cipher systems was, of course, Enigma; crucial information concerning German activity in France was also obtained from intercepted messages sent by Japanese diplomats in Europe.

By the summer of 1944, Bletchley Park was able to access a wide range of enemy communications. Before looking in detail at what was learned from these signals, we should explore exactly what material was coming in, and what systems the Germans were using for different functions; how much of this material was intercepted; what the processes were for handling it; and in turn how much of it could actually be read. And, finally, none of the decryption achieved by Bletchley Park would have been possible without analysis of the incoming material, to sort it into the relevant key groups and networks – a task known as traffic analysis (T/A). Quite apart from its importance to the codebreakers, T/A produced useful intelligence in its own right.

ENIGMA

The story of the Enigma family of encryption machines began at the end of the First World War. In 1918, Arthur Scherbius, a German electrical engineer, submitted a design to the German navy for a rotor-based encryption machine.

At the heart of the machine were three discs or 'rotors'. Each of these discs had twenty-six electrical contacts on each face, representing the letters of the alphabet. However, the contacts on one face were connected inside the rotor to the contacts on the other face in an apparently random sequence. This meant that a current entering one face of the disc at a particular letter would emerge on the other side as a different letter. When a key was pressed on the machine, the electrical current passed through all three rotors, with the input letter being transposed each time. Also, crucially, the first rotor would rotate one place each time a letter key was pressed. This would change the path of the current, and produce a different encryption for the next letter. Once the first rotor had moved through all twenty-six positions it would move the second rotor forward one position. The second rotor would in turn advance the third rotor one position after it had completed one complete revolution – in a fashion similar to an odometer in a car. This meant that, for each key-press, the current followed a different path through the rotors and the letter represented by the key underwent a different encryption each time. It would take 17,576 key-presses before the rotors returned to their original starting position.

As a result, the machine produced a 'poly-alphabetical substitution cipher' – that is, when typed into the machine, each letter of a message was 'permuted' to emerge as a different letter. The encrypted text could then be passed either by cable or wireless as Morse code to a recipient with a similar machine, who would reverse the permutation to recover the original message. The earliest machine looked and functioned much like a typewriter, but was both heavy and complex. The German navy was not particularly interested in his design, and nor was the German Foreign Office. Neither felt that they generated enough radio traffic to justify the expense.[6] Undeterred, Scherbius continued to develop his ideas. And, in 1925, he finally persuaded the inter-war German navy to adopt a version of the device. In 1927, the system was also adopted by the inter-war German army.

More than twenty different variants of the Enigma machine were produced, but the army's Enigma I (brought into service in 1932) had all the characteristic features of the machines used by the German armed forces throughout the Second World War (see Plate 10). These machines had three interchangeable encryption wheels, and are commonly known as 'three-rotor' Enigmas (although the three rotors used at any one time were selected from five available). Another important feature of these military machines was a 'plugboard': letters could be linked by double-ended plug cables to swap the two linked letters over, vastly increasing the complexity of the encryption.[7]

The German army and the Luftwaffe continued to use machines that were very similar to Enigma I until 1945. But, in 1934, the German navy adopted a version of the machine that differed from its land-based equivalents in several minor respects. It was known as the M1 (M = '*Marine*'). Slightly modified M2 and M3 variants followed in 1938 and 1940 (collectively referred to as 'M3').[8] The navy adopted the same three (later five) rotors as their land-based colleagues, allowing effective communication between the services. However, in 1939 it introduced three more rotors, exclusively for naval use. Both Enigma I and the naval machines (M1–3) were widespread in the respective German armed forces. While the machines were not suitable for low-level tactical communications, almost all significant headquarters units would have had an Enigma. In total, around 20,000 Enigma I machines were manufactured, along with a further 2,000 naval variants.[9]

By late 1941, the German navy was sufficiently concerned about U-boat cipher security to introduce a separate key network for U-boats only. This had the German codename *Triton*, and its intercepts became known at Bletchley Park as SHARK. In February 1942, a new four-rotor Enigma machine was introduced on this network (generally known as the M4). In fact, the fourth 'rotor' did not move during encryption; nonetheless it significantly increased the complexity of decryption, and Bletchley Park was unable to read this traffic for almost ten months. Although the Allies were eventually able to break back into SHARK and read U-boat traffic, the German navy's faith in the machine's security persisted, and the M4 remained the standard equipment for U-boats until 1945.

We have already mentioned Enigma 'keys'. These were fundamental to Enigma's operation – and to the breaking of the message traffic. Scherbius's invention was not secret: it had been marketed commercially – and, indeed, in the 1920s GC&CS had bought two such examples for examination. The German military version's wiring in each of its rotors was different from the commercial version's; but this wiring had largely been deduced by Polish codebreakers prior to the war, and GC&CS completed the picture when it seized several rotors in 1940. However, even a complete understanding of how the machine worked was not enough to break the cipher it created.

Auguste Kerckhoffs was a nineteenth-century Dutch cryptographer who in 1883 outlined a series of principles for successful encipherment.[10] His second (and most famous) principle was that a good cipher system should remain secure even if the system and the rules by which the cipher is created are known to the enemy: security depends on the secrecy of the particular 'key' used for any message sent via the system. Both Enigma and the Lorenz SZ40/42 (FISH) systems followed this principle.

In Enigma, Kerckhoffs's principle was reflected in the starting settings of the machine. Since the cipher changed every time a key was depressed, if a message was to be deciphered successfully it was vital to know the precise starting configuration: which rotors were in the machine and in what order; the position of the numerical 'rings' around the rim of each rotor; the position of the ten plugs in the plugboard; and, finally, the relative positions of the rotors as the first letter was enciphered. The number of encryption possibilities allowed by these variables is 103,325,660,891,587,134,000,000 (or 2^{77}): trying to find the correct settings simply by testing each possibility in turn is clearly not an option.

However, the same problem confronted the legitimate recipient of a message. Thus, each wireless station on a particular German communications network was issued with a set of 'keys' – printed sheets that provided groups of settings, each group valid for twenty-four hours. Typically, a month's worth of settings would appear on one sheet. These so-called 'daily keys' provided the rotor choices and the ring and plugboard settings for the machine. However, the final element of the setting – the position of the rotors at the start of encryption – was left up to the operator, and was selected at random for each new message. Along with the daily key, this 'message setting' (*Spruchschlüssel*) provided the full 'message key' that was required to unlock the message's content. Since the recipient of a message would have the daily key, but not the individual message setting for the rotors, the sender would choose a starting position for the rotors and simply write it (unencrypted) as part of the preamble to the message. He would then use this setting to encrypt a second starting position, which he would actually use for the message.[11]

For the codebreakers at Bletchley Park, the task each day was to find the settings for each key in use by the Germans on that day – and, having found each one, to use it to decipher all the messages sent that day using that key. Each key used by the German armed forces served a different group of units. Some were in widespread use across Europe; others served only small groups of specialist users. But each of them had to be identified each day by Bletchley Park and then attacked separately. Codenames were allocated by the British to each of the keys as they were encountered. In the early days of 1939–40, so few keys had been identified that it was enough to allocate a colour to each one. This reflected the simple practice of marking the raw intercepts in coloured pencil to show the key to which they belonged. One of the early keys – which remained a rich source for Bletchley throughout the war – was RED. This was a widely used Luftwaffe general-purpose key. Later, the codebreakers ran out of pencil colours and a series of additional codenaming conventions was introduced:

Insects	Luftwaffe air force units
Flowers	German air force regional commands (*Luftgau*)
Birds	Army
Fish	Navy
Vegetables	Weather and navigation

Other names were applied ad hoc, such as the use of the fruits ORANGE and QUINCE for keys used by the SS.[12] The first SS key – ORANGE – was broken while colours were still being used as codenames. When other SS keys were identified later, it was observed that ORANGE could also be a fruit, and so other fruit-based codenames were adopted. By D-Day, GC&CS had identified 128 separate keys in use every day by the German armed forces (excluding the navy). Unfortunately, resources did not allow for a full-scale attack on each of these keys every day; while some were judged to be of extreme intelligence value, others were rarely attacked. Some keys – either because they were easy to crack or because of their general usefulness – were routinely broken, RED being one example. Peter Calvocoressi, who worked in Hut 3 and was thus the immediate recipient of Hut 6's successful codebreaking, commented:

The importance of 22 May [1940] lay in BP's prompt surmounting of the new difficulties and in fact – not realised at the time – that we were never again to lose Red. It became the constant staple of Ultra for the rest of the war. From this point it was broken daily, usually on the day in question and early in the day. Later in the war I remember that we in Hut 3 would get a bit tetchy if Hut 6 had not broken Red by breakfast time.[13]

The overall effectiveness of the Enigma decryption operation at Bletchley can be gauged by looking at the number of intercepted messages coming in, the success rate in decrypting these, and the number of messages sent out. The precise figures available for the various parts of Bletchley are incomplete, and different teams collated their numbers in different (incompatible) ways. Nevertheless, we can get some idea of the effort.

The first set of information available concerns the identification and breaking of particular Enigma keys by Hut 6.[14] By June 1944, a total of 128 army, air force and SS keys had been identified, creating (in theory) a requirement for 128 separate breaks every day. The process was facilitated somewhat by the fact that the Germans frequently sent identical messages on more than one key.[15] Nonetheless the scale of the daily challenge is apparent.

How effective was Hut 6 in meeting this challenge? A separate set of data[16] suggests that, for the period with which we are concerned (the 273 days from January to September 1944), Hut 6 achieved 6,655 key breaks – that is, out of the 128 keys identified by D-Day, an average of 24 a day were being broken by Hut 6. Thus, on any given day, on average Bletchley Park was achieving breaks in around 19 per cent of the keys. Hut 6 might be said to have 'peaked' in the months immediately following the invasion: while the number of keys identified continued to rise throughout the rest of the war, the proportion of daily breaks achieved was never again as high as in July–September 1944.

Once a particular twenty-four-hour key had been broken, all messages sent on that key for the remainder of those twenty-four hours could be processed. During the period under examination, an average of 3,500 to 4,500 messages flowed through Hut 6 each day. In the period June–September 1944, 186,000 out of 430,000 messages (around 44 per cent) were decrypted – just over 2,000 a day. Keys used for large numbers of messages would always take priority. This explains why, even though only 20 per cent of keys were broken, 44 per cent of the traffic was decrypted.

Clearly, as a proportion of all the Enigma-encrypted messages transmitted on any given day by the German Wehrmacht, this was a drop in the ocean.[17] However, it still represents a very significant haul of intelligence: in terms of the volume of decrypted messages, roughly the equivalent of a bible (old and new testaments together) was being produced every twelve days in the latter half of 1944.

While Hut 6 toiled on army and air force Enigma, Hut 8 was almost as busy with naval Enigma traffic. Its work would make an important contribution to the security of the Allied invasion fleet as it crossed the Channel, as well as to the protection of the subsequent supply and reinforcement effort. No details of the volume of traffic handled by Hut 8 are given in the various histories of the hut, but some general figures are available. Hugh Alexander, who headed Hut 8 from 1942 until April 1945, wrote in his 'Cryptographic History':

Traffic steadily increased throughout the war, from about 300 messages a day in 1940 up to 1500–2000 messages in 1944 and 1945; despite the decrease in the area controlled by the Germans, traffic continued to increase almost to the very end, the record intercept being 2,133 messages on March 12th 1945. At the same time the number of keys in use also increased and whereas in 1941 we had one main key to deal with, Dolphin . . . there were about 20 keys in use by the end of the war, most of which we were either breaking regularly or had broken often enough to see that they were not worth further work.[18]

This figure of 'about twenty' keys broken by the end of the war tallies reasonably closely with the figure of twenty-five identified naval networks given by Hinsley. Possibly because of the smaller number of keys in use, Hut 8 was able to achieve a higher average rate of decryption than Hut 6. According to A.P. Mahon, Alexander's successor as head of the hut:

> Hut 8's accomplishment consisted in decoding during the course of the war about 1,120,000 messages; the total number of intercepts received was about 1,550,000. It is remarkable that since regular breaking began in the autumn of 1941 the situation has always been under control and no important key has ever ceased to be broken with the exception of Shark between February and December 1942.[19]

If accurate, these figures represent an average decryption success rate of 72 per cent. It probably took some time to build up to that figure, and indeed Mahon acknowledged the black-out of U-boat communications after the introduction of SHARK and the four-rotor Enigma in 1942. However, again it represents a very large body of intelligence material.

Thus, at the time of the Normandy invasion, GC&CS was producing up to 5,000 useable Enigma message decryptions every day. This was a substantial achievement, but (as we saw in the previous chapter) it was possible only through the investment of a huge amount of human and mechanical effort. In summer 1944, Hut 6 was employing 560 people just to process army and air force Enigma.[20] And that did not include the 1,737 Wrens and RAF technicians operating the bombes.[21] A further 144 staff were employed in Hut 8.[22] Thus, about 2,500 staff were working on Enigma – about one-third of the total GC&CS workforce.

LORENZ AND FISH: HEATH ROBINSON AND COLOSSUS

While Enigma has claimed much of the historical limelight, the non-Morse teleprinter intercepts known as FISH were at least as important in building the intelligence picture prior to the Normandy invasion. In the absence of any combat in the west, the German army in France provided little or no useful information through Enigma intercepts. FISH, on the other hand, provided a vital insight not only into the Germans' order of battle, but also into their high-level strategic thinking and their expectations of the likely invasion.

UK intercept stations started to pick up intermittent 'non-Morse' transmissions in the latter half of 1940. These first regular transmissions were on an experimental link established between Athens and Vienna.[23] At around the same time, a deciphered Enigma message made reference to a non-Morse cipher system (properly known as a *Geheimschreiber* or 'secret writer') using the codename *Sägefish* ('Sawfish'). On the strength of this, the new traffic was named FISH by GC&CS, and its variants were all given fishy names (for instance, the early Athens–Vienna link was christened TUNNY).[24]

By June 1941, the Research Section at Bletchley Park was reporting that up to 300 messages a week were being transmitted on the Berlin–Athens link alone, and some of these were up to 15,000 characters in length. The Germans also appeared to be having trouble with the system, as messages were often repeated verbatim several times.[25]

The signals were actually teleprinter messages which had been encrypted using the Lorenz SZ40 and SZ42 teleprinter cipher machines. The Lorenz SZ42 was only the latest in a family of cipher machines that dated back to 1918. These machines employed two pre-existing technical principles. The first was the Baudot teleprinter code, invented by Emile Baudot in 1874. In this code, each alphabetical character was represented by five 'bits'. Five bits per character provided 32 possible permutations: from XXXXX to OOOOO and all variations in between (e.g. A was XXOOO). Thus 32 characters could be distinguished. A character-shift enabled a further 32, providing for the letters A–Z, numerals and various other special characters. The bits could also be transmitted over cable or wireless as electronic pulses. Modified versions of this system became widespread in the 1920s, and by 1939 teleprinter communications were commonplace in government and business circles.

The second technical principle was the Vernam cipher. Gilbert Sandford Vernam (1890–1960) was an employee of the American Telephone and

Telegraph Company (AT&T) who, in 1918, patented a way of enciphering Baudot code. In essence, he realised that if the five bits of a randomly selected cipher-key character were superimposed onto the five bits of a plaintext character, a third – new – cipher character would be created. Importantly, all the recipient of the encoded message had to do to get the original plaintext character was to superimpose the cipher-key character on the new character.

If a truly random sequence of cipher-key characters is used – a sequence at least as long as the message to be transmitted – then this produces a completely secure cipher. The difficulty lies in creating a sufficiently long string of random key characters – and of securely transmitting it to the recipient.

The solution to this problem was identified in 1932 by Colonel Parker Hitt (1878–1971), a US Army officer who had been a senior army cryptographer in the First World War. In Hitt's machine, the random key letters were generated by two sets of five wheels, one wheel in each set operating on one 'bit' of the Baudot code: the five wheels operating together would produce one Baudot character.

Each wheel had a different number of adjustable teeth (or 'cams') which could be set to produce either an 'X' or an 'O' at each position of the wheel. As these wheels rotated, so they generated an apparently random pattern of characters, according to the settings of the teeth. As there were two sets of five wheels, this generated two characters which, added to the original plaintext character, made for a very complex cipher.

The Lorenz company in Germany was actually a subsidiary of ITT, which owned the patent for the Hitt machine, and indeed the Lorenz SZ40/42 operated on very similar principles.

It is clear that from the early 1930s, GC&CS took an increasing interest in all types of mechanical and electro-mechanical encryption. Surviving correspondence suggests that Denniston was aware of the trend towards machine encryption as early as 1932, and that he recognised the need for a new kind of codebreaker. In a letter to the Civil Service Commission in July 1932, he wrote:

The advent of mechanical methods of cyphering has opened up a new phase of the work and, as it develops, it is taxing our resources in men capable of conducting investigations on machines to test the security alleged for them by their inventors ... They tell me it is a type of clockwork mechanics, rather than anything to do with pistons or cylinders, which have to be studied. The question of a knowledge of modern languages appears to be of little account on this occasion.[26]

Denniston would be even more specific in 1936, when he wrote concerning new recruits to GC&CS: 'On this particular occasion we should give serious consideration to a candidate with a training in electrical engineering.'[27]

There is a tendency among those retelling the FISH story to suggest that John Tiltman and Bill Tutte, who were largely responsible for breaking the cipher at Bletchley Park, divined the encryption process and the physical character of the Lorenz machine from scratch, with no prior knowledge of its mechanism. For example, according to Michael Smith: 'Given that no-one at Bletchley Park had any idea what a Lorenz machine looked like, Tutte had achieved a near miracle.'[28]

There is no doubt that the work of the two codebreakers did represent an astonishing cryptanalytical feat, but it did not come out of thin air. It is reasonable to assume that GC&CS was aware of the Hitt patents and of the development of Vernam cipher machines in the inter-war period, and thus the attack on Lorenz from 1941 onwards would have been aided by at least some prior knowledge of these systems – even if the precise mechanism of the German machine was unclear.

The work of analysing Lorenz traffic was given to Bletchley Park's Research Section, under John Tiltman. Drawing on a standard codebreaking technique, he realised that they needed to identify two messages that had been composed using the same cipher key and that had similar content. When the characters in the two messages were put together, this would produce a string of characters where the cipher key had cancelled itself out; and the remainder would be a combination of the two sets of five 'bits' representing the two plaintext characters.

The crucial breakthrough came when just such a pair of messages was intercepted. After a great deal of work, Tiltman was able to extract the full content of the shorter of the messages; more importantly, he was able to reveal a 3,976-letter long sample of the cipher-key character sequence. Analysis of this key sequence had the potential to reveal the means by which this pseudo-random cipher was generated.[29] Unfortunately, after this breakthrough, work on the cipher stalled for several weeks. As was described at the start of this chapter, the task was handed over to one of the newest members of the section, Bill Tutte.[30] Tutte devised a method of analysing the cipher-letter string which allowed him to reconstruct the operation of the machine, including the positions of the various wheels and their inter-relationships. It took until spring 1942 to complete the work, but thanks to the insights of Tiltman and Tutte an almost complete understanding of how the Lorenz SZ40 cipher machine (and its successor SZ42) operated had been achieved.

As with Enigma, the breaking of Lorenz traffic relied on identification of various components of the 'key' used for each message. Again, this was in two parts: the first described the position of the adjustable cams on each of the wheels of the machine; the second indicated the position to which each wheel should be rotated before encryption began. Unlike Enigma, which had interchangeable rotors, Lorenz's cipher-wheels were in fixed positions; however, the cams (which determined whether a dot or a cross was produced at each position of the wheel) were adjustable. In the early days, the cam positions were changed by the German operators once a month; but gradually the frequency increased until after D-Day new cam patterns were being introduced daily. The process of working out these cam positions was known at Bletchley Park as 'wheel breaking'. Each message used an individual position for each wheel at the start of the message. Establishing these starting positions was known as 'wheel setting'.

During 1942, a number of pencil-and-paper 'hand' techniques for both wheel breaking and wheel setting were developed. The message settings for Lorenz traffic were identified to a sufficient extent that a mechanical analogue of the machine could be commissioned in April 1942. The first of these machines, also known as TUNNY (nothing to do with the Athens–Vienna link!), was delivered in June. In July 1942, a new FISH Subsection was created under the control of Major Ralph Tester, a thirty-nine-year-old former accountant who had worked extensively in Germany.[31] His 'Testery' was able to read a significant proportion of intercepted traffic. However, at the end of 1942 the Germans tightened up a number of their operating procedures and it became harder to use the hand techniques to break FISH traffic.

Further research by Bill Tutte revealed that it was possible to find the starting positions of wheels with known cam settings. A common code-breaking technique relies on the fact that in unencrypted German (or indeed any language) different letters appear more or less often: 'e' more often than 'q', for example. The technique is known as 'frequency analysis'. Tutte showed that a number of starting positions of the wheels could be tested. If the correct starting position of a wheel was used, the frequency with which the dots or crosses (representing the letters) appeared would change from a purely random frequency pattern to a pattern similar to that of unencrypted German. Thus settings that produced a partial decryption would stand out (statistically) from the totally random sequences generated when the wrong setting was applied. The problem was that the process was so laborious that even to break one message by hand would take an impossibly long time.

Max Newman, another Cambridge mathematician who had joined Tiltman's Research Section, reckoned that electronic methods could substantially cut the time needed to find the wheel settings to just a few hours.[32] In December 1942, he was tasked with devising a mechanical solution to the problem, and his department became known as the 'Newmanry'. Construction began in January 1943 of a prototype machine, christened 'Heath Robinson' after the cartoonist who depicted fanciful mechanical devices. Newman devised a system where the known wheel settings were punched onto a paper tape, and this was compared with a second paper tape containing an adapted version of part of the encrypted message. The number of dots and crosses which were produced when the two tapes were combined was counted electronically by the machine, thus allowing Tutte's frequency patterns to emerge and the appropriate wheel starting positions to be identified.[33]

The system worked, but there were a number of problems. First was speed: the tapes ran as fast as was mechanically possible around a pair of large pulley frames (known as 'bedsteads'); but, at around 2,000 characters per second, this still meant that the processing of one message might take several hours. Then the strain on the tapes meant that they had a tendency to snap – and, even if they stayed in one piece, they stretched, playing havoc with the precise timing required by the electronic counters. Despite these issues, Robinson worked and twelve production machines were ordered in February 1943. The machines continued to evolve – from 'Heath Robinson' to 'Old Robinson' and then 'Super Robinson'; two were still in service at the end of the war, and two more were under construction.[34] Nonetheless, a better solution was clearly required.

Enter 'Colossus', the name given to a series of machines developed from late 1943.[35] GC&CS relied for much of its technical support on the Post Office Research Station at Dollis Hill in London. This organisation worked on versions of the bombe machines devised for key finding for Enigma, as well as other projects, including Robinson. One of its principal engineers was Tommy Flowers, who had joined the Post Office in 1926.[36] Flowers's particular interest (some might say obsession) was with electronic valves and their broad application in communications technology. He devised a machine that would replace both the paper tapes in Robinson with valve systems – over 2,000 valves for each machine.

Flowers put his suggestion to Max Newman in February 1943, but at that stage Newman was happy with the tape-based systems. Undeterred, Flowers continued to work on his design at Dollis Hill, reining in his ambition and producing a machine that still used paper tape for the cipher text but reproduced the possible wheel positions with valves. This machine used 1,600 valves, but it could process 5,000 characters per second (later versions would use 2,400 valves and could process up to 25,000 characters per second). Flowers returned to Newman with the new design, and this time his idea was accepted. The machine was christened 'Colossus'. Flowers's diary for 1944 contains a simple entry for 18 January: 'Colossus delivered to B.P.' The machine was up and running at Bletchley by the beginning of February – a milestone that Flowers recorded on 5 February in a remarkably downbeat diary entry: 'Colossus did its first job, car broke down on the way home.'[37]

Once the concept had proved itself, more Colossus machines were commissioned. In total, ten would be delivered by April 1945. The second machine, which incorporated a number of improvements and was dubbed Colossus Mark II became operational on 1 June 1944. A number of commentators – not least Flowers himself – have remarked on the timing of this event:

June 1 was to have been D-Day. The fact that our first fully satisfactory Colossus was put into service on that day is no coincidence. I had been told in February that if it was not ready by that date it would be too late to be of much use.[38]

Flowers went on to suggest that the machine was used to decipher a message from Hitler to Rommel stating Hitler's belief that the Normandy invasion, when it came, would only be a feint before a larger attack in the Pas-de-Calais. According to Flowers, the delivery of this message to Eisenhower on 5 June prompted the US general to announce 'We go tomorrow!' Neat as it is, there are a number of problems with this version of events – not least the fact that the invasion fleet had sailed on 4 June, ready to invade on the morning of the 5th, but had been delayed by the weather for twenty-four hours. Also, rather than a FISH decryption, the last-minute revelations of Hitler's views on the 'real' invasion are widely attributed to the decryption of a message sent by General Ōshima, the Japanese ambassador to Berlin, after a meeting on 27 May.[39] Even with Colossus in action, FISH decryptions could take days or weeks. It seems likely, therefore, that Flowers either embellished or misremembered the story in later life.

According to historian Jack Copeland, Colossus was 'the world's first large scale electronic digital computer'.[40] However little it resembled what we regard nowadays as 'a computer', there is nevertheless some truth to this. But, the technological legacy of Colossus should not lead us to over-estimate its wartime significance. It must be remembered that, during the Normandy campaign, the Newmanry was running four Robinsons (installed in November and December 1943, and January and March 1944). Colossus I was up and running in February 1944; Colossus II was operational in June; Colossus III would arrive in July; and the fourth machine would come in August.[41] Thus, for much of the build-up to the invasion and for the earlier part of the campaign, it was the Robinsons that were taking most of the strain.

But one area where Colossus was undoubtedly significant was in 'wheel breaking'. In July 1944, instead of changing the cam settings on the wheels of Lorenz only every month, the Germans started to reset the wheels daily. By the beginning of August, this was widespread across the whole FISH network. Not only did the wheels need to be 'broken' daily now, but also many of the previous techniques – which relied on accumulating a number of messages over several days and looking for 'depths' (i.e. several messages composed using the same cipher key) – became redundant. Fortunately for Bletchley Park, two members of the Newmanry, Jack Good and Donald Michie, had developed a technique in early 1944 whereby Colossus could be used to find these wheel cam settings, and thus 'break' the wheels directly. This concept was incorpo-rated into the design of Colossus II and by the end of the war three of the ten machines delivered were permanently occupied with wheel breaking, rather than wheel setting.[42]

In order to operate the growing fleet of machines, the first Wrens were introduced to the Newmanry in April 1943, and their numbers were to grow as the section expanded. Although the Wrens were never formally promoted to management positions, they rapidly became expert in their work, and supervision by cryptanalysts became increasingly redundant. Newman encouraged informality with the use of Christian names (except his own), and promoted 'comments books' for new ideas and brainstorming sessions to improve procedures.[43] He himself is variously described as either very friendly or quite reserved, especially in the presence of women (who over time made up an increasing proportion of his staff). One anecdote was told by Wren Catherine Caughey, who one day found him disconsolate on Bletchley station platform. He had lost his ticket. When Caughey suggested that he should simply explain this to the guard, he replied that the real problem was that he couldn't remember whether he was going to Oxford or Cambridge.[44]

Whatever Newman's immediate destination, by the time D-Day dawned his section – and the FISH operation as a whole – had become organised and mechanised. In contrast to the sketchy data available for Enigma, quite a detailed picture of the effectiveness of the GC&CS attack on FISH can be gained from documents in the archives, some declassified as recently as 2004.[45] In all, fifty-five separate FISH links were identified by GC&CS between June 1942 and May 1945. The first of these was the experimental TUNNY link (see above), which operated between Vienna and Athens from June until October 1942. This then shut down, but a growing number of operational links started up: two by the end of 1942; nineteen by the end of 1943; and twenty-one by the end of 1944.

As has been noted, up to the end of June 1944 the cams of the Lorenz machine wheels were reconfigured once a month; this basic monthly key was then made more secure by changing the start position for the wheels for each message. There was thus one basic key to break each month (wheel breaking) and a starting position to be identified for each message (wheel setting). If we look at the nineteen networks in use by the Germans at the end of 1943, at least one monthly wheel break was achieved on all but two of the links. Furthermore, if the number of monthly keys used on each link is counted, this results in 108 'link/months' to be attacked in 1943. Of these GC&CS was successful in 67. This is a reasonable wheel-break success rate. Of course, a further 'wheel setting' had to be achieved for each message. However, without the basic monthly wheel breaks, individual message breaking would have been impossible.

But, from July 1944, some thirty times as many wheel breaks were required each month. The Testery and Newmanry teams focused their limited resources on a few specific links that were considered most important – particularly links to fighting fronts where British or Allied forces were involved. Thus BREAM, the link to *Oberbefehlshaber Südwest* (*O.B. Südwest* or Commander-in-Chief South-west) in Italy, was a priority (indeed, that link recorded the highest number of daily wheel breaks – twenty-one in March 1945). Other priority links included JELLYFISH (the link to *O.B. West* – Commander-in-Chief West – in Paris), GURNARD (the link to *O.B. Südost* – C-in-C South-east – in Greece) and two Eastern Front links – WHITING and STICKLEBACK (which linked to the *Heeresgruppe Nord* (Army Group North) and *Heeresgruppe Süd* (Army Group South), respectively, in Ukraine). By contrast, no effort was expended on either TURBOT (Denmark) or MULLET (Norway), and no breaks were achieved on either of these links at any point in 1944. The efforts against BREAM and JELLYFISH were the most significant for the Normandy campaign.

The 'History of the Fish Subsection', also gives data on the number of messages processed and the levels of decryption success achieved between 1942 and 1945. The intercept station at Knockholt was collecting large numbers of messages, each of which had to be relayed to Bletchley with extreme accuracy. During the first three months of 1944, 8,000–10,000 messages were being intercepted each month. This amount of data swamped both Knockholt's capacity to pass the material on and Bletchley's capacity to process it. As a result, a new system was introduced whereby Bletchley Park would 'order' messages of a particular type to be passed on, according to its needs. This was necessary, as different types of message were required, in terms of both length and other characteristics – first for the wheel-breaking process and then, once the wheels had been broken, for actual decryption. The incoming message load was thus reduced to a more manageable 2,000 per month. Nonetheless, at its peak Knockholt was maintaining ten separate teleprinter lines to Bletchley Park and was transmitting up to 400,000 characters of cipher text per day.[46] Of these messages, about half were deemed 'possible for cryptography'; of those, about half again were decrypted and issued. This resulted in around 400 messages on average being decrypted each month during 1944. This tallies with a passage in the 'History of the Fish Subsection' from May 1944:

> At this time the section was decoding on the average 15 Jellyfish and 60 Bream transmissions each week, out of an average number of suitable transmissions intercepted of 78 Jellyfish and 180 Bream, i.e. 20% Jellyfish and 33% Bream.[47]

As a proportion of the total number of messages intercepted, the number decrypted was always very low: only in two months of 1944 (June and November) were more than 3 per cent of intercepted messages actually decrypted, and the average for the whole war was only 4.1 per cent. This reflects just what a monumentally complex task the breaking of FISH was. That any messages were ever broken is remarkable.

The total volume of FISH decrypted and read by Bletchley Park between 1942 and 1945 is recorded (with impressive precision) as 63,431,000 characters – the equivalent of about twenty bibles – over thirty-one months, or about one bible every six weeks (about a third of the output of Enigma from Hut 6). Analysis of the figures suggests that between 10 and 15 such messages might be produced each day, working out at around 60,000 characters (compared to 2,000 messages and around 250,000 characters of Enigma).

The nature of the FISH messages was, however, very different. FISH messages of more than 10,000 characters were not uncommon, whereas Enigma messages tended to be short. Also, Enigma messages typically reflected routine communication at the divisional and corps level within the German armed forces: small snippets of data from individual messages were aggregated to produce a larger intelligence picture. FISH messages, on the other hand, could contain complete high-level intelligence in a single message: a strategic appreciation by von Rundstedt or the tank states of an entire division. Thus, it is hard to overestimate the importance of FISH to the Allied intelligence picture before and during the Normandy invasion. Hinsley summed this up in his official history: 'From the point of view of its operational importance GC&CS regarded the solution of Jellyfish as its most significant cryptanalytic achievement during 1944.'[48]

JAPANESE DIPLOMATIC CODES

The last important group of codes and ciphers broken by Bletchley during the Normandy campaign were the Japanese diplomatic systems. It may seem counterintuitive that a codebreaking effort focused on the war in the Pacific could be useful in France, but that was indeed the case. This was because of the Germans' habit of sharing with Japan, their closest ally, details not only of their physical defences, but also of their strategic plans and appreciations of the Allied effort. Japan had a number of embassies in Europe, the most significant of which was that in Berlin, and in addition had staffs of attachés associated with their various other diplomatic posts. All of these representatives communicated frequently with Tokyo, reporting what they had learned from the Germans. Interception and decryption of these messages provided a rich seam of intelligence for the Allies.

Most of the communications emanating from the Japanese in Europe were sent to Tokyo by wireless. As diplomatic traffic, UK interception of these messages fell within the remit of the Foreign Office, and was carried out at intercept stations run by the GPO on its behalf at Brora in Scotland, Sandridge (near St Albans) and Whitchurch in Shropshire. Traffic was also collected at intercept stations in overseas embassies and at points around the empire, including Canberra, Abbottabad and Bangalore. Further intercepts were obtained by the Canadian navy at its intercept stations at Winnipeg and Point Grey Vancouver.[49] The Japanese armed forces used a wide range of code and cipher systems, which were attacked by both the US and the UK. However, in the context of Operation OVERLORD, it was the Japanese diplomatic ciphers that were the most significant. Of these, three could be regarded as the most important: two machine-based ciphers, PURPLE and CORAL, and the Japanese Military Attaché code (known as JMA).

By the end of 1940, a US team was able to break PURPLE traffic with great efficiency, the resulting intelligence being christened 'MAGIC'. In due course, this knowledge was shared with GC&CS. The first group of US personnel to arrive at Bletchley in February 1941 – the members of the Sinkov mission (see above) – brought with them a PURPLE analogue machine as a gift for their British counterparts.[50] PURPLE traffic would continue to be broken throughout the war, and indeed a US study of 100 randomly selected intercepted messages from November 1944 has shown that the average decryption time was 1.5 hours. Discounting 4 messages that were garbled, the average fell to 42 minutes.[51] Thus messages could be read almost as quickly by the Allies as by their intended Japanese recipients.

The PURPLE decrypts that were of greatest significance to OVERLORD were those from Japan's ambassador in Berlin, Ōshima Hiroshi. General Ōshima had been born in 1886 into a diplomatic family. He graduated from the Japanese military academy in 1905 and went on to hold several posts abroad as military attaché. He was first posted to Germany in 1921, and returned in 1934 after the Nazis had come to power. He spoke perfect German and rapidly developed a close relationship not only with Ribbentrop, the Nazi foreign minister, but also with many members of the general staff, and indeed with Hitler himself.[52] Ribbentrop wrote of Ōshima that he enjoyed 'the complete confidence of the Führer and the German Army'.[53] In 1938 he was promoted to ambassador.[54] Ōshima left Germany in 1939, after the invasion of Poland, but returned again as ambassador in 1941. From that point until the end of the war, he would become a vital source for the Allies. General George C. Marshall, chief of staff of the US Army, described his importance:

> Our main basis of information regarding Hitler's intentions in Europe is obtained from Baron Ōshima's messages from Berlin reporting his interviews with Hitler and other officials to the Japanese Government.[55]

Ōshima was able to have frequent conversations with those in the highest echelons of Nazi power, and was taken completely into their confidence. He aligned himself very much with their ideas and objectives, to the extent that the journalist William Shirer, a US correspondent in Berlin, described him as 'more Nazi than the Nazis'.[56] A slightly more revealing description of him was provided in a report by a British military attaché in Berlin:

> Gen. Ōshima is a typically courteous and polite Japanese officer of undoubted intelligence and considerable personality. The German War Office have a high opinion of his attainments. Unlike many of his countrymen he is a gregarious creature and enjoys society. This is probably mainly due to the fact that he drinks like a fish.[57]

From 1941 onwards, Ōshima would be a frequent correspondent back to his home government. In that year, 75 of his messages, varying in length from one to thirty close-typed pages, appeared as MAGIC decrypts. In 1942, the figure would rise to 100; in 1942, 400; and in 1944, the year of OVERLORD, over 600 of his messages were read by the Allies.[58]

Perhaps the only drawback of Ōshima's prolific communications was his extreme sympathy for the Nazis, which meant that he was not always a completely objective observer of German activity. He was not, however, the only Japanese source providing intelligence to the Allies. The Japanese developed two other machine ciphers using similar principles to PURPLE. The first of these was codenamed JADE. This machine was solved by the US Navy codebreakers at OP-20-G in August 1943. The solution of JADE gave added impetus to the effort to break its close cousin CORAL (also known as JNA20 by the Allies), used by Japanese naval attachés around the world, including those in Berlin and accredited to the French Vichy government. A limited number of decryptions followed containing key intelligence about the German forces in France in 1944.[59]

One of the key users of CORAL, from an Allied point of view, was Vice Admiral Abe Katsuo. Abe was a former chief of Japanese naval intelligence who had been appointed naval attaché in Italy in early 1941. He was reassigned to Germany in spring 1943 as Japanese naval representative on the Tripartite Military Commission and chief of all Japanese naval attachés in Europe.[60] Abe followed German defensive preparations in the west in great detail and faithfully reported back to Tokyo all that he learned. After CORAL was broken in March 1944, the intelligence derived from his reports was so reliable that the cryptanalysts at OP-20-G christened him 'Honest Abe', in a play on the nickname of former US President Abraham Lincoln.[61]

The third system carrying significant intelligence from the Japanese in Europe during 1943 and 1944 was the code used by the Japanese military attachés, JMA. Rather than being a mechanical letter-substitution cipher, this code was book-based and used two-letter 'digraphs'. These letter pairs were written into a grid known as a 'conversion square' in a complex pattern and then transcribed out of the grid in a different order. As a further level of security, these new letters were then replaced with new letters generated by a 'literal additive' process, where letters from a separate table would be combined with the initial cipher text to create a 'super-enciphered' text for transmission.[62] JMA was introduced in 1941, and was tackled by John Tiltman at Bletchley Park in early 1942. He was able to discern the way the code was constructed. This information, combined with a large number of 'depths', allowed him to break into the system.

In June 1942, Tiltman established a Japanese section within his own Military Section at Bletchley to work particularly on JMA. This operated in parallel with the larger Japanese Naval Section.[63] Staff for the new section were taken from recent graduates of Bletchley's six-month rapid Japanese language course, established (again on the initiative of Tiltman) in Bedford in February 1942. Much of the traffic was of little intelligence value: embassy gossip and matters concerning the personal lives of the attachés; however, the material did also contain useful items. And some – such as the description of the Berlin attaché's visit to Normandy in late 1943 – were pure intelligence gold. The role of Japanese intercepts before and during the 1944 campaign has been summed up by American historian Carl Boyd, in his account of the breaking of General Ōshima's messages:

> Earlier in the war MAGIC intelligence was probably never crucial in the ETO [European Theatre of Operations] or used decisively in the operational conduct of the war. But this changed dramatically during the planning for the invasion in the spring [of] 1944 of northwest Europe, Operation Overlord. Ōshima's role became seminal.[64]

The same might be said of a number of the ambassador's diplomatic colleagues.

TRAFFIC ANALYSIS

Finally, a survey of the incoming material exploited by GC&CS would be incomplete without reference to traffic analysis (T/A). In the early years of Bletchley, traffic analysis was rather underappreciated. It was carried on by a variety of disparate sections, with little liaison with the cryptana-lytical teams proper. However, by 1944 this situation had been rectified and T/A was to play a huge part in painting the intelligence picture of the German forces prior to the invasion.

In essence, traffic analysis is very simple. As well as its enciphered message text, every message intercepted by the Y stations possessed a number of other characteristics, such as the frequency on which it was transmitted and the time of day. The distinctive keying styles of enemy wireless operators could also be detected, allowing individual operators to be identified. And the location of the transmitter could be discovered by taking multiple bearings on the transmission – a process known as direction finding (D/F). The enemy operators were also prone to communicating in what was effectively plain language prior to the transmission of cipher text, often using the internationally recognised Q Code, where three-letter groups beginning with Q were used to exchange information (for example, QSA – 'What is my signal strength?'). Lastly, all messages were prefaced by call-signs for the sender and recipient. In German Enigma traffic these were encrypted, typically using a regularly changed three-character alphanumeric code. Careful analysis of the codes used allowed GC&CS to build up its own nearly complete understanding of call-signs early in the war. The Germans abandoned call-signs altogether in late 1944; but for much of the period under consideration here their call-sign system was fairly well understood.[65]

All this information was passed to teams of 'log-readers', whose job it was to try to categorise the messages (without being able to read the actual content), identifying who was communicating with whom and when. This process was rarely referred to at the time as 'traffic analysis'; more commonly it was known as 'log-reading' or 'wireless telegraphy intelligence'. In the early years of the war, efforts at log-reading were dispersed across a number of organisations, chief among these being No. 6 Intelligence School (6IS), based at the Y station at Beaumanor. There was also relatively little appreciation among the cryptanalytical departments of GC&CS of its usefulness. Over time, however, as the number of German networks and keys being intercepted proliferated and the decryption task became ever more complex, the value of T/A became more apparent. One of the early converts was Gordon Welchman, head of Hut 6, who observed in July 1941:

It may eventually be possible to work out the entire battle order of the enemy from a study of the callsigns, provided that we have broken enough traffic to give the callsigns used by each unit on some days in the past ... This callsign development revolutionises our ideas about what is worth breaking.[66]

As a result, and partly at Welchman's instigation, most of the functions of 6IS were moved to Bletchley Park in May 1942. The organisation was further rationalised in late 1943 and integrated with Hut 6. Later, in February 1944, the department adopted the title SIXTA, which it retained for the remainder of the war.[67]

SIXTA veteran James Thirsk described the nature of the work. The log-readers were issued with pro-forma sheets on which they would draw out diagrammatically each week the networks they had identified. For each enemy station or call-sign, lines and arrows showed the direction of communications and the volume in each direction. The resulting patterns reflected the structure of the German command networks. Two common types were the 'Star' (*Stern* in German), where a central HQ node had links radiating out to subsidiary stations, and the 'Circle' (*Kreis*), where a series of stations of broadly equal status were linked in a loop.[68] The diagrams were sent to the Fusion Room in Hut 6, where they were compared with decryptions of the traffic concerned, and further intelligence inferences were drawn. Somewhat unhelpfully (but in keeping with the general compartmentalisation at Bletchley), the log-readers were not told that any of the traffic was actually being deciphered and read. Only in January 1943 was it decided that they could be let in on the 'big secret', and Gordon Welchman was able to brief the log-readers on the success of the decryption operation. James Thirsk described the experience of this revelation: 'It was a memorable day for all of us, since our log-reading had been a boring occupation. Now we had a new zest for the work, with access to a wealth of information about the German networks we were studying.'[69]

By the time of D-Day the two sections – SIXTA and Hut 6 – had become highly integrated, and the various log-readers' diagrams were collated on large wall charts, where the separate 'Stars' were linked together to produce a schematic map of the whole of the enemy communications network. These schematics were known as 'Morrison Walls', after their inventor and the head of the group responsible for them, Major Morrison (see Plate 6). The process was further streamlined by the creation in November 1943 of a 'D/F exchange' in SIXTA, allowing the T/A teams to task the remote direction-finding stations with concentrating on particular enemy stations, in order to pinpoint their geographical locations.[70]

Traffic analysis was extremely successful in mapping the order of battle of German signals units and, by inference, their parent formations. Prior to the invasion, little operational traffic was sent by the German army by wireless. But it did hold regular anti-invasion signals exercises, where all the links in a particular network would switch on and send dummy communications. Monitoring of these exercises revealed a huge amount about the German communications arrangements. A second key function of T/A was to identify patterns and routines in the enemy's messages. While routine daily signals might not hold much intelligence information, their stereotypical character made them ideal for developing cribs – predictable phrases used in message content – for codebreaking. James Thirsk again:

> We were asked by the cryptanalysts to look out for messages at regular times in the mornings or evenings. These were usually situation reports, which often had standard opening phrases like 'Morgenmeldung' (morning report) in cipher. This could help the cryptanalysts to decrypt the message by providing a crib.[71]

Finally, once a key had been found, simply being able to identify and list which messages were likely to have been sent using that key was vital to efficient decryption. The T/A log-readers were thus an essential and (by 1944) integral part of what Frank Birch described as the 'Army Air Force German Enigma Complex'. By the summer of 1944, SIXTA employed 348 staff.[72]

*

The description above is of necessity brief, and has not touched on the many 'low-level' codes and ciphers that were being attacked by Bletchley Park during 1944. In particular, a huge effort was made against Luftwaffe 'medium-grade' ciphers – both those used in the air and those on the ground. Much of this focused on the German air defences and night fighter control, and was intended to assist the strategic bombing campaign over Germany. However, it also informed the OVERLORD planning process. Nor have we looked in much detail at the ciphers used by the German intelligence services – these will be examined more thoroughly later. However, the scale and success of the operation against the various German code and cipher systems (as well as against those of their allies) is evident. It now remains to see how all of this incoming data could be converted into useful intelligence, and then disseminated to those who could use it.

CHAPTER THREE

OUTGOING INTELLIGENCE

A t the start of 1942, Bletchley Park's Hut 3 was not a happy place. It was responsible for distributing intelligence derived from German army and air force Enigma messages, yet it was presided over by a naval officer, Lieutenant Commander Malcolm Saunders, one of its founding members. Supposedly acting as advisers to Saunders were two men – Wing Commander 'Harry' Humphreys from the RAF and Major Curtis from the army. These two men were not keen on the hut engaging in joint operations; instead, they felt that German air force traffic should be the preserve of Humphreys, and German army traffic the domain of Curtis. Both were fiercely protective of the partisan interests of their respective ministries and sought to outflank Saunders and subvert his authority as head of the hut. They also scorned the work of the civilian watchkeepers in the hut on the grounds that they were not formally trained intelligence officers. By late 1941, the tension had reached breaking point.

In early 1942, the Air Ministry sent someone to investigate the problem. The man chosen was Squadron Leader Eric Jones, who was neither a career military man nor an intelligence officer. He did not even speak German. In the twenty years since leaving school (at the age of fifteen) he had worked first in his family's textile business in Macclesfield, and then later in his own textile agency. He only gave up his business interests in 1940 to enlist as a reservist in the RAF, taking up a post in Air Ministry Intelligence. Thus, he knew a lot about how to run a business – and how to manage people. Jones produced a report on the problems in Hut 3 which so impressed the head of Bletchley Park, Edward Travis, that in 1943 Jones was promoted to group captain and placed in charge of the hut.

The skills that Jones brought with him in management and organisation signalled a revolution in Hut 3. A modest man who respected the skills of his colleagues and subordinates, he was very well liked, and would go on to be head of GCHQ after the war. Peter Calvocoressi, who worked for Jones in Hut 3, described him:

> He was unlike other senior people in the Hut, neither don nor schoolmaster, neither professional man nor intellectual. He came from the north Midlands where he was believed to have had something to do with biscuits [sic]. He respected and probably admired the intellectual qualities of his subordinates, but was not intimidated by them and showed that since whether they approved or not, he had been appointed to govern them, he would do so.[1]

As Jones was not a 'university man', the intellectual snobberies of Bletchley Park worked against him. As the GCHQ website observes, 'some senior colleagues, at Bletchley and beyond, referred to him, somewhat sniffily, as "the Manchester Businessman". It was not meant to be complimentary.'[2] However, he was a success among those of whom he was in charge. As Ralph Bennett put it, under his 'enlightened despotism'[3] the flow of intelligence out to battlefield commanders would become a well-regulated and highly productive machine.

Hut 3 would come to lie at the heart of Bletchley Park's support for the Normandy invasion, and much of that success was due to the skilful leadership of Eric Jones, the textile agent from Macclesfield. A tribute to Jones's success as a leader can be found in the 'History' of the hut, which records the morale of the organisation:

Here over five hundred and fifty individuals, of widely differing ages, gifts, and characters, men and women, service and civilian, British and American, formed with all their variety one welded whole; working – often overworking – together, year by year, with unpretentious skill and pertinacity, gaiety and irony, and with less time wasted in intrigue than one could easily have thought possible in this too human world.[4]

*

In the previous two chapters we examined exactly what data, in the form of intercepted signals, was flowing into Bletchley Park, and in what quantities. We also looked at how the encrypted portions of this material were deciphered and their contents extracted in plain language. The next obvious questions are: where did all this data go? And what was done with it? The traditional answers have tended to be that the information contained within the decrypted messages was redrafted and sent out to government ministries and field commands as ULTRA. However, this was only the tip of the very large iceberg of Bletchley's intelligence effort before D-Day. In addition to this daily, urgent flow of information to commands, a much longer-term and deeper intelligence analysis operation was being carried on – and Hut 3 lay at the heart of it.

AN INTELLIGENCE AGENCY IN ITS OWN RIGHT

As with so much of the GC&CS organisation, the origins of Hut 3 were modest and relatively informal. When Luftwaffe Enigma messages first started to be broken successfully, in January 1940, a team was created to read, translate and pass on the contents of the decrypts to the relevant government ministries. This became known officially as the German Army and Air Force Enigma Reporting Section, but was soon known more commonly as 'Hut 3'. This first building was indeed a small hut (now demolished) on the lawn immediately to the north-east of Bletchley Park mansion. The section would subsequently move from there to a new, larger 'Hut 3' farther from the mansion; and finally, in February

1943, to still more spacious accommodation in Block D. A veteran described the rather forbidding aspects of this new building after life in the huts:

> We then moved from Hut 3 into this great enormous building which had a long corridor where we all had to hang our coats, it was very damp and smelt of raincoats. The place was very dark with the black-out, we kept the windows closed so as not to let out even a peep of light and the electric light didn't give very good illumination at all. There was no romance in it, I liked the old huts.[5]

By 1944, Hut 3 occupied the six westernmost spurs in Block D – about half of the block (the eastern end being filled by Huts 6 and 8, and parts of SIXTA).

The section started off with a team of just four officers – one from each armed service and one from the Foreign Office – supported by three or four female clerk-typists. Despite the fact that virtually all the material being decrypted originated with the Luftwaffe, the section was provided with an RAF officer who did not speak German, which cannot have been an ideal arrangement.[6] The official function of the hut was 'to translate and annotate high grade German signals (Enigma and non-Morse), and to report the results to Ministries and Commands in the field'.[7] What was both controversial and 'a revolutionary innovation' was that the team took it upon themselves not simply to pass on the decrypted material *en bloc*, but to sift it for both value and urgency. The material judged most urgent would be passed to the relevant ministry by teleprinter; the bulk of the remainder by bag; and some – deemed worthless – not passed on at all. As GCHQ's 'History of Hut Three' comments: 'The Hut 3 party thus became the judges of the Intelligence value of the messages.'[8] This move was very unpopular with the Air Ministry in particular, which had a very narrow concept of Bletchley's role as a decryption – not an intelligence – agency; however, it was eventually to lose this battle, and GC&CS continued to sift and categorise material.

The sorting process was quite simple. As traffic was received, it was sorted into 'piles'. Pile 1 required urgent translation and redrafting for transmission to ministries as soon as possible. Pile 2 could wait four to eight hours before following the same route. Pile 3 would be processed and sent by bag within twenty-four hours. Pile 4 was 'Quatsch' (the German word for 'nonsense'), which would be examined only when all the other piles were empty. It was later estimated that up to 40 per cent of the decrypts arriving from Hut 6 ended up on Pile 4 because of corruptions in transmission and decryption, because their content, taken out of context, could not be understood, or simply because they didn't say anything very interesting.[9] From these relatively simple systems, Hut 3 would grow into an organisation of over 500 people, carrying on a wide variety of intelligence analysis functions and producing an equally wide range of product, from urgent teleprints to multi-page long-term assessment reports. This is perhaps one of the least well understood parts of Bletchley, but was undoubtedly one of the most important, lifting GC&CS from the position of merely a decryption and translation service to the status of what would be considered in more modern terms an 'intelligence agency' in its own right.

The various departments within Hut 3 can be seen most clearly if we follow the path of a message through the hut.[10] The first room encountered was the Reception Point. This was served by a conveyor belt at ceiling height from Hut 6 (at the other end of Block D), which brought in decrypted messages.

The messages were sorted and logged before passing through a hatch into the 'watch'. This was the heart of the hut. Here the 'Number 1' of the watch would skim-read the incoming material and distribute it to his watchkeepers, who would perform the initial translation and 'emendation' of the message (resolving corruptions, elucidating abbreviations and so on).

The English translation would then be passed to the air and military advisers, whose job was to determine what should be done with the message and, if necessary, draft an outgoing signal, to be teleprinted out to a ministry or command. This process was overseen by a duty officer, who occupied an adjacent office and was responsible for the final verification of the content of these outgoing signals.

Once he was happy, the signals were passed to a dedicated Hut 3 teleprinter room, where they could be sent to SIS at Broadway Buildings or to the various ministries. These links could be made in plain language; but if material was to be sent further afield – to commands overseas – it was first passed to the hut's own cipher office, where the information could be re-encrypted before transmission.

Each of the advisers was part of a larger section that related to their particular arm of service: thus there was an Air Section (3A), a Military Section (3M) and a small Naval Section (3N). Although Hut 3 was principally concerned with the battle on land and in the air, a certain proportion of material derived from naval traffic was relevant to the land war, and so a few naval personnel were useful. This had been particularly significant earlier in the war, as Bletchley Park's ability to read Italian naval ciphers had made it possible to monitor (and attack) the flow of supplies to North Africa, thus impacting on the land battle in the desert. The D-Day invasion would, of course, also be an amphibious operation, with an enormous and vital naval component, and so this additional expertise was crucial to the work of the hut.[11] Various other specialist advisers were also present; for example, such was the volume of SS traffic intercepted that full-time specialists were appointed to deal with that material.[12]

These sections backed up the work of the watchkeeping advisers, and also handled liaison with their respective ministries, dealing with inquiries and making sure that the flow of information remained smooth. Also (and contrary to some accounts of Hut 3), the 'HQ' section for each service was charged with keeping up to date with the current operations of its service and with future plans. As 'The History of Hut Three' put it:

The service of information from Hut 3 to ministries and (especially) to commands could only be operated with maximum efficiency if

Hut 3 was aware, at any rate in outline, of current Allied plans (including deception-plans) and of any subjects to which an exceptional amount of attention was being paid, since only then could the comparative importance and urgency of the various items be assessed.[13]

It was also policy that any appreciations or summaries produced by the ministries that included ULTRA intelligence were copied back to Bletchley. This meant that not only could Hut 3 follow the thinking of the ministries, but it could also keep an eye on how its material was being interpreted and distributed. The 3M HQ would also produce weekly summaries for internal circulation within the hut; these provided a precis of the battlefield situation, as well as upcoming operations and priorities, so everyone knew where the focus of their efforts should lie.[14]

After the watches had carried out the immediate task of reporting urgent information, copies of the messages were passed on to the 'backroom' parts of Hut 3. Perhaps the most important of these were the Air and Military Indexes, which occupied two large rooms; there was also a smaller Naval Index. These served as the 'memory' of the hut. Each message was scrutinised for any items of useful intelligence – names, places, military units, types of equipment – and everything was recorded on small index cards. Thus the significance of any new fact could be checked against previous information, and the larger intelligence picture assembled. For example, if a message indicated that a particular German officer was associated with a particular unit, a card would be created under his name, recording his association with that unit; but the card for that unit would also be updated with a reference to him, and a geographical place-name card might be annotated to show where he was. Thus huge numbers of cards had to be created, as a single intelligence snippet might need to be recorded in four or five different places; but the result was a vast store of readily accessible information – and, more importantly, a system for recording the inferences and connections that linked all the individual facts into a coherent whole.

The system was not without its faults. For example, when the indexes were first begun, some information was recorded on differently sized cards. Later, when the system was reorganised and card sets were amalgamated, this caused problems. However, by and large the indexes worked. This was mostly thanks to the quality of the indexers – generally women, typically chosen from university graduates with a good knowledge of German and (perhaps equally importantly) with legible handwriting. Their role was to judge what needed to be recorded on which card from each incoming message, and to answer inquiries from the watch and from other members of the hut. Such was the complexity of the system that it was not possible for advisers themselves to look up information: inquiries had to be routed through one of the indexers. Many of these women became expert in the material they were handling, and several were promoted to fully fledged intelligence positions as the hut grew.[15]

One such indexer was Doreen Tabor, who was directed to the Foreign Office in 1941, after completing a degree in French and German at Victoria University in Manchester. She went on to the Air Index in Hut 3, under its then head, Squadron Leader Reginald Cullingham, known as 'Cully':

Cully introduced me to my work, which was on the Air Index. I was told how shift work was organised, with five girls per shift, three shifts in the day and one shift spare for holidays. I was allocated to a shift and went on from there. The Air Index was a magnificent work. Cully had a very beautiful flowing hand and he had set up the index because he used to work for Kelly's Directory [a pre-war directory of businesses, a bit like the later Yellow Pages] ...

Once I went to Cully and said 'I'm sorry Mr Cullingham I just don't know anything about the German Air force, and here I am being asked to do aircraft markings and things like that, I really must have somebody to tell me.' He just smiled and he told me. He didn't say 'I'm too busy now' or 'So and so will let you know'. He did it himself kindly and not in a hurry, you would think he'd nothing else to do, which I thought was wonderful man management.[16]

Despite her early ignorance, Doreen was able to master the Air Index sufficiently well for her to be promoted to head the section in 1942. Her account describes how she several times complained to management that frequent promotions of her 'best people' were affecting the efficiency of the section, but the new recruits who arrived were generally of good quality:

> They then started sending recent graduates to me from the Scottish, Irish and English universities, but not Oxford or Cambridge. They were very good girls, not at all the sort of thing you read about in the early days when there were many debs, one or two of whom I met, but the index was hard, serious work. I was very fond of these new girls; they were very young and made me feel very old at the age of 23.[17]

Much has been made of the electro-mechanical devices employed at Bletchley (the bombes and Colossus, for example) and their contribution to the codebreaking process. But, from the point of view of absorbing, storing, retrieving and processing data in large quantities, it could be argued that the legacy of the indexes is just as important for modern knowledge-based organisations. And their work was all done by hand, with pencils, cards – and a great deal of patience and expertise.

Behind the service sections of Hut 3 and their indexes was 3G, a multi-service, long-term research section. It consisted of small teams that concentrated on developing a detailed understanding of particular intelligence problems. The tasks were many and varied. For example, one team worked on the interpretation of German cover names. It was commonplace for intercepted messages to use codewords to disguise units, place names and pieces of equipment. If these references were collated over time, it was often possible to identify by inference which town (for example) a particular cover name referred to – or which tank or gun, or wireless set. Similarly, enemy supply or unit-strength reports were often intercepted in highly abbreviated form, the messages often consisting simply of numbers, in lettered columns. These 'pro-formas' were dealt with by a dedicated team. Geographical information and such apparently mundane items as railway movements (in fact, fundamental to military operations) were also closely studied. Often these tasks were undertaken more in hope than expectation, but surprising discoveries were sometimes made. Earlier in the war, the study of German railway movements had given GC&CS clear hints (later shown to be correct) of the upcoming German invasion of Russia in June 1941.[18]

It was this scrutiny of tiny details over time which often 'paid dividends' in terms of intelligence.[19] Indeed, the authors of the hut's 'History' suggested that in many ways this was the more important of Hut 3's activities:

> Indeed, one may say without serious error that much of the red-hot tactical Intelligence could have been jettisoned without irreparable harm: but the long-term things, nearly always less spectacular, often individually very trivial, were yet indispensable and unique in the history of Intelligence.[20]

The 'History' went on to suggest that the material produced by Bletchley was mostly used for advance planning, rather than as a source of up-to-the-minute tactical intelligence:

> As the war progressed, in particular from ALAMEIN onwards, it became ever clearer that Ultra Military Intelligence was most valuable in the planning periods between battle rather than during the battles themselves. This meant that the [military adviser] besides being a master of quick decisions in time of battle, had to be a master of details, in particular those that might give clues to intentions.[21]

As we shall see, this was particularly true of the Normandy campaign. Indeed, it could be said that Bletchley Park's most significant contribution to that operation was in the eighteen months before the first troops landed, rather than once they were on the battlefield (at which point tactical SIGINT, developed locally by units in France, became more important). The importance of FISH in developing this advance picture of the enemy is also relevant here, as the nature of the material and the complexities of its decryption meant that it was 'seldom urgent or operationally red-hot, but was often of great strategic importance'.[22] Thus the 'back rooms', just as much as the watch, were fundamental in Bletchley's contribution to OVERLORD.

The final large section within Hut 3 was 3L (Liaison). This section was led by Squadron Leader (later Wing Commander) Oscar Oeser. Born in Pretoria, South Africa, to German parents, he was an unlikely candidate for employment at Bletchley; remarkably, his middle name was Adolph. By the start of the war he had acquired a degree in physics in South Africa and a PhD in psychology from Trinity College, Cambridge, as well as a further DPhil from Marburg University in Germany.[23] Perhaps it was his Trinity contacts that brought him to Bletchley Park in 1940, as a reserve officer in the RAF, working in Hut 3, within Section 3A.

Oeser was responsible for studying the overall flow of intercepts from Hut 6, and latterly from the FISH Subsection. He and his team performed statistical analyses on these messages and were able to determine which keys and frequencies were most productive in terms of intelligence at any particular time. This was important, because the volume of material being broadcast by the Germans always outstripped the capacity of GC&CS and the Y Service to intercept it. Similarly, once the material was received at Bletchley, time on the bombe machines was also limited, and so decryption priorities had to be established. Oeser set up links to the other teams, in particular Hut 6 and SIXTA, as well as to the Y Service and the ministries in London. He was then able to prioritise the efforts of all these different operations to bring in the maximum useful intelligence to Hut 3. Regular contacts with the ministries also ensured that he knew which operations were forthcoming and what intelligence questions were taxing the ministry intelligence teams at any particular time. He held daily meetings with Hut 6 to establish bombe priorities, and after November 1943 did the same with Knockholt and the FISH Subsection.[24] Weekly lists of priority Enigma keys were also produced. In 1944, knowing that the invasion of Europe was imminent, Oeser gradually re-tasked the Y stations onto western Enigma keys as the year progressed and, on 1 June as the invasion fleet sailed, released a specific list of stations to be listened to most closely.[25] This is another example of the intelligence 'feedback loop' which existed between Bletchley and its customers and suppliers, and which allowed the whole SIGINT process to operate with maximum efficiency.

Bletchley's relationship with its customers also grew closer in the run-up to OVERLORD. Previous experience in the Mediterranean during 1942 and 1943 had shown that greater coordination was required between those planning future operations and those developing intelligence for them. When the planning body for D-Day – COSSAC (standing for 'Chief of Staff to Supreme Allied Commander') – was established, this was considered early on. In May 1943, the Y Board, which was responsible for the management of SIGINT, suggested that it should be directly represented on COSSAC. At that time, it was felt that this would risk compromising the security of the codebreaking effort. Later, however, this opinion changed. When COSSAC merged with SHAEF (Supreme Headquarters Allied Expeditionary Force – the headquarters body that would command the actual operation) in January 1944, meetings started to be held between GC&CS and the director of military intelligence at SHAEF. At these meetings, the operational planners were able to give the codebreakers a full brief on the proposed operation, and then there was discussion on how best SIGINT could support it. Constant close liaison continued between Bletchley and SHAEF up to the invasion. This culminated in May with a visit to Bletchley Park by the intelligence staff of 21st Army Group to present a map briefing on the operation, including phase lines and daily objectives. Hut 3 could not have been better informed of its customers' intentions.[26]

FEEDING THE MILITARY HIERARCHY

Not only were ULTRA signals to commands only a portion of the output of Bletchley, the forms in which the intelligence was actually distributed also varied hugely – and each of the dissemination channels had an impact on the planning and execution of OVERLORD in different, inter-connected ways.

Starting 'at the top', Hut 3 delivered some of its intelligence daily, direct to the prime minister. Winston Churchill had always been a keen consumer of intelligence material, ever since the First World War, when, as first lord of the admiralty, he had access to the SIGINT product of the navy's codebreakers; his interest continued in the inter-war period.[27] When he became prime minister and was made aware of the work of GC&CS, Churchill resumed his demands for intelligence. In September 1940, Churchill's personal assistant, Desmond Morton, wrote to 'C', the chief of SIS (now Colonel Stewart Menzies, Admiral Sinclair having died in 1939): 'I have been personally directed by the Prime minister to inform you that he wishes you to send him daily all the ENIGMA messages.'[28]

In this respect, the prime minister was a little behind the times – there was no way an individual could read all the Enigma decrypted every day, even in 1940. He was, however, appeased by the production of 'Headlines', which were sent to him each morning from SIS. From that time on, a system was instituted whereby a despatch box would be delivered to him daily from 'C' containing a precis of recent intelligence and, where appropriate, copies of messages. Menzies is quoted as saying: '[A red box] was deposited on the [PM's] bed each morning, within it all relevant reports and intercepts obtained by GC&CS over the previous 24 hours.' (Morton suggests that the box was actually placed on Churchill's desk, rather than on his bed; but either way the information was made available.) These boxes typically contained a series of items: a covering note from 'C' himself and summaries of German army and air traffic, plus individual items of traffic where relevant. A similar set of 'Naval Headlines' (from Naval Section in Hut 4) and a sample of diplomatic cable intercepts (known from the colour of the file as 'Blue Jackets' or 'BJs') were also included.[29]

'Hut 3 Headlines', copies of which are in the Bletchley Park archives, listed the messages considered most important in the day's traffic, and corresponded to the individual messages passed to the prime minister in his box. Not being included in the files actually passed to Churchill, the exact purpose of these 'Headlines' is not clear; but they formed part of the process whereby Hut 3 suggested to SIS in London what material might be included for the prime minister. Each issue of 'Hut 3 Headlines' consisted of a list of sample messages, the serial number of each message and a further distillation of its original contents, and included times and dates. So, in 1941, between four and six 'Headlines' were generated each day, each with a series of message summaries. It is possible that they were produced in line with shift changes in Hut 3. By late 1942, the pattern had changed: individual 'Headlines' were generated each time a significant piece of intelligence data was acquired. As a result, some 'Headlines' could be separated by as little as an hour; in one period of nine days, 300 'Headlines' were issued. They were compiled by Hut 3 staff, typically by the air and military advisers, but after March 1942, when duty officers were appointed in Hut 3, it was their responsibility to compile the 'Headlines';[30] whoever carried out the work would place their initials at the end of the sheet, meaning the compilers could potentially be identified.

Churchill came to rely heavily on the reports from 'C', and as a result a close relationship developed between the two men.[31] The prime minister liked to attend meetings being better briefed than his subordinates, and SIGINT was one way to do that. Unfortunately, Churchill's understanding of the material was not always very nuanced: he tended to use it as a stick with which to beat his generals, rather than acknowledging the often vague and complex intelligence it actually represented.[32] Nonetheless, keeping up a steady flow of information to the prime minister was one of the key responsibilities of Hut 3.

The next most senior rungs of the military hierarchy serviced by Hut 3 were the Air Ministry and the War Office (and occasionally the

Admiralty). As we saw earlier, perhaps 60 per cent of the whole daily volume of decrypted traffic eventually made its way to the ministries, either by urgent teleprint, by slower daily teleprint service or by bag.[33] Hundreds of messages a day were passed on. Initially, an attempt was made to produce a coherent summary of the material, and short descriptions of individual messages were provided in a typed report, divided into sections relating to different theatres of battle, and to army, air and naval activity. However, by 1944 pressure on the hut meant that this was not always possible.

The daily files surviving in the National Archives typically each have three summary reports, corresponding to the watches in the hut; but also a number of 'undigested' messages attached, for which there was no time to prepare a summary. The files held at Kew appear to be the Bletchley Park copies of this material, for internal use rather than circulation, as each file has a front page giving a detailed list of the frequencies and keys used to send each of the messages.[34] For recipients, however, the fiction was maintained throughout the war that the 'source' was one or more human agents working within the German military hierarchy. Reports derived from SIGINT obtained at Bletchley were given the same serial number prefix 'CX' as were SIS reports released to other government departments which contained information gained from human agents. Plausible descriptions were added to the messages regarding how they had been obtained. For example, a transcript of one of *Generalfeldmarschall* von Rundstedt's periodic appreciations of the situation in the west, written on 21 March 1944, appears in the file with the words 'Source has acquired an incomplete copy of a document dated 21/3 addressed to C.-in-C. South West'. The transcription continues, with breaks in interception or decryption noted:

> The enemy harassing effort against airfields continued. However in this connection the scale of effort was (WORD ILLEGIBLE) than before ... (SMUDGE) night attacks were made on industrial and supply factories ...[35]

It is remarkable just how 'smudged' German secret documents seemed to become in their journey through GC&CS. A similar C-in-C appreciation from 25 June 1944 carries the note:

> Source has now seen the final portion of this document, some lines at its beginning had however been torn away. The signature on the document was C.-in-C. West.[36]

Other conventions included 'Found in the file of ...' or 'Marked with the stamp of ...'[37] By 1944, it is questionable how many people at the ministries remained fooled by these deceptions, but the pretence was maintained and no reference was ever made outside Bletchley to SIGINT; the only term ever used was the wonderfully uninformative 'Source'. The actual source of both of these C-in-C appreciations is clear, however, as the Bletchley file copies of both are marked in pencil at the bottom 'BREAM', indicating that they originated on the FISH link to *Generalfeldmarschall* Kesselring's headquarters in Italy.

The final, and most widely known, output from Hut 3 was, of course, messages to commanders in the field. However, it is worth emphasising that this represented only a small portion of the decrypted material. In the 211 days between 1 January 1944 and the end of the Normandy campaign, 25,500 messages were forwarded as ULTRA to ministries and commanders – an average of 120 a day.

The mismatch here is obvious: as we saw above, up to 5,000 incoming Enigma messages were successfully decrypted each day (plus a smaller number of FISH), and yet only around 120 went out. Clearly only a small fraction of the incoming material was considered sufficiently time-sensitive to be forwarded to commanders as urgent ULTRA.

The question also arose of how this material could be delivered in secret to the commanders and how its circulation at the receiver's end could be controlled so that it did not fall into the wrong hands or get misused. Furthermore, not only were many of the recipients overseas, but they were also potentially mobile, as their headquarters followed the ebb and flow of battle. At first, decrypted messages were passed via SIS to the relevant ministries' intelligence sections, and this information was then passed on to field commanders. This system was flawed for several reasons: first – and the problem of greatest concern to Bletchley Park – was that this placed the security of the traffic in the hands of a long and potentially unreliable signals chain: material could be lost, could fall into the wrong hands or become available to those who were unaware of its sensitivity. The second problem was simply one of efficiency: conveying information to battlefield headquarters by this circuitous route introduced a significant delay.

In 1940, SIS already had access to its own wireless network, established before the war to allow clandestine communication between SIS personnel in Europe (most of whom were operating under diplomatic cover as 'Passport Control Officers' in various UK embassies and consulates) and the home base at Broadway Buildings in London. This operation, which formed part of SIS Section VIII, was moved briefly to Bletchley Park in 1939, before becoming permanently established at nearby Whaddon Hall at the start of 1940 (see above).

It was around this time that Frederick Winterbotham became involved in the story. Winterbotham was a former Royal Flying Corps pilot who, after being shot down in 1917, learned German as a prisoner of war. After the war, he joined SIS as air adviser to 'C' – at that time Admiral Sinclair. He also spent much of the 1930s successfully ingratiating himself with a number of senior Nazis in the course of a series of semi-official visits to Germany, learning in the process a good deal that was of interest to British intelligence about German plans for the Luftwaffe. He described his own part in the establishment of the system for the distribution of signals intelligence in his book *The Ultra Secret*, published in 1974. According to Winterbotham, he made a pitch to Stewart Menzies (who would replace Sinclair as 'C' in 1939) that suitably trained officers should be placed at each headquarters, and that signals intelligence should be passed to them direct over SIS's own wireless network. These officers would then control the security of the material, showing it only to the appropriate senior officers and then destroying it. As most of the intercepted material at that time was from Luftwaffe networks, Winterbotham suggested that these officers should be selected from his own service, the RAF.[38]

Winterbotham also claimed to have invented the specific security classification for the material: 'ULTRA SECRET' or simply 'ULTRA'. Initially this term had quite a narrow meaning, referring only to the messages sent out to commands over the SIS network; however, in due course it would broaden into a cover term for all SIGINT produced by GC&CS. This version of events has been contradicted by Patrick Beesly, who during the same period was working in the Admiralty Operational Intelligence Centre (OIC) in Whitehall. He attributed the name ULTRA to one of his OIC colleagues, one Commander Colpoys, who 'suggested that they be given the designation Ultra, about the only Latin he could remember'. Beesly also described the more specific usage of the term by the navy:

> The word Ultra has now come to be used in a generic sense for all information available to the British in the last war derived from cryptanalysis, whatever the nation or service of origin and whatever form it took. This usage is incorrect and in the Navy, at least, it was only applied to outgoing signals and documents as a security grading and the actual information itself was always referred to as 'special Intelligence' or 'Z' because this letter was used as a prefix in the telex messages from [Bletchley Park].[39]

Whatever the truth of the matter, ULTRA was born at around this time, as the first sporadic decryptions started to flow from Bletchley Park.

Winterbotham went on to describe how, during the campaign in France in the summer of 1940, he provided units to the headquarters both of Lord Gort, commander-in-chief of the British Expeditionary Force, and of Air Vice Marshal Barratt, commander of the RAF Advanced Air Striking Force in France. Both units were provided with a liaison officer, chosen by Winterbotham from among his 'trusted personal friends' in the RAF, along with a wireless unit and two or three RAF cipher sergeants.[40]

It is possible that this was an informal arrangement put in place by SIS, since, according to the internal history written by GC&CS at the end of the war, material was still flowing to France in 1940 via the service ministries, and it was not until later that a specialist arrangement was instituted:

> A lesson had been learnt from the battle of France when information from GC&CS passed to GHQ [General Headquarters] through the ordinary service signals channels. These had failed to provide a satisfactory service when open warfare and the disruption of the front had occurred. It was decided that for future campaigns special signal and cipher units, responsible to and in direct contact with GC&CS through SIS should be established.[41]

Either way, the first official unit was created in April 1941. This was Special Signals Unit (SSU) No. 1, and it was despatched to Egypt, where hitherto ULTRA had been handled by the Combined Bureau Middle East, an offshoot of the Bletchley Park codebreaking operation. SSU No. 1 was commanded by Major J.K. Macfarlan, with a staff of one army and one RAF officer, and 36 mixed army and air force signallers and cipher clerks. These were supported by six drivers, with four wireless telegraphy (W/T) vans, a staff car and a couple of motorcycles. The unit was based initially at Abbassia near Cairo, and had two outstations, one serving the British headquarters in Jerusalem and one at Bagush, supporting the headquarters of Eighth Army and the Air Headquarters Western Desert. The former was closed fairly rapidly but the one at Bagush would stay open, following the Eighth Army across Africa and on into Italy, right up to 1945.[42]

Decrypted messages were selected by Hut 3 to be sent directly to this unit via a dedicated wireless connection through the SIS station at Whaddon Hall. Typically, the messages were re-enciphered using a one-time pad, which was one of the most secure cipher systems available; however, after 1942 and the increase in traffic, Typex cipher machines were also allocated to the units. The signals were teleprinted to Whaddon, before being transmitted onward by wireless. The surviving teleprinted copies reveal that, as the number of stations increased through the war, so the list of recipients for each individual message grew longer.

The structure of the organisation was later further refined, with each unit divided into a Special Communications Unit (SCU), responsible for the practicalities of signalling, operating the wireless sets and for transport of the unit as a whole, and a Special Liaison Unit (SLU), responsible for the decryption of incoming messages and their secure circulation to the appropriate officers. It was also possible for the SLUs and their contacts to send questions back to Hut 3 via the same route; but the balance of traffic was 80 per cent outbound, with relatively few returning messages.[43]

By the time of OVERLORD, the SCU/SLU system had become a tried-and-tested means of delivering ULTRA to field commanders. Intercepted traffic had been delivered successfully throughout the campaign in North Africa, as well as through the invasions of Sicily and mainland Italy. The direct service from Hut 3 had also been extended to US Army and USAAF commanders during 1943. This was a significant development, as it would have been perfectly possible for the US Army, once it had 'boots on the ground' in North Africa in 1942 and in Italy in 1943, to set up its own strategic SIGINT operation. However, the climate of cooperation between the Allies was such that a service to US commanders was established on exactly the same basis as to their British colleagues. This would continue during OVERLORD and beyond.

With the invasion being planned, it was clear that a number of SCU/SLU units would be needed for the invading forces, and a special organisation – SLU8 – was set up at Hamilton Terrace, in St John's Wood, London. This remained the headquarters of the unit. A series of outstations was set up with the various ULTRA customers involved in OVERLORD.

By June 1944, nearly all the component formations at Army level and above had been supplied with an SLU. Thus, in addition to the supreme commander at SHAEF, Montgomery's 21st Army Group had one, as did his two subordinate armies, the British Second and the First United States Army. Subsequently the Third United States Army (under General Patton) and the First Canadian Army were also equipped with an SLU.

The air force headquarters attached to each of these formations had an SLU of its own. For the first six months of 1944, all these stations remained in the UK and were served by teleprinter links direct from Hut 3; but, from the outset, each was provided with a wireless-equipped SCU, in anticipation of them moving overseas after the invasion. The staff of the SCUs were kept in training by the delivery of dummy traffic, code-named 'Chocolate'.[44] Several operators later recalled sending messages to chocolate-themed recipient call-signs such as 'Fry', 'Cadbury', 'Terry' and 'Rowntree', unaware that the ciphered groups they were transmitting were actually meaningless.[45] This was also a security measure, as it produced a steady volume of traffic; when the dummy messages were replaced by 'real' messages, there would be no detectable spike in signals traffic. In May, as the planning sections of SHAEF at Norfolk House were closed down, its SCU staff moved to the headquarters of the Allied Naval Commander Expeditionary Force (ANCXF), Admiral Ramsay, in Portsmouth. A total of fifteen stations were open by the time of the invasion; of these, seven would move to France within six weeks of the landings.[46] The first unit to land in France, on 7 June, was the SCU/SLU attached to the British Second Army and the RAF's 83 Group. This unit supported Montgomery's forward headquarters for the first month of the battle. Non-British Allied commanders were equally well served: the station for the First US Army arrived at Omaha Beach on 10 June, followed in early July by a station supporting the Canadian First Army.[47]

Despite their close proximity to the headquarters that they served, a deliberate distance was maintained between the SCU/SLU teams and their host headquarters. It was important that local intelligence staff (or anyone else, for that matter) should not interfere in the work of the teams or in their security arrangements. The need to keep their communication lines clear for ULTRA meant that they firmly resisted any effort to encroach on their resources, to send messages on their networks on behalf of other units, or to borrow or steal personnel and equipment. It was firmly emphasised to all 'indoctrinated recipients' (the term used to describe those individuals who had been let in on the secret of Bletchley Park) that: 'The [officer commanding] SCU is subordinate and responsible direct to A.I.1(c) in London, representing "C" and the Directors of Intelligence for all administration and operations of his unit.'[48]

This principle was jealously defended by the commanders of SCUs, despite the fact that they were often of significantly junior rank to those who might be trying to interfere with their work. Each indoctrinated recipient was issued with a lengthy set of written rules governing their relations with the SLU, and was expected to sign a consent to abide by them. Much of this responsibility devolved on the individual SLU commander, and recruiting the right men with an appropriate mix of tact and firmness was key. 'The History of Hut Three' outlined the qualities required: a liaison officer should 'know how to indoctrinate new recipients in sufficiently impressive style', but at the same time should be 'able to refuse access to material; if possible, without giving offence.'[49]

Thus, a robust system was in place for the delivery of SIGINT direct to field commanders prior to the Normandy invasion. However, the effectiveness of intelligence relies not only on its delivery to battlefield customers, but also on how effectively the information is exploited by those commanders. The attitude of the commanders to the value and credibility of the intelligence is vital. One of Frederick Winterbotham's responsibilities as head of the SCU/SLU organisation was to 'indoctrinate' potential recipients, briefing senior commanders on what they would receive and the associated security arrangements. His impressions of the reaction of a number of these key figures is revealing of their attitude to the intelligence with which they were about to be provided. Some commanders were immediately receptive to the idea. Winterbotham recalled his interview with Patton in 1943:

He greeted me with a broad smile and a cheery welcome and a 'Now young sir, what's it all about?' He was delighted at the idea of reading the enemy's signals, but when I got on to the security angle he stopped me after a few minutes. 'You know, young man, I think you had better tell all this to my Intelligence staff, I don't go much on this sort of thing myself. You see I just like fighting.'[50]

Others were much less enthusiastic. Montgomery, for example, did not create a good impression on Winterbotham:

> Over the years I was to get the impression that Montgomery did not like Ultra primarily because he knew that Churchill and the Chiefs of Staff would also be getting the same information. According to Menzies there had been a row when he first told Montgomery about Ultra in London. Montgomery had insisted that he alone should have the military information. This was of course impossible and Churchill told him so. As a result Montgomery never appeared to recognize the Ultra source as such.[51]

This unfortunate situation (at least in Winterbotham's eyes) persisted after Montgomery and 21st Army Group had moved to France. Winterbotham visited the field headquarters of the army group and observed:

> Montgomery himself was not available. I'd already got used to the formula, but as I only wanted to check up with Bill Williams [Montgomery's chief of intelligence] that he was fully satisfied and that the SLU had no complaints on security matters, it was just as well. The latter, poor chaps, on instructions from the C-in-C himself, had been banished to a solitary spot in a little quarry some half a mile away. It meant a long walk at night. I complained to Major-General Graham – the G3 [Montgomery's senior operations officer] – but apparently the C-in-C was adamant.[52]

He was even more outspoken in an interview given to the Imperial War Museum in later life, commenting on Montgomery that 'He didn't like air force blue on his campus' and 'These poor chaps [the SLU staff] they were treated like mud by Montgomery.'[53]

Fortunately for Winterbotham, Montgomery's subordinates, including his chief intelligence officer, Edgar 'Bill' Williams (an historian who would go on to edit the *Dictionary of National Biography*), was an avid consumer of ULTRA and was able to counterbalance the lack of interest from his boss. Indeed, Williams was warm in his praise for Bletchley Park and maintained a close relationship, through his SLU, with the team in Hut 3 supplying him with intelligence:

> We made it our business in Normandy to send a daily [intelligence summary] from 21 Army Group [to Bletchley] saying what we thought was happening in front of us and in general attempting in a friendly and unofficial fashion to keep the Park aware of what we were trying to do. The whole series of signals was conversational. One felt one was talking to friends.[54]

There is no evidence that Montgomery's attitude to ULTRA had a significant impact on the conduct of the Normandy campaign, but it shows that the intelligence process could depend as much on personal relationships and attitudes as it did on cryptanalytical skill or wireless technology. This applied equally at both ends of the SIGINT chain: the fact that Eric Jones ran a 'happy ship' in Hut 3 was no doubt a major factor in its success, but that would only work if the 'customers' receiving the intelligence had faith in what was being sent to them – and in the wisdom of those sending it. By and large, this seems to have been achieved. Perhaps, in spite of some of the less-than-credible cover stories spun around the intelligence itself, 'Source' was delivered effectively to all levels of command that required it. It now remains to see exactly what information was passed on, and what Bletchley Park was able to reveal about the Germans in the west.

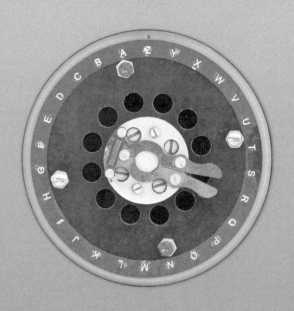

PART II

PREPARATIONS FOR INVASION

CHAPTER FOUR

INVASION PLANNING IN 1943

THE WESTERN FRONT COMMITTEE

O n 10 October 1942, a small group of officers from Air Section met in Room 149 on the upper floor of Block B, a large brick and concrete office block only recently completed in August 1942, adjacent to Bletchley Park's ornamental lake.[1] The group was chaired by Professor T.S.R. Boase, an Italian specialist who had spent over a year in Cairo before returning to Bletchley Park and, in March 1942, becoming deputy head of Air Section.[2] Also present were Arthur 'Bill' Bonsall, head of the German Air Subsection, Captain Jack Brown, an Intelligence Corps officer working as a subsection head with SIXTA,[3] and Squadron Leader Oscar Oeser, head of 3L.

The purpose of the meeting was made clear by Boase: 'The question was raised by the chairman as to whether there was any military Battle Order available for the Western Front.' Of course, at this time the Western Front – France, Belgium and the Low Countries – was not the scene of active fighting; however, large numbers of German troops were massing there. They were also protected by the fortifications of Hitler's Atlantic Wall, the construction of which had begun in earnest in the summer of 1942. These troops and defences reflected the Germans' recognition that at some point, in order to win the war, the western Allies would eventually need to reinvade continental Europe, and a seaborne landing on the western coast was the most likely scenario.

This conclusion had also been reached on the Allied side. If such an invasion were to go ahead, it would be imperative for the Allies to know what they were up against. The collection of that information – the compilation of a detailed 'order of battle' for the German defending forces – would be a vital intelligence task, and one in which Bletchley could play a key role. Thus, while no one at Bletchley knew exactly when – or even if – the invasion would occur, the rapid collection of as much relevant intelligence as possible seemed like an urgent priority.

Captain Brown told the professor that the maintenance of such a 'battle order' was normally the responsibility of Home Forces – a task for Military Intelligence, rather than GC&CS – but he would see what he could find. Meanwhile Oeser was able to report that the air advisers in Hut 3 were keeping an 'Air Map and Battle Order', recording information about the German air force based on Bletchley decrypts.

The group, which christened itself the 'Western Front Committee', decided that henceforth GC&CS should compile its own orders of battle and collate all other information relevant to an invasion. If all these individual strands of information could be brought together and combined, Bletchley had the potential to work out the nature of the German forces in the west in great detail. It would take time and a lot of work to piece together fragmentary facts and hints from different sources; but it was possible.

It was decided that Room 149 should be taken over permanently for this purpose, with filing cabinets for intelligence reports and a series of large wall maps which could be updated to reflect both military and air information. These would show the geographical location of units, their wireless networks and other details. A secretary would be needed to look after all this material and update the maps. The following week, the committee appointed Diana Pares, a Foreign Office civilian working in Air Section. Dinah, as she was known to her friends, had arrived at Bletchley Park earlier in 1942. She was probably recruited for her knowledge of German, acquired while teaching in schools in Germany before the war. She had also gone on to teach at Gordonstoun, the Scottish public school. Her time 'north of the border' seems to have influenced her off-duty activities at Bletchley, since she was also the secretary of the Scottish Country Dancing Club.[4]

The group agreed to meet every Saturday morning, and at Oeser's suggestion 'it was also agreed that each meeting should include a short statement of any relevant piece of intelligence derived from material dealt with by members of the committee'.[5] These snippets of information, recorded in the weekly minutes of the meeting, would form the building blocks for Bletchley Park's understanding of the German defences in the west.

By the time of the committee's next meeting, on 17 October 1942, additional members had joined:[6] Captain A.L. Gadd, head of traffic analysis in Hut 3 (and later liaison officer between SIXTA and Hut 3); Captain Alan Pryce-Jones from 3M; and Mr Handel Edwards, an Air Ministry civilian responsible for German air force tactical codes.[7] At this meeting, it was also announced that a regular supply of 'Martian' reports had been obtained. These were weekly reports produced by a specialist intelligence section of GHQ Home Forces in London.[8] They contained a wealth of information about German activity in the coastal areas, drawing largely on reports from members of the French Resistance and air photography.

Each weekly report was lavishly illustrated with maps, diagrams and reproductions of aerial photographs. The origin of the cover-name 'Martian' is not known, but it may have been a playful reference to the fact that the reports were intended as preparation for an invasion. A key focus of the Martian reports was the beach defences of the Atlantic Wall itself, and these were recorded in meticulous detail. This information would be a useful complement to the SIGINT identified by the committee; for example, information supplied by the French Resistance on German troop movements could be correlated with intercepts; divisional signs on vehicles might reveal the identity of a unit whose location had been established via wireless direction finding; or a divisional move reported via Enigma might be confirmed by direct observation of railway movements. This ability to cross-check the conclusions derived from decrypts would prove vital to the development of Bletchley's understanding of the German forces.

The last intelligence report produced by the Western Front Committee was circulated on 5 June 1944. After that, once battle had commenced, its role in preparation for the invasion was overtaken by the mainstream work of Bletchley Park's huts and sections. However, the committee's work over the twenty months between October 1942 and June 1944 on German order of battle and strategic intentions would form Bletchley Park's most direct contribution to success on D-Day.

*

Having seen in some detail how work was carried out at Bletchley Park, we now need to examine the fruits of those labours. Just what information about the forces facing an invasion was revealed by all those thousands of intercepts?

The purpose of intelligence is fundamentally to provide information about the enemy: *who* he is, *where* he is and *what* his strengths and weaknesses are. It is therefore the first task of intelligence providers to create and maintain an 'order of battle' for the enemy. This should contain details of what enemy units are present on the intended field of battle, as well as what units can be expected as reinforcements at a later stage. Details of the personnel, equipment, standard of training and morale, and the command structure of each of these units is required. Not only does such an order of battle need to be created, but it also needs to be constantly updated and checked against new information. A second, equally important strand is to determine the enemy's intentions: *what* does he plan to do, and *where* and *when* does he plan to do it? In the case of an enemy who is strategically on the defensive, as was the case in Normandy, this principally concerns details of how he is likely to react to various eventualities, including attack.

At the beginning of 1943, the leaders of the western Allies met at the Casablanca conference. Here, UK Prime Minister Winston Churchill and

US President Franklin D. Roosevelt thrashed out their plan for the future conduct of the war. Churchill sought to dissuade the Americans from an immediate plan to invade north-west Europe, arguing in favour of developing the campaign in the Mediterranean. He also felt that insufficient Allied forces were available to sustain an attack on France. In the end, the Americans were persuaded, and the invasion of north-west Europe was postponed until spring 1944. Meanwhile alternative plans were developed to exploit the situation in North Africa and the Mediterranean, including the invasion of Sicily and mainland Italy.[9]

A further decision was taken that for the 1944 invasion a 'supreme commander' of the two principal allies' forces would be appointed. It was broadly agreed that the nationality of this officer would be determined by the nation providing the majority of the invading forces; thus, it was expected that the general appointed would be British. In the event, it was the American Dwight Eisenhower who would be formally assigned to this post, but that did not occur for nearly a year. In the meantime, a planning staff was created under the command of the Chief of Staff to Supreme Allied Commander (COSSAC), British Lieutenant General Frederick E. Morgan. Morgan was empowered to create a joint UK/US planning staff and to begin preparations for the 1944 invasion, as well as contingencies for an earlier strike if circumstances permitted. This organisation, which also became known as COSSAC, would be the focus of planning efforts for the remainder of 1943. Once Eisenhower was appointed Supreme Allied Commander, his headquarters – Supreme Headquarters Allied Expeditionary Force, or SHAEF – took over planning in January 1944, and COSSAC was absorbed into it.[10] During 1943, then, COSSAC was formed of five branches: three of these were operational, representing the army, navy and air force elements of the Allied armies; the remaining two were an Administrative Branch and an Intelligence Branch, providing support to the three operational branches. The Intelligence Branch, under its British head, Major General P.G. Whitefoord, would be the main consumer of intelligence product from Bletchley.[11]

Prior to the actual landings, it would be the job of GC&CS to provide as much information as possible to the Allied planners. This would require the meticulous scrutiny of many thousands of intercepted messages, as well as the comparison and collation of all this information over the longer term into usable intelligence (the task undertaken by the Western Front Committee, as described earlier). This is at variance with the widespread perception (reinforced by Ralph Bennett in his account) that GC&CS was some kind of 'news service', providing information only on what the enemy was doing on any particular day. That latter task was, of course, vital; but it was only one piece of the puzzle. Indeed, since the invasion had yet to take place, the amount of urgent actionable intelligence concerning the Western Front was minimal.

PRE-INVASION INTELLIGENCE

GC&CS, of course, was not alone: several Allied organisations were engaged in supplying information to the planners, including the service intelligence branches. Of particular importance was MI14, the branch of the War Office's Directorate of Military Intelligence that was tasked specifically with studying the German armed forces. As the invasion approached in 1944, SHAEF and 21st Army Group also developed their own intelligence capabilities. GC&CS would feed information gained from signals intelligence to these other organisations, but it also received information back from them. This exchange was essential and allowed comparison of Bletchley's own SIGINT material with intelligence obtained in various other ways, including from agents in France, POW interrogations, and air reconnaissance and photography. This extra material significantly helped the staff at Bletchley, and enriched their understanding of the intercepts which formed their main task.

Ever since the evacuation of the British Expeditionary Force from France in 1940, there had been an expectation that British forces would at some stage return to continental Western Europe. This intention had been confirmed after the entry of the US into the war, at the Arcadia Conference in Washington DC, on 31 December 1941. At that meeting, a 'Germany first' strategy was agreed between the two (now allied) powers, the UK and the US. The possibility of an invasion of Germany via France was also agreed in the conference communiqué:

> It does not seem likely that in 1942 any large scale land offensive against Germany, except on the Russian front, will be possible ... [but] in 1943, the way may be clear for a return to the continent across the Mediterranean, from Turkey into the Balkans, *or by landings in Western Europe*. Such operations will be the prelude to the final assault on Germany itself.[12]

Meanwhile, as Captain Brown noted at the Western Front Committee meeting, British Army Intelligence had been studying German activity on the French and Belgian coast in detail since 1940–41, when the UK was threatened with invasion. It was a simple matter to alter the focus of this study from defensive to offensive. Back in October 1941 the group was given specific responsibility for collecting intelligence on the area from Den Helder in the Netherlands in the north, to the mouth of the Loire in the south, and up to 30 miles (50km) inland. It was later joined by the Naval Intelligence Division, which was tasked with studying the coastal fortifications of the Channel (many of them manned and operated by the German navy rather than the army). Together they became the Combined Intelligence Section (CIS) of GHQ Home Forces.[13] Thus, when the Western Front Committee at Bletchley Park became formally involved in the collection of intelligence relevant to an invasion, the CIS had already been at work for about a year.

In October 1942, the Western Front Committee decided that henceforth GC&CS should compile its own orders of battle and collate other information relevant to an invasion. All these individual snippets of intelligence brought to the committee were reported in the minutes of their meetings, revealing how this small group grew into a larger organisation that was able to synthesise information gained from intercepts and intelligence feeds from other external sources to produce a focused intelligence product devoted to a particular purpose (in this case, the invasion of Western Europe). This is a far cry from the image of Bletchley Park depicted by Ralph Bennett, who described the various 'research' sections working in Hut 3, but minimised their importance:

> These research departments had some contact with the world of non-Ultra intelligence outside Bletchley Park and were able to utilise information thus gained to assist and accelerate their work. But they were alone in this. Hut 3 existed to purvey pure Ultra, not to adulterate it with anything else. No teleprint or signal ever bore footnote or comment derived from anything except Hut 3's own card-indexes ... No hint of forthcoming Allied operations normally reached the Hut, so that we remained 'pure'. It was an exception to this rule when a few of us were given details of Overlord a day or two before the landings in order that we might keep an eye open for anything bearing on them.[14]

As we have seen, the contents of ULTRA were only the tip of a very large iceberg of information held at Bletchley. To presume, as Bennett and others have done, that the contents of ULTRA signals represent the totality of GC&CS's understanding of the enemy is to significantly understate the depth of knowledge. As a watch officer, Bennett would clearly have been concerned with the daily production of ULTRA, rather than wider matters. Also, given the highly compartmentalised world of Bletchley Park, it is understandable that he was unaware of the more general intelligence assessments being carried out. But, far from remaining 'pure', GC&CS was actually preparing in detail for the invasion of Europe more than eighteen months before the event. Also, as has been described, liaison with the planners at COSSAC and SHAEF would become increasingly intimate through 1943 and the first part of 1944.

RECORDING THE GERMANS

In February 1943, the Western Front Committee decided to meet only fortnightly, but members would submit in advance any new intelligence information they wished to offer. This would be typed up into a formal report, which would be reviewed and approved by the committee, before being distributed to a limited number of people around Bletchley Park. The first such report, 'Record of Western Front' (No. 1), was produced for the committee's meeting on 20 February 1943.[15] To get the ball rolling, it included a full three-service order of battle, intended to cover the whole front, from France to northern Norway, though admittedly at this stage only the section for France was anything like complete. Over the next sixteen months, the order of battle would go through eleven further revisions.[16] Henceforth, the reports would also include a significant quantity of naval information, provided by a new committee member from the Royal Navy. The report for 20 March 1943 also records that the committee meeting was attended (as a 'non-member') by Harry Hinsley, later official historian of British intelligence.

The first 'Record' had relatively little to say about the German army in the west, commenting only that:

> In recent weeks a considerable number of divisions have left France and the Low countries for Russia. This departure has been partially counter-balanced by the arrival of a smaller number of divisions in the west.
>
> . . . Information, however is deficient, especially along the Channel Coast and Brittany, and the present War Office total of 40 divisions (of which two are unidentified) is tentative only.[17]

This view reflects the difficulties faced by Allied intelligence organisations in the spring of 1943. By this time, the German field army (excluding the home or training forces) comprised over 300 divisions. There was also a wide range of other units that were not permanently part of any one division, but could be attached temporarily to a division, greatly enhancing its strength. In addition, there were the combat formations of the Waffen SS, as well as an increasing number of Luftwaffe 'field divisions' (ground combat troops). These formations were deployed on a number of fronts, and rotation between the various fronts was frequent. The German army at this point in the war did not retain a strategic reserve in Germany; rather, non-active fronts were used as areas to rest and refit divisions that had suffered in combat in other theatres. New units in training were also assembled in the same areas. Thus, France was used to rest a number of units on rotation from the Eastern Front, and also as a training ground for new formations. It was intended that these formations would serve as front-line combat units in the event of an invasion in the west, but they were not part of a structured defensive plan. February 1943 in particular marked the climax of the German debacle at Stalingrad, where *Generalfeldmarschall* Paulus's *6. Armee* had surrendered en masse and the Germans had suffered nearly 300,000 casualties (almost 100,000 of those becoming prisoners of war). Lacking a central reserve to replace these losses, forces had to be reallocated to Russia from other fronts. Units that had suffered heavily were also withdrawn from the east and sent to France to recuperate and absorb new equipment and personnel.

On the fighting fronts in Russia and North Africa, where radio communication was a necessity, wireless interception produced a steady flow of organisational and strength information for decryption and analysis at GC&CS. But on the inactive fronts, particularly in the west, where landline communications were good, the German army committed very little information to the airwaves. The result was that, as Harry Hinsley described, 'Sigint still provided only fitful intelligence.'[18] The Allied intelligence agencies were forced to rely on fragmentary information supplied by the Soviets, open source information gained from the German press, POW reports and a large but often unreliable volume of agent reports.

Nonetheless, the first months of 1943 saw a significant shift of units out of France to both Russia and Tunisia. MI14, the branch of Military

Intelligence concerned with the German order of battle, produced a summary of these troop movements between September 1942 and January 1943, in a report produced on 21 February. The contribution of SIGINT to this overall understanding of the Germans can be measured in this report: of the twenty-five divisional movements mentioned by MI14, ten were either identified or confirmed high-grade intercepts provided by GC&CS.[19] The fact that this intelligence came from Bletchley Park SIGINT was mirrored in the 'Records of Western Front'.

As the months passed in 1943, the amount of SIGINT-based order-of-battle intelligence that GC&CS was able to provide to MI14 increased steadily. For example, in March an Enigma decrypt revealed that the remnants of two named panzer divisions which had suffered heavily at Stalingrad were being moved to France from Russia for rebuilding.[20] This information was included in the 'Record of Western Front' (No. 5) in April.[21]

In addition to the location of formations, the Western Front Committee was also accruing detail on each of them: 'Record' (No. 6; 8 May) contained a list of the names of German commanders at army and army group level, and of five corps and fifteen divisional commanders.[22]

Of particular relevance to the battle to come in 1944 was the identification and analysis of the so-called 'static' divisions of the German army, which would be the first line of defence on the Normandy beaches. These formations were described at Bletchley as the '700 Series', because their divisional numbers all began with the number seven. They were intended from the outset as garrison units for the west and for the Balkans. Fifteen such divisions had been raised, starting in April 1941, initially from men with a lower level of physical fitness and older men (the average age in *709. Division* was 36). They were poorly equipped, having virtually no transport; and what anti-tank and heavy guns they did have were typically from obsolete or captured stocks. These units were increasingly mined for their fitter men, to reinforce units on the Eastern Front. Those transferred were replaced by less-able individuals and by *Volksdeutsche* – ethnic Germans recruited from outside Germany, in particular from the occupied territories in the east. Later on, they were to be reinforced by whole battalions of former Soviet POWs and other troops of dubious fighting quality.[23]

The '700 Series' divisions were first addressed by the Western Front Committee in the 'Record' (No. 8) for 5 June 1943:

> Their personnel was known to include a high proportion of men aged 30 and older, together with younger men of relatively low medical category; and they have been described by some observers as *Landesschuetzen* [equivalent to Home Guard or Reserve] divisions. From the first the majority of them have been retained in coastal sectors in FRANCE and the LOW COUNTRIES or in NORWAY, though five have been in the BALKANS (including GREECE and CRETE) and one on the L. of C. [line of communications] in RUSSIA.

The full divisional structure was also outlined (two regiments of three battalions each) and the absence of an anti-tank battalion was noted.[24]

Another formation that was to play a significant role in the fighting in 1944 was *21. Panzer-Division*. This unit was well known to both GC&CS and the wider British public, having formed one of the two panzer divisions in Rommel's famous *Deutsches Afrikakorps* during the fighting in Libya and Egypt in 1941–42. The division had gone on to fight in Tunisia until it more or less ceased to exist as a cohesive fighting unit. In June 1943, the title was passed on to a new armoured formation created in France for anti-invasion duty. The unit then came to the attention of GC&CS again in October 1943, 'Record' (No. 17) reporting that '21 Panzer Division "destroyed" in TUNISIA is now reforming in North-West FRANCE.'[25]

Knowledge of the German army's order of battle could also be important from the political standpoint. In August 1943, COSSAC prepared an outline plan for operation OVERLORD, which was then submitted to the Heads of Government conference that month in Quebec. Having calculated the probable Allied forces available for an invasion, COSSAC also calculated the maximum number of German divisions that that force could reasonably expect to defeat:

> On the target date, if the operation is to have a reasonable chance of success ... the German reserves in France and the Low countries, excluding divisions holding the coast [the '700 Series' divisions], and GAF [German Air Force] and training divisions, should not exceed ... twelve full-strength, first-quality divisions. In addition the Germans should not be able to transfer more than fifteen first-quality divisions from Russia or elsewhere during the first two months.[26]

This precondition for a successful invasion probably originated as a working assumption on which the planners at COSSAC could base their estimates. However, it became highly political. Both the Americans and the Soviets suspected that it was a delaying tactic, introduced by the British as an excuse for deferring or cancelling the invasion, and it was repeatedly discussed both in Quebec and later, in October, at the Heads of Government meeting attended by Stalin in Tehran. What was never questioned in these discussions, however, was the ability of Allied intelligence to identify the locations of the German divisions concerned: the quality of German order-of-battle information available to COSSAC was simply assumed. Indeed, on a visit to Moscow in October 1943, Foreign Secretary Anthony Eden told Stalin's aide Voroshilov 'We are constantly and accurately informed of the whereabouts of all German first-quality divisions.'[27] This remark, while flattering to the work of GC&CS and the other Allied intelligence agencies, was perhaps rather indiscreet.

While the German forces could rely on landlines for much of their day-to-day communication, it was still necessary for them to practise their wireless routines in preparation for mobile operations, should an invasion occur. These wireless exercises provided GC&CS with the ideal opportunity to analyse and reconstruct the communications networks involved and to record call-signs (which often, as mentioned above, used simple forms of encryption). This was the job of Bletchley's traffic analysis specialists in what would eventually be known as SIXTA. For example, 'Record' (No. 10; 3 July 1943) reported on an exercise that had been conducted by *26. Panzer-Division* (based near Amiens) in early May.[28] The level of detail given is quite striking. The German units concerned had used frequencies with which they were not usually associated, and the 'Record' noted that the Germans were probably 'deliberately working off-frequency for camouflage reasons'. Later, in August, *26. Panzer-Division* was intercepted again – this time in Italy, where the unit had been transferred in response to the Allied invasion of Sicily. It was transmitting on the same frequencies as had been used during the exercise in France. As the committee observed: 'It is possible that the exercise was to test the frequencies to be used in its new theatre.'[29]

As well as the rebuilding of German army divisions, 1943 was notable for the substantial expansion of non-army formations, in particular from the SS and the Luftwaffe. The SS had started life as a small paramilitary wing of the Nazi party, but by 1943 it had grown to include what was effectively a second German army – the Waffen SS – fighting alongside the regular forces of the German army. During 1943, the Waffen SS expanded significantly: from around 230,000 men in December 1942, it had nearly doubled in strength to 430,000 by July 1943, rising further to 600,000 by July 1944. Initially, the three older Waffen SS divisions – *Adolf Hitler, Das Reich* and *Totenkopf* – were upgraded to become *1., 2.* and *3. SS-Panzer-Divisionen* respectively, while two further panzer divisions – *9. SS (Hohenstaufen)* and *10. SS (Frundsberg)* – were formed in January 1943. By the end of August 1943, a total of thirteen SS divisions had been identified.[30]

The *Adolf Hitler* and *Das Reich* divisions had been posted to France in mid-1942, when Hitler first became seriously concerned about an Allied invasion in the west.[31] Subsequently both the *Hohenstaufen* and *Frundsberg* divisions were formed in France, and these were followed by *12. SS-Panzer-Division (Hitlerjugend)*, which was assembled and trained in Belgium. Unlike the German army in the west, the Waffen SS made substantial use of Enigma-encrypted wireless communications. GC&CS

was thus able to follow the activities of Waffen SS units quite effectively, since the SS Enigma ORANGE key was broken as early as December 1940. Subsequent SS keys ORANGE II (used for communications between SS HQ in Berlin and divisions in the field) and QUINCE (a general SS key) were broken in February 1942 and August 1942 respectively, and would continue to be read until the end of the war.[32]

Interceptions of the QUINCE network were quick to reveal the existence of *9.* and *10. SS-Panzer-Divisionen*, and the locations of their headquarters and training areas. This intelligence was recorded in the 'Record of Western Front' (No. 3) on 20 March 1943:

W/T Networks

On the main E/Quince frequency, two new callsigns appeared simultaneously at the end of February; one of these is now D/F'd [located by direction finding] at Angouleme, and, by analogy the other is probably also in France. It appears very likely that the callsigns represent S.S. reception depots at Angouleme and Chalons-Sur-Marne, which served S.S. Div. Totenkopf and the Korps generally while they were in France, and now serve S.S. Divs 9 and 10 which are in the process of formation in that country.

This frequency which is controlled at Berlin now links the main S.S. stations on the Eastern and Western fronts.[33]

Such was the quantity and quality of information about front-line SS units that in September 1943 GC&CS appointed a full-time adviser within Hut 3 to work on decrypts concerning these formations.[34] This officer was able, by concentrating on SS material, to understand fully the unique structure of the organisation. In the months leading up to the invasion, he produced a summary of SS intelligence every ten days for circulation within Bletchley. He also worked as a specialist liaison officer with MI14 on matters concerning the SS.[35]

The German fighting strength in France also consisted in part of air force personnel in the so-called Luftwaffe 'field divisions' (see above). In

September 1942, Hitler had suggested that the German air force be sifted to remove its excess personnel, who would be transferred to the army. Hermann Göring, as head of the Luftwaffe, was zealous in guarding his airmen, whom he considered to be better Nazis than their more traditional conservative army counterparts. He proposed instead that the Luftwaffe form its own ground fighting formations. This was approved in October 1942, and in due course over 200,000 men would be transferred into these units.[36] Twenty such divisions had been raised by January 1943. British Military Intelligence not only identified many of them, but also assessed their fighting qualities quite favourably, reporting that some were not just defensive formations, but were capable of mobile warfare and were 'potentially of great value'.[37]

While little wireless traffic was being intercepted from German army sources, the Luftwaffe had always been more active in its use of wireless – and more lax in its adherence to security procedures. This resulted in a rich harvest of Luftwaffe-derived SIGINT for GC&CS, beginning with the breaking of the RED key in 1940 and continuing throughout the war. Thus the Luftwaffe field divisions were quickly identified. They first appeared in Record (No. 6), from 8 May 1943, when one field division was reported as arriving in the Paris area from Russia:

> This consists of Air Force personnel trained to fight as a normal infantry formation, though having far lower establishment than an infantry division ... In this connection a single reference to 'IV Luft. Feldkorps' which has been D/F'd in the PARIS-ETAMPES area, may be recalled.[38]

Two weeks later, 'Record' (No. 7) was able to expand on this information, reporting that the division identified near Paris had moved to Alençon, and that the headquarters of another two field divisions had been reported – one in Brittany and one in Amsterdam.[39] The presence of four Luftwaffe field divisions was confirmed the following month, and 'Record' (No. 8) was able to identify one specifically as the 17. Luftwaffen-

Feld-Division, located at Auray in Brittany, since it had been 'mentioned in correspondence'.[40] This was followed in July by a two-page resumé of all the information known about Luftwaffe field divisions, including their origins, recruitment and training, internal structure and manning levels.[41] Information from Luftwaffe intercepts concerning the location and activities of Göring's field divisions would continue to flow in during 1944, up to and after the invasion.

By summer 1943, the Western Front reporting system at Bletchley Park was getting into its stride. 'Record' (No. 7; 22 May) reported on its first page that 'Enigma sources have produced a considerable volume of detailed Western Front information' over the previous fortnight.[42]

Hinsley summarised these developments:

Sigint was making an ever growing contribution to MI's [Military Intelligence] familiarity with the German order of battle in all theatres including, indirectly, France. From the summer of 1943 Enigma and Army Y [battlefield wireless interception units] provided all but exhaustive intelligence about the formations engaged in Sicily, Italy, and the Balkans, while the intelligence obtained from Enigma and Fish traffic about those on the Russian fronts was steadily expanding. These developments substantially improved MI's understanding of the situation in the west, though the Enigma and Fish keys in use in that area were not to be broken before the spring of 1944.[43]

Hinsley is correct about the western FISH keys; and, if his remark about Enigma is taken to refer only to army keys in the west, he is broadly also correct on that point. However, it is clear that both SS and Luftwaffe Enigma were already a fruitful source for GC&CS at this time.

In early October 1943, the Western Front Committee gave a summary of the overall situation in the west in 'Record' (No. 17). In it, they presented a picture similar to that which had prevailed for much of 1943. Many if not all of the German formations in France and the Low Countries were under strength, and the 'Record' suggested that '700 Series' divisions mostly had around 10,000 men out of a theoretical establishment of 12,000, while the more mobile '300 Series' units had only 12,000 out of 14,000. It was noted that mechanised units had only around half of their establishment strength of vehicles and equipment. Mention was also made of the rising proportion of non-German personnel in these units – up to 25 per cent. The 'Record' concluded:

> If at normal strength a force of forty divisions might be estimated to amount to over a million men. At the moment it is doubtful whether total GERMAN strength in personnel in the west is much more than 850,000. Including G.N. [German Navy], G.A.F. [German Air Force] and administrative personnel.

It went on to add that 'This paints an unfavourable picture of the present enemy forces in the west. *But it must be remembered that invasion is NOT at present expected*.'[44]

Frequent troop rotations from France to the Eastern Front and the removal of units to fight in Italy showed that during much of 1943 senior German commanders were not prioritising garrisoning of the west. However, this situation might change rapidly if the Germans had reason to fear an imminent invasion.

In late October and early November 1943, the German view of the situation in the west altered. *Generalfeldmarschall* von Rundstedt, commander in the west, produced an 'appreciation' on 28 October, in which he laid great emphasis on the probability of an Allied invasion in the coming year and on the need to make every effort to strengthen the forces available to him. This viewpoint clearly chimed with opinions in Berlin, as on 3 November Hitler produced his Führer Directive No. 51, in which he predicted:

> The threat from the East remains, but an even greater danger looms in the West: the Anglo-American landing! In the East, the vastness of the space will, as a last resort, permit a loss of territory even on a

major scale, without suffering a mortal blow to Germany's chance for survival.

Not so in the West! If the enemy here succeeds in penetrating our defences on a wide front, consequences of staggering proportions will follow within a short time. All signs point to an offensive against the Western Front of Europe no later than spring, and perhaps earlier.[45]

The directive went on to list a series of measures that should be taken, including the allocation of new tanks and anti-tank guns to units in the west, and completion of the full equipping of both *12. SS-Panzer-Division (Hitlerjugend)* and *21. Panzer-Division*. How realistic these proposals actually were is open to question, but the refocusing of German effort was significant.

Hinsley has stated that 'neither Sigint nor any other source disclosed' the contents of the Führer Directive to the Allies.[46] He took a similar view on von Rundstedt's October 1943 appreciation.[47] However, there is evidence that both of these documents were available to the analysts in Hut 3 before the end of 1943.[48]

Several of von Rundstedt's later appreciations were also intercepted and read by Bletchley Park, and the 'Record of Western Front' (No. 20), issued on 4 December 1943, included direct quotations from von Rundstedt:

<u>Enemy appreciation of Invasion Prospects</u>

34/. An appreciation of the situation on the Western Front by C. in C. West is worth quoting in full:

35/. 'Although it was not possible to establish in England any new or immediate indications of an imminent attack, it must be pointed out that our air recce can hardly be carried out over the relevant areas on account of the weather and the strong defence.

36/. The withdrawal of landing craft from the Mediterranean towards England (Chiefly B% [*sic*] LCT) continued, though not in especially large numbers. It is certain that the enemy is methodically and on the largest scale proceeding with his preparations to attack. This makes it necessary therefore for C. in C. West to press on with his counter measures in every sphere with the utmost exertion of all forces.'[49]

According to Hinsley, this transcript came from a Luftwaffe Enigma decrypt, which was circulated on 15 November.[50] This is supported by a 'Hut 3 Headline' from 19 November, which included the verbatim quotations 'methodically and on the largest scale' and 'with the utmost exertion'[51] – clearly suggesting that von Rundstedt's appreciation was in the hands of Bletchley by mid-November.

At the same time as these high-level decrypts were being obtained, GC&CS was also able to draw inferences from apparently insignificant pieces of information contained in intercepted messages. In December, a detail that the leave of the commander of *II. SS-Panzer-Korps* needed to be (and had been) approved by von Rundstedt himself was sufficient to confirm the move of that corps to the Western Front. This was duly reported in 'Record' (No. 21) of 18 December.[52]

The status of the German army in the west at the close of the year was assessed in a full divisional order of battle (described as the 'Fifth Reissue'), included in 'Record' (No. 20) produced on 1 December 1943.[53] It listed 39 divisions in France and the Low Countries. Thus, a picture of increasing preparedness on the German side of the Channel was starting to develop.

INTERCEPTING THE JAPANESE

It was not only German material that was informing GC&CS's understanding of the German order of battle. In November 1943, Bletchley Park received, via the US, the first of what would become a string of highly revealing intercepts of messages from Japanese diplomats reporting on German anti-invasion preparations. We have already looked at the role of the Japanese ambassador in Berlin, Ōshima Hiroshi: thanks to the breaking of the PURPLE cipher, his insights into the minds of the Germans had been followed closely by Washington and London since 1940. Now, at the end of 1943, this source also provided information relating to the proposed invasion.

Between 24 October and 1 November 1943, Ōshima, accompanied by two embassy secretaries and an assistant military attaché who was a liaison officer with Wehrmacht High Command (*Oberkommando der Wehrmacht* – OKW), toured the defences of the Atlantic Wall. Their visit focused on the defences from Brest as far south as Bordeaux, and was followed by a stay in Paris. They also had personal briefings on the wider situation from both von Rundstedt and his chief of staff.[54] On his return to Berlin, Ōshima composed a series of messages to Tokyo reporting on what he had learned. The first of these was intercepted on 9 November and passed to the US Army's Signals Intelligence Service at Arlington Hall, Virginia. Over the next few days, further signals completing the message were received, and the process of decrypting and reconstructing the whole transcript was completed by 9 December.

One of the cryptanalysts involved at Arlington, Henry F. Graff, described the excitement of the moment when the Signals Intelligence Service team realised what they had received:

[I] was on duty when that report on the inspection trip began to come in from the signal corps intercept stations around the world ... When I picked up the first intercept I was not sure what I had because it was not part one. But within a few hours as ... [more] of the message came in the magnitude of what was at hand was apparent. I could scarcely contain my excitement, but working, as I was, late at night, it was not until the morning that my superior officers, alerted by me, alerted in turn the appropriate 'Higher headquarters' – Special Branch in the Pentagon ... and, I was told, General Marshall's office and the Map Room at the White House headed by Admiral William Leahy. I remained on duty throughout much of the day, continuing to translate along with colleagues who had pitched in to complete the work. I was too electrified to sleep. In the end we produced what was veritably a pamphlet, an on-the-ground description of the north French defences of 'Festung Europa' composed *dictum mirabile* by a general.[55]

The resulting decrypt was passed according to the normal procedure to Special Branch Military Intelligence Service, where officers would compile summaries of the intelligence to be passed to US Chief of Staff General George Marshall. He would then request the intercepts themselves, if required. Officers compiling summaries were sent the raw traffic and an accompanying indication: 'Note' (i.e. read and file) or 'Write' (i.e. redraft and send on). No doubt the Ōshima message would have been marked 'Write'.[56]

Churchill was the first of the leaders to receive the news, in the form of a report from MI14, delivered to him on 8 December.[57] For him, the crucial information contained in the ambassador's report was the number of divisions, both coastal and mobile, available to the Germans in France in the event of an invasion. These included thirty-one coastal divisions, of which eight were in *7. Armee* in the Normandy area, backed up by a reserve of six infantry divisions, four panzer divisions and five motorised divisions. Though getting close to it, these numbers were still just below the upper limit estimated by the Allied planners for the invasion to be feasible (see above). This was a relief to the prime minister, as only the week before, in Tehran, he had agreed with Stalin and Roosevelt that the invasion would be mounted in May 1944. He ordered the report to be 'shown to the President' as soon as possible.[58]

The report from Ōshima was supported by a similar (but even longer) message from Major General Komatsu, the Japanese military attaché in Berlin. Komatsu was very close to Ōshima, and apparently shared both his taste for alcohol and his pro-German sentiments.[59] Komatsu had conducted his own tour of the Atlantic defences, and provided a detailed, 32-part report on what he had observed. Unfortunately, in the second half of 1943, changes to the procedures used in composing messages using the Japanese Military Attaché code had greatly interfered with the ability of Tiltman's team at Bletchley Park to read these messages. As a result, although eleven parts of the message were deciphered by the end of 1943, other parts proved more stubborn and the report in its entirety was not available until June 1944. Nonetheless, as Hinsley describes, the parts which were read

> gave a detailed and extremely valuable account of the numbers and sites of every element in the coast defence [CD] system, from the heaviest CD battery down to grenade throwers, with comments showing how 'enormously' the system had been improved since an earlier visit in February 1943.[60]

This problem with changes to the JMA code would recur in May 1944, when a new 'conversion square' was introduced by the Japanese (see above, Chapter 2). However, on that occasion GC&CS was able to get around the problem quite effectively. When the change was introduced, the details were not passed to the Japanese attaché in Tangier (which was at the time a neutral city, albeit under Spanish military occupation). The attaché cabled his counterpart in Madrid, asking for a copy of the code to be sent to him. GC&CS was then able to use a local contact to steal the relevant telegrams from the Tangier cable office.[61]

More information became available in December 1943 from a third Japanese source: the military attaché to the French Vichy regime government. In particular, this related to *Generalfeldmarschall* Rommel's move from Italy to France in November 1943. Rumours of the move were already circulating in Allied intelligence, along with the question of whether he would replace von Rundstedt as commander-in-chief or take on some other role. A message was intercepted on 13 December, again transmitted in JMA code, which confirmed that Rommel was indeed to move to the west, but in a subordinate role – as commander of reserve forces. A further message was intercepted from the same source in February 1944 which confirmed the existence of *Heeresgruppe B* (Army

Group B) under Rommel's command, encompassing *7.* and *15. Armeen* in France, as well as the German forces in the Netherlands.[62]

*

By the beginning of 1944, it was clear that a cross-Channel invasion was likely within the year. Both the Führer Directive and von Rundstedt's own appreciations indicate that the Germans expected an attack in the spring or summer. Having been a rest-and-training area for German troops, with only a theoretical likelihood of attack, France and the Low Countries now became a prospective battle zone, and both von Rundstedt and Wehrmacht High Command began defensive preparations in earnest. 'Record of Western Front' (No. 21) observed on 18 December 1943:

> Finally, 17 SS Pz. Gren. Div. (Goetz von BERLICHINGEN) has been transferred from NUREMBERG to TOURS. *It may be, therefore, that the foundations of an anti-invasion force are at last being laid.*[63]

But Allied intelligence had already gained a comprehensive under-standing of the German forces in the west. Detailed orders of battle for the roughly forty enemy divisions present in theatre had been created, and movements in and out of France (often to and from Russia) were being monitored more or less reliably. Both the structure of the forces in the west and the chains of command in the event of battle had also been elucidated (the latter largely thanks to traffic analysis).

GC&CS had played a significant part in assembling this intelligence. By reading what little signals traffic was available from France (and by drawing inferences from the much larger flow of data from other theatres), Bletchley Park and the Western Front Committee had been able to contribute substantially to the intelligence picture. Significantly, the committee had been able to pool information from multiple sources and – despite the high level of compartmentalisation and secrecy at Bletchley – to compile this information into a coherent whole. This reve-lation of GC&CS as a centre for analysis and intelligence production is at odds with the traditional view of Bletchley Park as effectively a decryption and translation service, with no interest in the ultimate meaning or usefulness of its product.

At the start of the war, GC&CS had to fight to convince the service intelligence branches first of all that its raw intelligence product was credible and should be taken seriously, and then later that its role should include analysis, as well as decryption. By the end of 1943, both these battles had largely been won and Bletchley Park was able to develop its own analyses, as well as to 'trade' intelligence material freely with other parts of the invasion planning machine (in particular MI14). The following year, that process would only speed up and become more complex still, as Bletchley started to supply SHAEF and 21st Army Group directly with intelligence, and as the breaking of FISH in the west provided a vast new store of information. However, the foundations laid in the thirteen months since the founding of the Western Front Committee would serve the organisation well in meeting this challenge.

CHAPTER FIVE

INVASION PLANNING IN 1944

SHAEF AND JELLYFISH

Donald Michie was at home for the Christmas school holidays in 1941. Recently turned eighteen, there would be another two school terms before he took up a scholarship place to study classics at Balliol College, Oxford. But Donald yearned for a more active role in the war. Following a tip his father had picked up in the City, Donald presented himself at an address in Bedford. Here, it was rumoured, they were secretly teaching people Japanese. To what purpose was unclear, but it sounded more exciting than university.

In fact, the Japanese course had yet to start; but the mysterious officer Donald met in Bedford enrolled him on a cryptanalysis course commencing the following Monday. Six weeks later, Michie arrived at Bletchley Park, and in June 1942 he was transferred to the newly formed Fish Subsection under Ralph Tester.

Michie found himself installed in a room 'filled to capacity by members of the Women's Auxiliary Air Force'. His initial hopeful enthusiasm was crushed when he discovered that 'those whose boyfriends were on active service felt only contempt for an apparently fit young male in civilian attire. Some of them had lost boyfriends in the RAF and many had boyfriends still alive but in daily peril.'[1]

Michie settled down to his new life as a codebreaker, but 'For all the attractions of the new life, or perhaps because of them, I could not drop from my mind the initial "white feather" impact of that roomful of WAAF girls.' He still yearned for the glamour of active service. His father, too, was baffled and embarrassed by the mysterious nature of his son's occupation. Having had to negotiate some awkward questions at his golf club as to his son's role in the war, he hinted to Donald that maybe he should consider a more active occupation.

Michie presented himself to one Colonel Pritchard in the Testery and asked for a transfer to the Western Desert, where the war was then in full swing, with Rommel's panzers closing in on Cairo. But Pritchard was having none of it:

> I have to instruct you to return to duty. You see, Mr Michie, we have a war on our hands. Inconvenient but unfortunately true. Unless you have further questions you are free to return at once to your section. And by the way, I do not expect you to raise such matters again. Either with me or anyone else.

With this rebuke ringing in his ears, Michie returned crestfallen to his work in the Testery. But his loss was Bletchley's gain: Donald Michie was to go on to become one of the leading lights of Lorenz cipher breaking. In concert with Jack Good, he would develop a technique whereby Colossus could be used to perform both 'wheel breaking' and 'wheel setting'. After D-Day, this technique would become vital, as the Germans started to change their wheel cams daily, rather than monthly.

Michie took up his place at Balliol at war's end. After obtaining his doctorate, he moved into the field of machine learning, becoming a pioneer in what is now known as artificial intelligence. Without his wartime brilliance, the output of FISH intelligence would have been vastly reduced, if not cut off entirely.

*

On 15 January 1944, Supreme Allied Commander Dwight D. Eisenhower arrived at Supreme Headquarters Allied Expeditionary Force.[2] Initially based in Central London, SHAEF moved to Bushy Park, near Hampton Court, that March.

By the beginning of 1944, in addition to the normal delivery of SIGINT via the service ministries and the Combined Intelligence Section, ULTRA signals were being sent direct to headquarters. The first message sent direct to SHAEF was on 26 January and contained the relatively mundane information that a particular German bomber squadron had moved from southern France to Italy.[3] Many more messages, of far greater import, were to follow.

However, as was discussed earlier (Chapter 3), despite the new direct link, by no means all the available ULTRA intelligence was passed to SHAEF in the form of urgent teleprinter messages. This was the material later available to Ralph Bennett for his analysis, and such gaps in the sequence of ULTRA messages have distorted previous understanding of the true depth of the developing intelligence picture. But if we compare the reports produced by the Western Front Committee, the weekly MI14 intelligence summaries and the Martian reports we can see how information was flowing between the various bodies 'behind the scenes', with each exploiting information gained by the others. One example of this comes from late January/early February 1944 and concerned the SS in Belgium.

On 5 January, a Martian report included the information (presumably acquired from human sources) that large numbers of 'young' SS men had been noted in the Antwerp–Brussels area, probably reflecting the presence of *12. SS-Panzer-Division (Hitlerjugend)* in the area.[4] This same information appeared in 'Record of Western Front' (No. 23), covering the period 7–9 January.[5] It is likely that the Western Front Committee took this information for its own report straight from the Martian document. A little later, on 12 February, the MI14 weekly appreciation reported that:

A Most Secret report dated 26 Jan locates I SS Pz Corps at BRUSSELS. The appearance of this Corps at BRUSSELS probably explains a statement by a Belgian source that a second SS Pz Div is in Belgium.[6]

The 'Most Secret report' is likely to have been an intercepted message, as this terminology is often used as a cover for such material, while the 'Belgian source' is probably the same human agent as in the Martian report. This exchange is referenced directly in the minutes of the Western Front Committee for 3 March 1944:

Captain Pryce Jones said that the Military Party had discussed chiefly Order of Battle and Railway movements. They were particularly interested in any inferences drawn from W.T.I. [Wireless Telegraphy Intelligence, i.e. traffic analysis] which might confirm agents' reports. In particular they wanted details of the whereabouts and organisation of SS formations, Army Corps and now divisions.[7]

This is only one small incident in the much larger intelligence-gathering process, but it shows the level of exchange and cooperation between the various agencies, and the multi-source analysis that was taking place within each organisation. This is a far cry from the portrait of monastic isolation and SIGINT-only 'purity' that is often painted for Bletchley Park.

Indeed, the contact extended beyond the exchange of material: the head of 3M (Military Section in Hut 3) would actually visit MI14 and other intelligence branches in person, as is described in 'The History of Hut Three':

The Head of 3M or a deputy toured the relevant sections of the War Office once a week. Sometimes there was business to transact, sometimes not. It was, however, only by regular visits that good liaison could be maintained at all levels.[8]

The 'History' went on to describe the importance of War Office data in the maintenance of Bletchley Park's own orders of battle (compiled in the 3M Index Section):

> Indexing was done from Ultra only, with the single exception of notes made from periodical W.O. Location and Order of Battle lists. The checking of these lists continued throughout the career of the Index; on occasions where 'Source' [i.e. intercepts] had lost sight of a formation for some time, this War Office information was often of great use.[9]

After November 1943, the practice of making personal visits was also extended to individual commands that received ULTRA. This was no doubt helped by the fact that at the time SHAEF and 21st Army Group were based in the UK, unlike Bletchley's earlier customers, who had been in North Africa or Italy. A more subtle, but nonetheless important, benefit of these regular personal visits lay in building trust and confidence between the different organisations:

> But perhaps the greatest benefit of visits was intangible. The security barrier of the earlier part of the War was such that customers dared not query service in any way. A series of visits established not only friendly relations but a mutual confidence. Customers now knew the Ultra material was passed to them by <u>human beings</u>, whose principal energies were directed towards serving them. They were able still further to trust the comments and rely on the accuracy of signals. They were able too to acquire more knowledge of the potentialities of Ultra, to help themselves by asking questions, and to help the Hut by sending back information about the enemy and about Allied intentions. This liaison was a delicate plant and had to be carefully tended. It could only be kept alive by regular visits.[10]

This close relationship had not always existed, and indeed it had taken four years of war to develop fully. But by the time of D-Day the 'delicate plant' was in flourishing good health.

NAMING SOURCES

The extent of the collaboration in 1943 and the first months of 1944 can only be inferred indirectly. But from March 1944 we can get a detailed insight into the precise contribution of SIGINT to the understanding of the Germans in the west, and of the feeds from other agencies into GC&CS, from the Western Front Committee 'Record', starting with issue No. 27 (covering 4–10 March 1944). In previous editions of the 'Record', information about German activity was listed, but the source was not typically recorded; however, the minutes of the meeting on 10 March include an instruction that henceforth 'source of all items of information should be indicated'.[11] Starting with 'Record of Western Front' (No. 27), a new section on 'Sources and Contributors' was added to each report, listing who was responsible for contributing the information in each numbered paragraph in the 'Record', and what source had provided the primary information.[12] For example, No. 27 includes sixteen items (paragraphs) of information in the section on 'The German Army in the West'. Of these, the first ten were provided by Captain Pryce-Jones of 3M. Some were derived from Hut 3 decrypts of Enigma and FISH traffic; others were supplied by Martian reports. The remaining paragraphs (eleven–sixteen) were derived from traffic analysis and supplied by Captain John Manson, an Intelligence Corps officer working in SIXTA.[13] This detailed content means that, for the twelve weeks preceding D-Day, it is possible to identify the exact contribution made by each intelligence source to Bletchley's picture of the Germans in France, and to assess the type and frequency of the information each supplied. While this is only a snapshot of a much longer process (beginning in late 1942), it portrays the most crucial period in the build-up to the invasion. It also allows a direct comparison between what Bletchley Park *knew* at each stage and what it *sent out* to SHAEF and 21st Army Group in the form of ULTRA messages.

Perhaps the biggest surprise is the paucity of army Enigma, already alluded to in the previous chapter. The source notes in the 'Records' for March–May 1944 do not indicate *any* specific intelligence items derived from decryption of German army Enigma networks based in the west (except via traffic analysis of exercises). As mentioned above, the German army in France was well provided with landlines and made little use of Enigma-encrypted wireless for important communications. This is acknowledged in the 'History of Hut 6', produced by GC&CS after the war; commenting on the pre-D-Day period, the writers observe:

> The German Army was well trained in the first golden rule of cipher security, that no traffic should be sent over the air unless it is absolutely necessary. Consequently the history of Army keys everywhere is a story of spasmodic bursts of traffic with long periods of silence.[14]

They went on to add: 'Unlike the Air keys, the Western Army Keys passed virtually no traffic of significance before D-Day.'

Wehrmacht transmissions in other theatres, however, did produce occasional nuggets of information. For example, during the week of 10–17 March, information associating *Panzergruppe West* with the town of Meaux in France was acquired from a message on the GANNET network (a high command network in Norway).[15] Later, during the week of 15–21 April, parts of both *2.* and *17. Panzer-Divisionen* were identified in Russia, even though other sources suggested that the units were being rested in France. This information was derived from the NUTHATCH Enigma key connecting Berlin with Belgrade, and from VULTURE, an Army High Command key used on the Eastern Front.[16] Another key that provided occasional information was FALCON: it was used by the German military administrative districts and dealt with administrative, personnel and supply matters on behalf of field units nominally drawn from those areas. This key appears five times in the sources quoted in the 'Records', identifying particular divisions present in France.[17]

As in 1943, the SS key QUINCE continued to be a fruitful source for the Western Front Committee. Information about the location of *2. SS-Panzer-Division (Das Reich)* was obtained from this key in early March.[18] The following week, QUINCE intercepts also revealed the presence of the tank regiment from *5. SS-Panzer-Division (Wiking)* at the tank training area at Mailly le Camp. This division was (and would remain) fighting in the east, but it was not unusual for individual units from armoured formations in Russia to spend time at Mailly, either training or converting to new equipment. This formation would, in due course, return east before D-Day; but, from the point of view of GC&CS, it could equally well have been the first stage in the transfer of the whole division to the west. The same week, QUINCE provided information confirming the upgrading of *10. SS-Division (Frundsberg)* to full panzer division status.[19] Later, in April, the network would confirm the location of *2. SS-Panzer-Division (Das Reich)* at Montauban in the south of France.[20] And, in May, two QUINCE messages located the headquarters of *I. SS-Panzer-Korps* at Epône-Mézières to the south-west of Beauvais.[21] Such snippets, combined with other sources, produced a fairly complete picture of the locations and strengths of the SS units in the west prior to the invasion.

Although little specific intelligence was gained from German army networks it should not be inferred that they were silent during the pre-invasion period. On the contrary, many demonstrated periods of intense activity, primarily in the form of communications training exercises. These were closely monitored, and both Hut 6 and SIXTA were engaged in extensive traffic analysis, mapping the networks concerned, logging call-signs and frequencies and, using an outline order of battle, mapping these radio networks onto the ground formations concerned. This would provide a huge advantage when the invasion took place and the networks all lit up with real operational traffic.

This process was described in the 'History of Hut 6':

Before D-Day there was very little operational Enigma Army traffic in the West. There was, however, a series of extensive W/T practice manoeuvres. The traffic intercepted was carefully studied in the light of D/F [direction finding], discriminant, and Order of Battle evidence, and it was found that key areas corresponded, as was to be expected, with the areas of the four Western armies known from agents' reports etc. These practice manoeuvres gave us valuable information on the type of W/T communication to be expected, the locations of head-quarters, and in very general outline, key distribution.[22]

One of these exercises was conducted in the last week of February and the first week of March 1944. 'The Record of Western Front' observed that the exercise appeared to have concluded on 2 March, as after a period of intense activity traffic volumes had diminished substantially; however, one network was of possible significance:

> One wireless network intercepted during the exercise, tends by D/F to equate with S.S. formations. The main station is in the MEAUX area, for which nothing is known from the Order of Battle. The next two important stations on this group are located by D/F at BRUSSELS and ALENCON areas, where I and II S.S. Pz. Korps are respectively located.[23]

The intercepts from this network had in fact revealed the existence of the headquarters of the newly formed *Panzergruppe West*, created on 24 January under *General* Leo Freiherr Geyr von Schweppenburg to command the bulk of the armoured forces in the west, including at that time both *SS-Panzer-Korps* (*II. SS-Panzer-Korps* would return to the east in April 1944, before coming back to France after the invasion).[24] This identification was confirmed by further traffic analysis the following week, when *Panzergruppe West* was specifically mentioned in connection with these and other SS units in France.[25] As will be discussed, the *Panzergruppe* was of particular significance in shaping the German strategic defensive plans against an invasion, and so early identification of its existence was an important achievement by GC&CS.

In addition to the networks used by the German army and the SS during this period, the Luftwaffe continued to make widespread routine use of wireless, and this provided information about ground units as well as those in the air. The Luftwaffe RED key, consistently broken daily throughout much of the war, provided incidental identifications and locations for a number of army units during this period. In addition, these networks also provided more significant information. As well as the field divisions, from 1943 the Luftwaffe also had responsibility for parachute troops in France. These were of much greater fighting potential than the field divisions. British and US forces were already engaged against *Fallschirmjäger* (paratroop) units in Italy during spring 1944, and *1. Fallschirmjäger-Division* would become famous for its tenacious defence of the abbey at Monte Cassino. Meanwhile, in the west, the steady build-up of new parachute forces was followed via intercepted messages on Luftwaffe networks. Two new divisions, the *3.* and *5. Fallschirmjäger-Divisionen* were formed in France through the latter part of 1943 and early 1944. Based around cadres of veterans from units that had suffered heavily on the Eastern Front, these two divisions would go on to form *II. Fallschirm-Korps*. This formation would play a significant role in the fighting in Normandy, and would be almost entirely destroyed in the Falaise pocket.[26]

This training and development process was identified during the week of 8–14 April via intercepts of the Luftwaffe SNOWDROP key, and was reported in that week's 'Record':

5 Para Div. is being formed and is destined for the West; 91 Air Landing Div. is somewhere near STRASBOURG; and Para. Training and Ersatz Div. is to be set up in HOLLAND. These new identifications may partly account for a spate of reports of parachutists in the West. Parachute School I appears at LYON whereas the school has previously been associated with TROYES and DREUX.[27]

By May, the locations of these parachute divisions were well known. But GC&CS would overstate the number of units ultimately present. In the 'Record' for the week of 6–12 May, an identification of *1. Fallschirm-Armee* was made at Nancy.[28] An army-level formation would imply two corps, each consisting of two parachute divisions (i.e. a total of four divisions). In fact, only *II. Fallschirm-Korps* was present (i.e. two divisions). This confusion is understandable: several battalion-sized units serving on the Italian front were withdrawn to France, but it was difficult to tell whether this reflected a move of their parent division to the new sector or merely periods of rest and recuperation before a return to Italy.

Intelligence concerning ground forces in the west was not only derived from land and air force Enigma. The Western Front Committee 'Record' also shows that information was acquired from naval decrypts. In particular, two entries in the 'Record' of 1–7 April 1944 list 'Nile' as the source.[29] 'Nile' was a broad term used in Hut 8 to distinguish traffic using the naval Mediterranean Enigma keys, which included PORPOISE (a general Mediterranean shore installation key) and GRAMPUS (used in the Black Sea). Both of these keys used an old encryption procedure to communicate their Enigma machine message settings. The technique – which left traffic particularly vulnerable to decryption – had long been abandoned by the rest of the German armed forces.[30]

The messages in question related to the recent departure of *II. SS-Panzer-Korps* from France to the region of Tarnopol on the Eastern Front, taking *9.* and *10. SS-Panzer-Divisionen* with it. If true, the information was highly significant as it would represent a substantial decrease in the strength of German armoured forces in the west. Examination of the relevant ULTRA messages reveals how the movement of these SS units came to be reported by the German navy. An ULTRA message of 6 April 1944 reads, in part:

> According to Naval liaison staff Rumania and Rumania [names were repeated in ULTRA for clarity] . . . Second Sugar Sugar Panzer (Strong indications Corps) with Ninth and Tenth Sugar Sugar Divisions was on the march to the south in the area of Rohatin (comment forty miles southeast of Lvov and Lvov) . . .[31]

This one example demonstrates the depth of penetration of German communications systems achieved by GC&CS by 1944. But it also shows that monitoring of even the most apparently obscure source – in this case, the German naval liaison officer in Bucharest – could reveal important intelligence that might relate to a front many miles from the original source of the transmission. Furthermore, Bletchley's systems allowed that information to flow from the original naval translator in Hut 8 to the intelligence assessment teams in Hut 3 – and, ultimately, via ULTRA, to SHAEF, 21st Army Group and other intelligence customers.

THE VALUE OF FISH

By far the most significant source of information about the German forces in the west from March to June 1944 was a series of intermittent but highly valuable decrypts of FISH messages. These were transmitted by encrypted teleprinter on two networks, codenamed BREAM and JELLYFISH at Bletchley Park.

BREAM was the teleprinter link between Berlin and *Generalfeldmarschall* Kesselring, *O.B. Südwest* in Italy. Although these messages did not directly concern preparations in France, they often made reference to units in France and the Low Countries (interchange between units in the two theatres was common – for example, the above-mentioned move of experienced parachute units from Italy to bolster new units in France). The 'Record of Western Front' (No. 28) indicated in March that intelligence had been received about a cadre being taken from *1. Fallschirmjäger-Division* and sent to Brest, possibly as the kernel of a new unit within *3. Fallschirmjäger-Division*. The 'Record' also indicated that this information was derived from a BREAM intercept.[32] The continuing presence of *3. Fallschirmjäger-Division* in Brittany into April was confirmed in 'Record' (No. 33; 22 April 1944), again with the source listed as a BREAM intercept.[33]

Information about higher-level formations was also obtained from this source. Though the first hints of the existence of *Panzergruppe West* were obtained via traffic analysis, this was followed in early March by more concrete information. Hinsley quotes an ULTRA message sent to SHAEF on 11 March 1944,[34] and attributes the source of the information to Enigma: 'Enigma decrypts established on 11 and 18 March that the

HQ of Panzer Gruppe West was at Paris.'[35] However, 'Record' (No. 27; 4–10 March 1944) stated that 'Pz. Gruppe WEST has been identified in the PARIS area, presumably in control of training units or units in process of refitting' and gave the source note for this as BREAM.[36]

The same source was able to clarify further the role of this formation, thanks to several decrypts obtained in late April and early May. 'Record of Western Front' (No. 35) reported:

> In an exceptionally valuable BERLIN Bream message, OKW reserves in the West have been specified as 1 SS Pz. Corps with 1, 12, and 17 SS Divisions, and Pz. Lehr Division when it returns from HUNGARY.[37]

And 'Record' (No. 36) stated:

> Pz. Gr. West (Gen. GEYR) the equivalent of a reinforced Corps staff, is probably destined as the mobile H.Q. for tank warfare in N. FRANCE directly under RUNDSTEDT, and available to control tank reinforcements while leaving ROMMEL free to carry out immediate sealing tasks with semi-static infantry divisions in the coastal sectors.[38]

This was a remarkably accurate assessment of the role of *Panzergruppe West*, and was derived from BREAM. In total, twenty-two intelligence items attributed to this source – including individual unit identifications and locations as well as more strategic information – appear in the Western Front Committee 'Record' between March and June.

JELLYFISH was first detected by GC&CS in January 1944. This was the teleprinter link that connected *Generalfeldmarschall* Gerd von Rundstedt, *O.B. West*, with higher authorities in the Wehrmacht High Command. The OKW was led by *Generalfeldmarschall* Wilhelm Keitel, who reported directly to Hitler and who would translate the conclusions of the daily command meetings with the Führer into operational orders. These were issued under Keitel's authority as *Oberster Befehlshaber der Wehrmacht* (Supreme Commander of the Armed Forces). Officially, the

OKW served as the military general staff for the Third Reich, coordinating the efforts of the army, navy and air force on all fronts. In practice, however, as the war progressed, it found itself exercising more and more direct command authority over military units, particularly in the west. By 1942, the OKW had de facto command of western forces, while the Army High Command (*Oberkommando des Heeres* – OKH) had de facto command of the Eastern Front. Thus, JELLYFISH messages might concern the highest-level strategic discussions between C-in-C West and his political masters, but also significant amounts of administrative information concerning the supply states of units and other logistical matters. This meant that while these messages were extremely difficult both to intercept and to decipher, when this was achieved the results could yield significant rewards for Allied intelligence.

The first breaks into JELLYFISH were achieved in April 1944 and are recorded in the 'Record of Western Front' (No. 32) on 14 April. It contained a discussion of the effects felt by von Rundstedt, *O.B. West*, of the move of *9.* and *10. SS-Panzer-Divisionen* to Russia (as mentioned above, this move was actually identified at GC&CS through naval Enigma intercepts). As the 'Record' notes:

> That the abrupt withdrawal of two Panzer divisions and a Panzer corps has upset the precarious balance of Gen. GEYR's armoured forces may well be manifested by the troop movements now in progress.[39]

For the first time, the source reference for this paragraph is given as JELLYFISH. Much more was to follow.

One of the most spectacular JELLYFISH intercepts occurred on 20 April 1944, although it was not fully decrypted until 2 May, when the contents of the message were passed on to SHAEF in an ULTRA message:

> Information twentieth to Panzer Group West of itinerary for tour of inspection in France & France by Inspector General of Panzer Troops: . . .[40]

It went on to provide the full itinerary for a tour by General Heinz Guderian, inspector general of panzer troops for the German armed forces. The full list of units concerned was as follows:

Date	Unit	Location
24–25 Apr	654 Abt (Heavy Anti-Tank) (along with units of Grossdeutschland Division and 3 SS Division training from Russia)	Mailly le Camp
28 Apr	2nd Panzer Division	Amiens
29 Apr	12th SS Panzer Division	Evreux
1 May	21st Panzer Division	Rennes
2 May	17th SS Panzer-grenadier Div.	Thouars
3 May	273R/10th Panzer Division	Libourne
4 May	2nd SS Panzer Division	Montauban
6 May	155R/9th Panzer Division	Rennes
8 May	179R/116th Panzer Division	Paris/Melun

Although the tour was already half over by the time the message could be read, it provided GC&CS with an essentially complete list of the locations of armoured units in France. The 'Record of Western Front' (No. 35) observed that:

> Estimates of armoured dispositions made on the basis of air recce, and agent's reports have been substantially confirmed by a schedule for Gen. Oberst GUDERIAN's tour of Panzer installations in the west.[41]

On 3 May, a heavy bombing raid was mounted against Mailly le Camp by the RAF. It is unlikely that the raid was in response to this intelligence, as Mailly was already identified as a high-value target; however, GC&CS was able to quantify the results of the raid, since it was mentioned by von Rundstedt in one of his periodic 'appreciations' of the situation in the west, circulated via JELLYFISH and decrypted by 14 May. Unfortunately for the Allies, he reported that, while damage to buildings had been heavy and 400 casualties had been inflicted, damage to 'material' (i.e. tanks) had been minimal, since they had been dispersed around the site.[42]

Further extremely valuable information was to follow in late April and early May, although difficulties in the decryption of FISH messages meant a delay in the delivery of this intelligence – in some cases until the week after the invasion. The information was nonetheless of significant value to field commanders. Until April 1944, GC&CS and MI14 were obliged to base their understanding of the detailed internal state of individual German divisions on what few snippets of information were available from POW interviews, human agent sources, German press and radio reports, and the occasional inferences that could be made about units moving to and from the fighting fronts in Italy and Russia. The result was partial, and relied a good deal on guesswork.[43] But this all changed in late April.

As well as appreciations and orders from senior commanders, the ease with which long texts could be transmitted made the FISH links ideal for detailed administrative reporting. And it was a series of administrative returns transmitted in the weeks prior to the invasion that gave Allied commanders information in unprecedented detail about their opponents. The returns listed precise figures for the strength of units – how many officers, NCOs and other ranks – as well as tallies of equipment, ranging from pistols to tanks and trucks. Also included were lists of deficiencies and statements of serviceability for each type of equipment.

Unfortunately, the interpretation of these messages was often extremely difficult. As well as being encrypted for transmission, the information was highly abbreviated. Often the information was written into the columns of a pro-forma table and only the actual numbers were transmitted; or an alphabetical code referring to the column in the table might be used. As a result, the decrypted message might consist simply of letters, followed by numbers: 'A:21, B:46, C:110 . . .' It was only by careful and diligent teasing out of the formats used by these messages that their contents could be understood. This work was carried out by the indexers in Hut 3, as the 'History' of the hut described:

Proforma Returns.

The difficulty of these messages was one of <u>identification</u>. The messages themselves appeared as a chaos of letters and figures, rarely complete and often without preamble or signature. No use could be made of them until it had been determined (1) to what proforma already known (if any) the return belonged, (2) the probable meaning.[44]

Fortunately, by 1944, the staff of Hut 3 had gained significant experience of this process and their understanding of German methods was fairly good. Nevertheless, it did increase the delay in producing intelligible information.

Two messages concerning the state of the German *363. Infanterie-Division* were decrypted in late April. This unit was actually stationed in Denmark, but its condition provides a good barometer for the condition of other '300 Series' divisions stationed on other non-active fronts (of which there were several in France). The division reported a 'striking deficiency' of NCOs – a widespread problem in the German army, as soldiers with combat experience became casualties and new formations were forced to rely on cadres of less-experienced leaders. The division was also almost completely lacking in any motor transport, having to rely on horses for mobility and supply. And an outbreak of infection among the 8,000 horses in the division was severely hampering the training of the divisional artillery units.[45] A similar situation was reported for two infantry divisions in the west, both of which reported grave deficiencies in both NCOs and motor transport.[46]

A further series of FISH messages provided detailed strength returns for the armoured units in France. The first of these was intercepted on 20 April and was fully decrypted by 28 April.[47] A subsequent message was intercepted on 19 May and was broken in two parts, one on 25 May[48] and the other on 11 June.[49] These were followed by others on 25 May (broken 7 June)[50] and 11 June (broken 13 June).[51] The picture revealed by these messages was one of severe deficiencies in both manpower and equipment in the German panzer units.

The strength returns of the four SS divisions in France were reconstructed from these messages.

1. SS-Panzer-Division (Leibstandarte SS Adolf Hitler) reported a strength of 17,257 all ranks, deficient by 4,143 (19 per cent), most of the shortfall being NCOs. The two armoured battalions in the division had 41 *Panzer V* (Panther) and 45 *Panzer IV* tanks (out of a theoretical strength of about 70 each). Much personal kit was also missing: 'There are deficiencies in small arms, light infantry weapons, entrenching tools and camouflage suits.' And the division lacked training. To make matters worse, 1,685 members of the division were absent on training courses in the Reich. The division did, however, possess its full allocation of 42 StuG assault guns (turretless tanks).

2. SS-Panzer-Division (Das Reich) was in no better state. Two manpower returns were deciphered, showing the division with 17,025 (all ranks) on 20 April, rising to 18,930 on 19 May – still 1,582 under strength (again mainly NCOs). Tank states showed it to have 37 Panthers (a deficiency of 62) and 55 *Panzer IVs* (a shortfall of 46); however, all 42 StuG assault guns were present. There were complaints of lack of training and lack of all non-armoured motor transport.

12. SS-Panzer-Division (Hitlerjugend) was a new, as yet unblooded formation created in 1943 out of teenage members of the Hitler Youth organisation. Despite receiving cadres from *1. SS-Panzer-Division (Leibstandarte SS Adolf Hitler)*, this division also suffered from the perennial lack of officers: 488 were present (a shortfall of 182). The situation was even worse for NCOs: 2,004 were present (a shortfall of 2,500). It was, however, very nearly up to full strength with 19,920 other ranks. In April, the division had only 8 Panthers, but it was well supplied with 88 *Panzer IVs*. Non-armoured transport was again in desperately short supply, the division recording only 231 available trucks (out of the 2,000 it was supposed to have).

The fourth SS division, *17. SS-Panzergrenadier-Division*, listed its full complement of 42 assault guns, but it had no tanks. And it suffered a similar shortage of officers, NCOs, motor transport and spare parts.

(As an aside, it is clear from the figures just how much the German army and SS had come to rely on their StuG assault guns over the more expensive and complex panzers.)

Returns were also decrypted which provided snippets of data for *9., 11.* and *116. Panzer-Divisionen.* These showed a similar lack of motor transport and training. And on 19 May not one of *116. Panzer-Division's* allocation of 73 Panther tanks had yet been delivered.

The delay in the decryption of FISH traffic meant that some of this information was not available to commanders until after the invasion had begun. However, in many cases the information was available before the units in question were committed to battle in Normandy: *2. SS-Panzer-Division,* for instance, was stationed in the south of France and did not become involved in combat with the invading forces until August. Thus, Allied commanders had a detailed breakdown of the precise strengths and training and equipment states of the units they were facing (and would face) on the battlefield. This provided them with a huge combat advantage.

CONTINUING JAPANESE TRAFFIC

In the first half of 1944, interceptions of Japanese diplomatic traffic also continued to provide a key source of intelligence for GC&CS. With the success in breaking the CORAL cipher (JNA20) in March 1944, as well as ongoing decryptions of PURPLE and JMA material, the flow of Japanese intelligence through GC&CS concerning activity in Europe became significant. Such was the volume that it was decided to create a separate message series for this intelligence when passed to commands associated with OVERLORD and the ongoing campaign in Italy. This series was given the prefix/codename 'BAY'.[52] Much of the content related to German views on the likely timing and location of the Allied attack, and the debate within German high command over which defensive strategy should be adopted. This material is discussed in a later chapter, but some of the Japanese decrypts continued to provide detailed organisational and order-of-battle information.

One such was a report produced by the Japanese naval attaché in Berlin, Admiral Kojima, who had carried out his own tour of the Atlantic defences between 20 and 24 April 1944. The reports in which he described what he had seen were intercepted and disseminated between 8 and 13 May 1944.[53] These messages were redrafted in the normal way to disguise their source, before being passed on to commands. However, verbatim copies of the original translation of the Japanese signals also survive in the National Archives. The messages were considered of sufficient importance to be included in the daily 'Naval Headlines' passed to Churchill. In this case, the messages were provided in the form of verbatim translations. Written in the first person, they give a real sense of the raw form of this intelligence, complete with missing words – indeed whole missing sections – as well as guesses at translations. The level of detail can be gauged from this extract:

For example between OSTEND and BOULOGNE, counting Naval batteries alone, there is a total of 28 batteries, with a garrison of 16,000. Between BOULOGNE and LE HAVRE there is a total of 24 batteries. These principally consist of:

AT CALAIS: one 40cm battery (3 guns), one 38cm battery (3 guns), one 28cm battery (4 guns)

AT LE HAVRE: one 38cm battery (3 guns)

AT OSTEND: one 28cm railway battery (4 guns) and so on

For the seaward defence of OSTEND harbour there are:

Four 28cm guns, two 15cm guns, twelve 10.5 guns, four 5cm anti-tank guns, eight 7.7cm high angle guns, 20 machine-guns.

Two thirds of the above have an angle of fire of 120 degs. And the remainder can fire in any direction.[54]

The messages went on to describe details of minefields, anti-tank ditches, radars, the thickness of concrete on protective bunkers and the morale of the defending units. This information provided vital corroboration of the intelligence on German coastal defences gained from other (often human agent) sources and included in the Martian reports.

RELATIVE VALUE

The fact that from March to June 1944 the Western Front Committee was so rigorous in reporting the source for each item of intelligence placed before it means we can compare the various sources of intelligence available. Obviously not all these items of intelligence are equal: an important insight into German strategy provided by the decryption of one of von Rundstedt's appreciations was not the same as a Luftwaffe Enigma message reporting the movement of an anti-aircraft battery. However, it is possible to perform a simple count of the number of times each source is quoted in the appendices to the 'Records'. While this is a very crude measure, it does reveal certain broad patterns that probably reflect the balance of information making its way into Hut 3 and to the committee. It should be said at the outset that this count does not acknowledge the huge contribution made by traffic analysis to Allied understanding of the Germans in France. That intelligence source grew to have a large section of each 'Record' devoted to it. However, the count does reflect the information gained by the decryption and reading of the contents of enemy traffic.

What is immediately apparent is the major contribution made by FISH: twenty-two references to BREAM and the same for JELLYFISH (all after the first break into JELLYFISH traffic in April 1944). Thus, 44 out of 114 source entries are for FISH (38 per cent). This figure does not reflect the great value of many of these decrypts, but it is indicative of the success achieved in breaking FISH.

German army Enigma, by contrast, appears only four times in the appendices, and none of the keys listed were used by the German army on the Western Front. All of these intercepts were of networks operating elsewhere; only incidentally did they provide information about the west.

This reflects the almost total lack of significant Enigma-encrypted wireless communication by the German army in France prior to the invasion. On the other hand, the SS (as discussed) was more accustomed to communicate using its Enigma keys: there are eight references to QUINCE intercepts. The Bletchley codebreakers were assisted by the fact that the SS used only a small number of Enigma keys for all their communications on the various fighting fronts. The Luftwaffe provided the richest source of Enigma decrypts, appearing ten times in the appendices. Some of these were from keys used in the west: SNOWDROP and DAFFODIL, for instance, as well as RED, mentioned four times, and BROWN, mentioned twice. In other cases, however, relevant information about the west was recorded after being passed on keys used in other theatres: GADFLY, used by an air corps in the Mediterranean, appears once, along with BEETLE, used by Luftwaffe Command on the Eastern Front. Naval Enigma also made its contribution, with two references to intelligence about land-based units derived from *Kriegsmarine* intercepts.

Ironically, the highest number of references in the appendices of the 'Records' (eight instances) is to Martian – in other words, to intelligence information not derived from SIGINT at all, but provided by CIS. This shows the degree to which GC&CS was happy to accept and integrate non-SIGINT information, and illustrates the vital role that close liaison with the other intelligence agencies also working on invasion planning played in the work of Bletchley Park. Only by synthesising all this information, applying it to analysis of the decryptions achieved and also feeding it back into the decryption process (for example, by providing material to inform 'cribbing') could the levels of success achieved at GC&CS be maintained.

ORDERING THE BATTLE

Another powerful tool for assessing the depth of understanding that GC&CS had of the Germans in France came in the form of the periodic orders of battle produced at Bletchley as part of the Western Front

Committee reporting process. The order of battle from 24 March 1944 is of particular interest, given that it not only recorded the German units and higher formations known to Bletchley Park at the time, but also stated how the information had been acquired (SIGINT or some other source, such as photo reconnaissance).[55] Thus it is possible to discern precisely which parts of the order of battle were derived from SIGINT (both via decrypts and via traffic analysis) and which parts came from information sent in to Bletchley by other agencies. At first glance, it would appear that SIGINT did not play a huge part in the supply of intelligence used in this document: only seventeen out of fifty-six divisional identifications are attributed to SIGINT sources. However, a more detailed examination of which formations fell into which category is quite telling: Luftwaffe and SS formations were readily identified via SIGINT; army formations, by contrast, appear to have left far less of a SIGINT footprint and were mostly identified by other means.

The second Hut 3 order-of-battle document available is No. 12, first issued on 21 May but including amendments issued up to 2 June.[56] This document is not annotated with sources, but when compared with the known historical German order of battle at the time of the invasion it gives an impression of the accuracy and depth of Bletchley's understanding of the German dispositions immediately before the attack. Apart from fine points of detail, all of the German armour in France had been correctly accounted for and its locations identified. Only one significant error appears in the order of battle: a '1st Parachute Army' is postulated (albeit with a question mark against its name). As has been discussed earlier, the movements of degraded parachute units from the Italian front into France had confused the picture for GC&CS. In fact, only two parachute divisions were present. All but two of the remaining 58 divisional identifications were correct.

When (between 1977 and 1979) Bennett analysed the extent to which these forces had been 'identified' through their appearance in ULTRA messages to commands, he inevitably produced only a limited picture. He described how, of the twenty-eight divisions present on the coast between

Amsterdam and Brest on 6 June, ULTRA messages had mentioned fifteen at least once by the end of May. Similarly, of those from Brest to the Spanish frontier, five out of seven had appeared in a message; and on the Riviera – four out of seven.[57] He went on to point out that both *709. Infanterie-Division* (static) on the Normandy coast and the more capable *352. Infanterie-Division* opposite Omaha Beach had been mentioned only once, while *716. Infanterie-Division* (static) had not appeared at all in messages sent to SHAEF and 21st Army Group. While he does not state so explicitly, Bennett's phrasing – 'Ultra was even less well informed about 352 Division's right hand neighbours in the British landing area, 716 and 711 Divisions'[58] – suggests that he equated the appearance of a formation in an ULTRA message with knowledge of it at Bletchley Park. As has been demonstrated, this was by no means the case: Bletchley Park had a much wider grasp of the enemy order of battle than analysis of just these messages would suggest.

GC&CS was not purely a news service, reporting only current activity, but it was the responsibility of Bletchley Park to report change to commands. If a new formation had been identified, or an existing one had moved or altered its status in some other way, this would be reported. Units that did little would feature infrequently (if at all) in ULTRA messages. In this context, the fact that *716. Infanterie-Division* in Normandy did not appear in any messages to SHAEF or 21st Army Group in the first half of 1944 did not reflect ignorance on the part of GC&CS. Bletchley had been fully aware of the division's location since 1942, but the formation simply did nothing of reportable interest during that period. This can be contrasted with armoured units which, in many cases, redeployed on a number of occasions (or in the extreme case of *9.* and *10. SS-Panzer-Divisionen*, travelled from France to Russia and back again). Any such moves would naturally be immediately reported in ULTRA messages.

*

The intelligence picture provided to Allied commanders at the start of June 1944 was not perfect. The assessment included some details that were not correct (and there will be more on this later). Overall, however, the intelligence effort was largely successful. As Hinsley wrote: 'In the end . . . it enabled the Allies to make an all but totally accurate assessment of the German order of battle in the *Overlord* area on D-Day.'[59]

This was a significant – and unprecedented – achievement, and SIGINT developed by Bletchley Park had played a decisive role. That role was not limited to the interception, decryption and onward transmission of enemy signals: Bletchley played a much larger part in analysis and maintained a much closer and more reciprocal relationship with its intelligence 'customers' than has perhaps hitherto been appreciated. Indeed, that relationship – especially with MI14 and CIS – went from being one of 'delivery service' and 'customer' to being one of intelligence partnership and collaboration.

CHAPTER SIX

UNDERSTANDING GERMAN EXPECTATIONS

I n the summer of 1941, one of Bletchley's senior codebreakers, Dilly
Knox, was applying himself to the ciphers of the *Abwehr*, Germany's
intelligence service. Knox had led the early British attacks on
Enigma, including on both the commercial and the military variants. His
team in the former stable yard at Bletchley Park had also been successful
at breaking Italian naval Enigma traffic. In summer 1941, however, an
increasing amount of *Abwehr* traffic was being intercepted and, while
much of it was enciphered using simple pencil-and-paper methods, a
portion of it clearly used machine ciphers.

The format of these messages, with two groups of four letters at the
start of each message, suggested that they were enciphered using variants
of Enigma different from the models previously investigated. Knox had
developed a number of techniques for attacking these 'message indica-
tors' (as the letter groups were termed), as well as the cipher texts themselves, in order to figure out the workings of the machines. Complex
mathematical methods were needed to deduce the internal wiring of
each rotor, and thus work out what encipherments would be produced.
Knox turned to his team of female staff to perform these calculations. Of
the dozen or more women in his team, only two spoke the necessary
German. One was Margaret Rock.

Her father was a Royal Navy surgeon who had been killed in 1917, when she was just fourteen years old, after his ship hit a mine laid from a German U-Boat off the Irish coast. His letters to Margaret at boarding school had urged her to pursue her studies as far as possible and to take up a worthwhile career – in stark contrast to the general expectations of women in the early twentieth century. She had taken her father's wishes to heart, graduating in 1921 from Bedford College in London, at the time one of the relatively few institutions where women could obtain degrees. She became a business statistician, and enjoyed travelling widely with her brother John during her time off, in the course of which she learned German to add to the French she had learned at school. This combination of mathematical and linguistic skills led to her being recruited by Bletchley Park, where she arrived in spring 1940. She would go on to become one of the most senior and most trusted figures in Dilly Knox's team. She was older than the other women, and Knox considered her one of the half-dozen finest minds in the whole of GC&CS.

Long periods of tedious analysis and calculations led finally to Margaret and her younger colleague Mavis Lever being able to unravel the secrets of one of the most widely used *Abwehr* Enigmas. On 28 October 1941, Knox reported to Alastair Denniston, the head of Bletchley Park, that the prospects for breaking traffic on the so-called *Zählwerke* ('counter') Enigma were very good, and indeed the first decrypted message was issued on Christmas Day.

Bletchley Park would go on to issue over 140,000 *Abwehr* Enigma decrypts, from several different Enigma variants. However, Knox himself would play an ever-diminishing role: from December 1941, he was increasingly incapacitated by stomach cancer and was forced to work from home. For the next year, his main link with the other codebreakers was Margaret Rock, who frequently collaborated with him at his home and acted as his messenger. Dilly Knox died in February 1943, before he had the chance to see the fruits of his work on D-Day. Margaret, however, continued at Bletchley and subsequently worked with GCHQ until 1963.

Knox – a classical scholar – is reported to have paid tribute to Margaret and her colleague Mavis Lever in a paraphrase of a famous remark by Archimedes: 'Give me a Lever and a Rock and I shall move the Universe.'

*

In the previous two chapters we saw how completely Bletchley Park was able to understand the German order of battle prior to the invasion. After more than eighteen months of painstaking work, almost every enemy unit had been identified, and its location and strength mapped in detail. Its command and communications arrangements in the event of an attack were also well understood. However, while all this was of vital importance, there was another layer of information that was also required: what did the Germans expect to happen in 1944? And what were they planning to do about it? Thus GC&CS had a second key task, which was to penetrate the thinking of the German high command. The invasion plan itself relied at least in part on a measure of surprise, and so it was necessary to understand what the Germans were expecting. If they were able to identify the correct location of the attack, they might take measures to reinforce that area, and thus compromise the Allied plan. Equally, even if they did not know exactly where they would be attacked, it was important to know their likely responses to an invasion, wherever it occurred: how were they planning to deploy their reserves? Would they fight hard on the beaches, or were they planning to hold back and counterattack once the Allies were ashore? The task of finding the answers to all of these questions fell to the listeners, codebreakers and analysts of GC&CS.

First we should look at the Allies' actual plans and situation on the ground at this time, so that it can be compared to the picture that developed on the other side of the Channel.

ALLIED PLANS

In the years leading up to 1944, Allied planners had studied in detail the entire coast of Western Europe, from the Netherlands to the Spanish border. Each beach and port had been analysed for its suitability for a landing. At the same time, these planners had to keep various constraints in mind. The first of these was air power: the further the invasion beach was from the UK, the harder it would be to maintain air superiority over it; and that was vital to success. Secondly, the quantity of shipping required to lift the force would need to be larger if an extended sea journey was involved, as return trips would be longer. All of this favoured an attack on the closest part of the continent – the Pas-de-Calais. Yet this was the most heavily fortified part of the German Atlantic Wall defences, and the ports of Kent were too small to support the size of fleet required for the invasion.[1]

In the event, an attack on the Normandy coastline around Caen was selected, with the secondary objective of the rapid capture of the port of Cherbourg, at the tip of the Cotentin peninsula to the west. The difficulties created by the longer sea and air journey were mitigated by other factors, such as the character of the beaches and their hinterland, the smaller strength of the German defences, and likely weather and sea conditions.

The initial plan called for a beach landing by three divisions, with airborne attacks in support; but this was limited to the Caen area, with no landing on the Cotentin. This smaller operation reflected the fact that Allied resources of troops and aircraft were limited: in particular, dedicated landing craft of the types required were in critically short supply.[2] When the plan was presented to General Montgomery, then land commander of 21st Army Group, he was concerned that it lacked sufficient punch to succeed; and, when Eisenhower was appointed supreme commander, he agreed. Thus, the final plan, developed in January 1944, called for a five-division seaborne landing, with an additional two American divisions landing to the west (one at the base of the Cotentin peninsula) and the whole operation supported by three airborne divisions. This widened the attack front from 25 to 50 miles (40–80km). While this made sense in terms of the land battle, it presented the planners with a serious challenge in terms of the required maritime lift and landing craft. This could only be solved by reducing the number of vehicles for each attacking division from 3,000 to 1,450; but even that was not enough, and the date of the invasion had to be put back from 1 May to 31 May to allow for additional landing craft to be manufactured.[3]

The prospects of success of this attack were calculated on the basis of the known strength of the German forces in the Normandy area, and their capacity to reinforce the battle once it had begun. Thus, Eisenhower's final approval on 12 February 1944 was predicated first on the maintenance of secrecy, and second on the premise that the Germans did not make any radical changes to their defensive arrangements.[4] The monitoring of these two factors would fall to the Allied intelligence agencies, and to GC&CS. We have already seen how the strength of the German defences, in terms of the number of available divisions, was also a political factor, as the president and prime minister had agreed to the invasion on the basis of quite restrictive estimates of the strength of the likely opposition. In short, if Allied intelligence detected radical changes made by the Germans that had not been predicted by the planners, the invasion would be either cancelled or postponed.

THE NEED FOR DECEPTION

The British artillery officer and military historian A.H. Burne described a process for analysing historic battles which he called 'Inherent Military Probability'.[5] This was based on the idea that if he could place himself in the shoes of a past commander and consider all the factors at play in his decision-making – available forces, enemy, constraints of time, terrain, supply, etc. – the number of possible options open to that commander would be very limited, and thus his likely command decisions could be predicted. A very similar process is used by intelligence officers. If you know the objectives of your opponent, the means available to him and the challenges he faces, predicting what he is likely to do becomes much simpler. As Sherlock Holmes famously put it: 'How often have I said to you that when you have eliminated the impossible, whatever remains, however improbable, must be the truth?'⁶ This principle applied to the Germans in 1944: if they were able to assess all the options available to the Allies, as well as their resources and limitations, German intelligence could well reach the same conclusions about the 'Inherent Military Probability' of the various plans on the table – and thus accurately predict the likely invasion.

It was essential for the Allies, therefore, to conceal as far as possible not only their plans, but also their own order of battle and resources – and, wherever possible, to mislead the enemy about all of these things. This is where the various deception operations planned by the Allies would play their part.

There were two principal objectives to the deception. The first was to deceive the Germans about Allied capability: if the enemy could be persuaded that the Allies had many more troops and landing craft in the UK than they actually had, that would widen the range of 'probabilities' that the Germans had to anticipate and prepare for. They would spread their forces more thinly as they tried to account for every eventuality.

The second objective was to persuade the Germans that the invasion itself would occur in a location other than that actually proposed. This would be attempted at both a strategic level (encompassing possible attacks from Norway to Greece) and later on at a theatre level (creating the impression of attacks on parts of France other than Normandy). And, even if Normandy was identified as the target of the first landing, the enemy had to be persuaded that it would be followed up by a second, larger attack elsewhere.

The role of Bletchley Park in this endeavour also had two aspects. The primary task of the codebreakers was to try and ascertain what the Germans were expecting and how they planned to respond. That, of course, is bread and butter to any intelligence organisation in the build-up to a large operation, and would have taken place even if no deception had been attempted. Its secondary role was to identify how the enemy was responding to the deception operation in particular, and to provide information that would allow the deception operation to be nuanced in the light of what was believed (or not believed) by the Germans. Ralph Bennett summed this up:

> If a deception plan is to be of any practical use there must exist in parallel with it an intelligence service capable of relaying news of the enemy's changing moods and measuring the degree of credence he is attaching to the false tale from day to day.[7]

*

From the outset, the Allied commanders faced the problem of the inherent likelihood of their proposed operation: it would be reasonable for the Germans to expect an attack exactly where the Allies intended it, across the Channel to France. Thus, it was necessary to build expectations in other areas, such as the Mediterranean. Unfortunately, that theatre had been the focus of Allied activity in 1943, and thus much deception effort had been expended in drawing attention *away* from that region. As the military historian Michael Howard put it:

> For the past six months they had been trying to persuade the Germans that they faced a major invasion threat from the United Kingdom when in fact they did not. Now they had to persuade them that they did not face such a threat, whereas in fact they did.[8]

Initially, efforts were made to develop a Europe-wide strategic deception. The London Controlling Section, the body responsible for devising such operations, produced a plan codenamed BODYGUARD in January 1944. This was intended to persuade the Germans of three things: that attacks would take place in Norway and the Balkans; that land invasion was a secondary priority to reducing Germany by air attack; and that 50 divisions were required for a land invasion and these would not be available until late summer 1944 at the earliest.[9]

Unfortunately, it became evident in the early part of 1944 that the wider, strategic-level deception was unlikely to succeed, as the Germans already expected an attack on France or the Low Countries (as we have seen in Hitler's comments on this in his Führer Directive No. 51 in November 1943). As a result, the more detailed plan approved by Eisenhower on 23 February – Operation FORTITUDE – acquired a narrower focus. The threat to Norway was to be maintained, but the remainder of the programme focused on localised deception, promoting the possibility of an invasion in the Pas-de-Calais rather than Normandy, and spreading confusion over the timing of the attack. An additional aim was to sustain in the minds of the Germans the possibility of an attack at Calais for two weeks (or as long as possible) *after* the Normandy attack was under way.[10] In fact, the focus on Calais was helped by the fact that the Germans already considered this to be the likeliest route for an invasion, and Hitler himself certainly thought it the most probable option.[11]

Overall, however, the greater part of Allied deception concerned order of battle. If the Allies could convince the Germans that they had a much larger force available than they actually had, the enemy would have to consider the possibility of multiple landings in different areas. There were three principal ways in which the Allies could exaggerate their available forces: by physically creating dummy aircraft, tanks, camps and so on for German reconnaissance aircraft to identify; by producing the signals footprint of imaginary Allied units for German Y services to intercept; and by feeding false information via 'turned' German agents in the UK controlled by the 'Double Cross' operation.

The first of these options – the production of physical dummies – was pursued with some enthusiasm, and rows of inflatable tanks sprang up alongside fake landing craft in east-coast ports.[12] However, in 1944 German air reconnaissance over the UK was so limited that there was little opportunity to observe these targets; only thirty-two overland reconnaissance flights by the Luftwaffe were recorded in daytime in the first six months of 1944. Thus, the German high command received very little useful data from air reconnaissance in 1944.[13]

At the same time, the Germans were singularly ineffective at intercepting Allied radio traffic emanating from the UK. This meant that radio deception by the Allies failed: the Germans simply did not hear it – especially the signals deceptions carried out in Scotland and the north of England as part of 'FORTITUDE NORTH', the fictional operation against Norway.[14] As Hinsley put it:

> Neither these measures nor the Allied deception plan . . . would have suffced to keep the enemy guessing if he had been blessed with reasonably good intelligence. Far from having good intelligence, however, Germany in the weeks before D-Day lacked any source of reliable information.[15]

This left German intelligence analysts with very little to go on, other than information from *Abwehr* military intelligence and its ('turned') spy networks in the UK. This is where the work of Bletchley Park could potentially play a role.

GERMAN MISUNDERSTANDINGS

There is little doubt that the elements of the Allied deception plan which related to the Allied order of battle were largely successful. The Germans' estimates of the available invasion forces were consistently hugely exaggerated, and this cast a shadow over the accuracy of all their subsequent strategic appreciations. They were not able to produce the accurate assessments of Allied strength that would have allowed them to draw the correct conclusions about the planned invasion. The German organisations largely responsible for estimating Allied strength were the two principal military intelligence departments of the German general staff, known as *Fremde Heere West* (FHW – Foreign Armies West) and the equivalent *Fremde Heere Ost* (FHO – Foreign Armies East). These two organisations were created in November 1938 by then Chief of the German General Staff Franz Halder. Their task was to develop orders of battle for the Germans' potential enemies in the west and the east. In peacetime, this was carried out through attaché visits and by studying non-secret publicly available information. After 1939, both organisations switched to clandestine methods of obtaining their information, as well as air reconnaissance, POW interrogations and the other channels of military intelligence.[16] Earlier in the war FHW had achieved some notable successes; in 1940, it had successfully identified 122 out of the 123 British and French divisions operating during the Battle of France. But its work has been described as 'statistical' rather than predictive, in that it tended to limit itself to producing catalogues of enemy units rather than trying to discern enemy plans or predict future operations.[17]

From early 1943, FHW was commanded by *Oberst* Alexis Baron von Roenne. A former banker, highly intelligent and a devout Christian, Roenne was born into a German family in Latvia. As a result, he spoke Russian, and began his career in FHO studying the Soviet forces under the famous intelligence officer Reinhard Gehlen.[18] He was moved west in March 1943 and from then on was less successful. His team failed to predict accurately any of the Allied landings in the Mediterranean in 1943, a fact not lost on Hitler himself.[19] Nonetheless, it fell to them to produce the daily *Lagebericht West* (Situation Report West), apprecia-tions of Allied order of battle, as well as other assessment reports. Roenne consistently overestimated the strength of Allied forces, leading to many of the false conclusions reached by German high command prior to the invasion.

Roenne was later implicated in the July 1944 bomb plot against Hitler, for which he was tried and executed. It has been argued that he was a Christian anti-Nazi hero and that his falsely exaggerated intelligence assessments were a deliberate effort to undermine German military operations.[20] Another explanation for the exaggerations could lie in the attitude towards FHW on the part of the *Sicherheitsdienst* (SD), the secu-rity branch of the SS, which typically passed Roenne's estimates of Allied forces to the Führer. Some have claimed that the SD considered Roenne's estimates too high and defeatist and so routinely revised them down before passing them on, leading, so historian David Kahn has argued, to Roenne following a deliberate ploy from the middle of 1943 onwards of exaggerating the reports *even more* so that the correct information would get through. Kahn even provides evidence of a meeting between Roenne and his second-in-command, *Oberstleutnant* Lothar Metz, at which such a plan was discussed.[21] However, Michael Howard has challenged this view, pointing out that the SD did not take over FHW reporting until the summer of 1944, and that prior to that time FHW reports were passed direct to German high command. He argues that Roenne was trying to do his job honestly, but that the flow of information, from the *Abwehr* in particular, was so poor and so riddled with errors – some prompted by deliberate Allied deceptions – that he was ultimately led to the wrong conclusions.[22]

Either way, the result was the same: German high command developed an exaggerated estimate of Allied strength. As early as January 1944, one German estimate placed fifty-five divisions in the UK, when the real figure was nearer thirty-seven. By April, Roenne estimated an available invasion force of between eighty-five and ninety regular divisions and seven airborne divisions, when the real figures stood at thirty-two and three, respectively. More significantly, perhaps, the Germans also estimated that the Allies had enough landing craft to deliver up to twenty divisions in a first-wave attack. As we have seen, in reality it was an immense challenge to lift just five divisions.[23] This overestimation was to have profound consequences when the German commanders tried to predict what action the Allies were likely to take.

RECEIVING AND DECEIVING THE *ABWEHR*

Much has been made of the contribution of Bletchley Park to Operation FORTITUDE, as the deception operations were codenamed, based on its breaking of the *Abwehr* ciphers and capacity thus to follow the effectiveness of various deception activities. But attention has also been given to the huge amounts of false order-of-battle information that was fed back to the *Abwehr*, and on to FHW, via messages carried by the Double Cross programme of turned German agents in the UK. These operations were in fact not controlled from Bletchley Park (they were largely MI5's responsibility); indeed they did not even constitute the bulk of the work carried out by the specialist sections of GC&CS dedicated to following this clandestine traffic. Bletchley's role was in fact much wider: to consider the enemy's strategic thinking in the west as a whole and to understand the Germans' knowledge of the Allies' own order of battle and their appreciations of likely invasion locations. In turn, this was part of a broader imperative: Bletchley's role was not to *change* the minds of the Germans, but to *read* them, regardless of the conclusions those enemy minds might reach.

Bletchley's breaking of the *Abwehr* Enigma traffic played an important role in its gauging of German thinking. The *Abwehr* – in full, *Amt Auslandsnachrichten und Abwehr* (Department for Foreign Intelligence and Defence) – was, from 1938, the military intelligence department of the German high command. Directed from Berlin by its head, *Admiral* Wilhelm Canaris, it had sections (known as an *Abwehrstellung* or *Ast*) in each military district in Germany, and established additional *Abwehrstellungen* in occupied territories as war progressed. *Abwehrstellungen* were responsible for defensive counter-intelligence in their regions as well as hostile foreign intelligence gathering.[24] In neutral countries such as Spain, Portugal, Sweden and Switzerland, the *Abwehr* used diplomatic cover to establish outstations, known as *Kriegsorganisationen* (KO), which performed a similar intelligence-gathering function and ran smaller local offices in major cities and ports. Importantly, from the point of view of GC&CS, many of these individual sub-stations communicated with their parent offices – which in turn communicated with Berlin – via wireless, which made them vulnerable to interception.

Originally established by the War Office, under MI8, the Allied interception of *Abwehr* wireless signals began by using the GPO's intercept stations, which could pick up *Abwehr* traffic between its agents and stations on the continent. By 1944 this operation had passed to SIS control when the RSS (the Radio Security Section, later the Radio Security Service) came under its wing.[25] By this time it had grown into a large organisation, employing nearly 3,500 staff, including 1,200 so-called 'Voluntary Interceptors' – civilian radio enthusiasts who monitored the airwaves on their own wirelesses and reported traffic to their RSS handlers – by war's end. In addition to these interceptors, the RSS also maintained a series of formal Y stations, the largest of which was at Hanslope Park, in Buckinghamshire, only a few miles north of Bletchley.[26] A significant proportion of *Abwehr* traffic in the west was intercepted by the RSS and passed to Bletchley Park.

The *Abwehr* used two types of ciphers. Its individual agents and smaller outstations communicated with their controllers using pencil-and-paper hand ciphers, while the larger stations used several versions of the Enigma machine. The hand ciphers were first broken in 1940. GC&CS set up a section to deal with this material under Oliver Strachey, an old Etonian and veteran of GC&CS who had started his codebreaking career during the First World War. Strachey had actually been due to retire in January 1940, but the outbreak of war meant that his services were retained.[27] In typical Bletchley fashion, the section was christened 'Illicit Signals Oliver Strachey' or ISOS; although Strachey left at the end of 1941, the section continued to bear his initials for the remainder of the war.

Bletchley was also able to break several of the *Abwehr* Enigma machines, starting in December 1941. This work was carried out by another First World War veteran, the code-breaking genius Dilly Knox, who we saw recognising Margaret Rock's potential at the start of the chapter. The *Abwehr* machines differed rather from their military cousins, but Knox spotted certain recurring patterns which enabled him to break the machines.[28] A subsection of ISOS was created to deal with this traffic – 'Illicit Signals Knox' or ISK – a name that also persisted even after Knox's death in 1943.

ISOS remained the overarching organisation responsible for the distribution of intercepted *Abwehr* traffic. At its peak in late 1944, the ISOS section had grown to a total of 182 staff, with roughly half working on ISK (Enigma material).[29] By the end of the war, it had issued some 268,000 decrypts. In May 1944, it averaged nearly 300 messages a day.[30]

The principal customer for ISOS material was Section V of SIS – the section responsible for foreign counter-intelligence. Using both ISOS and other sources, it was able to build up an almost complete picture of the *Abwehr*'s structure and operations. This indeed was its main purpose, monitoring the activities of hostile spies and countering enemy acts of sabotage. A particular focus was the protection of Allied shipping in neutral ports against both enemy intelligence gathering and direct attack. As a result of Section V's work, a number of German spies around the world were identified and prevented from operating – often simply by blowing their cover to the authorities in the neutral countries in which they were working.[31] ISOS also led to the capture of spies working on UK territory and British overseas possessions: of the 115 enemy agents captured in the UK during the war, 17 were identified through ISOS; overseas, of the 164 agents captured and returned to the UK, ISOS material was responsible for 52.[32]

If counter-intelligence was the main purpose of Section V and of ISOS, ISOS material was also supplied to MI5 in support of deception operations through the Double Cross Committee. The role of ISOS and ISK in supporting FORTITUDE and deception in this way has been given prominent emphasis in several accounts of Bletchley Park.[33] But the question of how much information was passed to MI5 and how useful it was has been much debated.[34]

Material now available in the National Archives makes it clear that ISOS was indeed supplying material to the deception effort. A 1946 report entitled 'Use of ISOS by Section V during the War' contains the heading 'Control of deception', under which the following appeared:

> In order to plan and carry out a successful policy of deception it is necessary to know – apart from all strategic factors – how the mind of the enemy intelligence services is working and how efficient the proposed channel of deception is likely to be. For this ISOS was an invaluable guide.[35]

Why, then, does ISOS not feature more prominently in accounts of the deceptions? The answer to this must lie in part in the clandestine nature of the whole ULTRA project: very few people were let in on the secret of what Bletchley was doing, and those who did know were bound by confidentiality until long after the war.

One instance of this is provided by the chairman of the Double Cross Committee himself, John Masterman, who immediately after the war produced an account of the committee and its work, *The Double Cross System in the War of 1939 to 1945*. This remained secret until 1972, when Yale University Press published an edition that was nevertheless heavily redacted at the request of the British government, which still regarded ULTRA as highly sensitive. Fortunately, Masterman lodged a copy of the full version in the archives of Worcester College, Oxford, of which he was provost after the war, and which is now publicly available.[36] In it, Masterman is unequivocal in his appreciation of the work of Bletchley Park:

> The immense and unexpected advantage of 'Most Secret Sources' [Bletchley intercepts] permitted us to observe that the reports of our XX [Double Cross] agents were transmitted to Berlin; that they were believed; and that competing reports were not.[37]

He alludes throughout the work to 'Most Secret Sources' supporting the activities of his committee.

However, the claim that the Double Cross spies were 'believed' in 'Berlin' needs some amplification. Even if the information was swallowed by the *Abwehr*, that is not to say that it was believed at OKW or that it influenced overall German policy. Part of the problem is that the *Abwehr* was not a very efficient organisation. Nor was it involved in significant analysis of its intelligence product: on the contrary, the *Ast* and outstations tended to pounce on any snippet of potentially useful information and, rather than evaluate its intelligence value, pass it on to Berlin as evidence of their 'busyness' and as justification of their salaries and expense accounts. As Michael Howard put it:

The information gathered by the spymasters in Madrid, Lisbon or Hamburg, was passed on raw to the departmental heads in Abwehr I, who made little attempt to evaluate or collate the reports which passed over their desks. All was dumped, largely unsorted, in the in-trays of the unfortunate officers at OKH's FHW.[38]

Thus, instead of gaining useful insights into enemy activity, FHW and the German high command were simply overwhelmed.

As far as the Allies were concerned, this lack of discernment by the *Abwehr* actually made nuanced deception more difficult, as carefully nurtured fictions planted in agent reports by controllers in the UK were 'swamped by the noise generated by the mass of rumours, gossip, diplomatic indiscretions, and garbled reports that the Abwehr Asts and KOs collected and forwarded, largely unfiltered, to their head offices'.[39] Since the *Abwehr* outstations typically forwarded *everything* they heard from any source to Berlin, trying to spot where a particular lie from London was being given particular credence would have been potentially very difficult. Masterman himself highlighted a further issue surrounding the delivery of intelligence to Berlin:

> The system in the Abwehr was that any member could start and control an agent. Not unnaturally the prestige, and presumably the income, of many Abwehr personalities depended upon the reputation of their own particular agents. If then the reliability of a double agent was questioned by the enemy his chief defender always turned out to be his own spy-master who would go to almost any lengths to protect him against the doubt and criticisms of rival persons, or of Berlin.[40]

Thus, rather than taking a suitably sceptical approach to sources of information, the *Abwehr* adopted a 'the-more-the-merrier' approach, which was ultimately counterproductive.

The character of the feed from the *Abwehr* to FHW and OKW can be followed week by week through 1944, as from December 1943 notes on

Abwehr reports of both the likely invasion plans and the Allied order of battle were included in the Western Front Committee 'Record'. An examination of the intercepted reports of the German intelligence service contained in these files from January to May 1944 shows just how incoherent the reporting of Allied intentions really was. From messages intercepted in December 1943, it was clear in January that the *Abwehr* was expecting the west to become an active front in due course: intercepts revealed that it was strengthening its operations in Paris and Brussels.[41] In January 1944, instructions were relayed to *Abwehr* outstations instructing them to look out for intelligence in particular concerning an Allied invasion:

> Regardless of other commitments use all your resources for urgent exploration of the following questions:
>
> (i) For which time and at which places on the Atlantic and Mediterranean fronts (in particular northern France and on the Adriatic coast) are British-American landings planned?
> (ii) What are the operational objectives in view?
> (iii) What is the strength of the enemy forces (Army, Navy, Air Force) envisaged for the various landing-places?
> (iv) Present state of the landing-preparations (Army, Navy, Air force).
>
> Endeavour to communicate news with the least possible delay.[42]

It is notable in this message that a further amphibious operation in the Mediterranean was also considered a possibility.

By February, information was flowing in from all over the German intelligence network, providing a wide variety of conflicting opinions. Reports of possible attacks mentioned the south of France, Cannes/Marseilles, Biscay, Brest, Normandy, the Channel Islands, Dieppe–Boulogne, Calais, Dunkirk and Ostend and Hamburg – as well as 'Great events' launched from Scotland (presumably against Norway). In other words, intelligence supporting an attack anywhere from north Italy to the Arctic Circle was available. Possible dates were also offered, ranging from the (alarmingly precise) '5 February' to early March, April or even 'no attack in near future'.[43] Even the *Abwehr* itself was forced to admit that its record of predicting this kind of operation was not good. An appreciation produced at the end of January on likely invasion prospects commented:

> From experience of the Allied landings at NETTUNO and the former landings in SICILY and at SALERNO it emerges that it has not been possible to obtain either from safe sources or from ABWEHR reports any useable data concerning preparations for such undertakings.[44]

In March, the picture presented by the *Abwehr* was no clearer. Some slight emphasis was detectable in the reporting towards an attack on the south of France. But at the same time other reports mentioned the Balkans, Gascony, La Rochelle, Norway – and in one case 'without doubt Holland, Belgium, northern and southern France, but not Denmark'. Further suggestions included the assembly of landing craft in the Firth of Forth and the rather outlandish contrary suggestion that all US troops in the UK were about to be withdrawn for operations in the Pacific.[45]

The following three months show a similar picture, with the *Abwehr* keeping its options open, referring to the Balkans, the south of France, Denmark and Norway, as well as the Channel coast. One other intriguing suggestion was that a Brazilian military force was to invade Portugal at the end of April.[46]

While the most obvious strategic possibility – an attack on the Pas-de-Calais – does occur in the reports, it seems that the *Abwehr's* belief in the Atlantic Wall was such that it subconsciously shied away from the idea that the Allies would attack it directly. Thus, there were several reports that plans for a cross-Channel attack were a bluff, or that they were unpopular with Allied commanders, who would rather attack a weaker point.[47] In a similar vein, a report at the end of April suggested that the French Resistance in north-west France was opposed to a cross-Channel invasion: apparently, they were worried about the likely resulting destruction to civilian infrastructure and, as communists, they would rather wait for liberation from the east by their socialist cousins, the Soviets.[48] Even to circulate this idea – including, as it did, the implication of a total Soviet conquest of Germany, as well as of France – was potentially a brave move: such 'defeatism', even if theoretical, would not have been welcome.

Perhaps unsurprisingly, then, the *Abwehr*'s stock had started to fall during 1943, particularly when it was unable to predict accurately when and where the various Allied Mediterranean offensives would take place. There were also suspicions among loyal Nazis and the SS that some *Abwehr* officers were at best lukewarm in their support for the Führer. By the spring of 1944, the organisation was in serious trouble. The political power of the Wehrmacht High Command was gradually declining, as Hitler came to rely more and more on his Nazi party colleagues for opinion and support. As the OKW declined in influence versus the Party, so the *Abwehr*, as part of the military, lost out to Himmler's SD. Canaris was relieved of his post in February 1944, to be replaced by his subordinate, *Oberst* Georg Hansen. The *Abwehr* was finally merged with the SD on 1 June 1944. Initially, many *Abwehr* personnel remained in post, but the 20 July plot against Hitler – and the number of *Abwehr* officers implicated in it – saw all trace of the organisation being extinguished.[49]

Against this background, it is clear not only that it would have been very hard to tell from week to week what opinion the *Abwehr* held about any future invasion, but also that there are serious question marks over the extent to which the opinions of the *Abwehr* (such as they were) had any influence on OKW and German strategy in the west as a whole. As Masterman observed, 'Unfortunately in this war the prestige of the Abwehr was clearly very low, and the advice of the Abwehr had probably very little weight.'[50] The sheer variety and disorganisation of *Abwehr* reports to German high command meant that misinformation carefully planted by Double Cross spies could easily be lost in the profusion of often equally erroneous ideas put forward by the organisation itself. At the same time, knowing what the *Abwehr* thought or predicted about any subject was not equivalent to knowing the thoughts and predictions of German commanders. For this, other more reliable sources were required.

A CLEARER VIEW

Fortunately for Bletchley Park and the Allied planners, listening in on the *Abwehr* was not the only means by which German strategic thinking could be discerned. A significant quantity of information was available from other SIGINT sources, in particular FISH and the communications of the Japanese ambassador and his attachés. When this material is examined, a much more consistent picture of German expectations emerges.

At the end of 1943, it started to become clear that the Germans were expecting the Allies' next move to be a cross-Channel attack. FHW produced an appreciation in December which presented the appointment of Eisenhower as supreme Allied commander as evidence of the 'manifest decision of the enemy command to concentrate the main effort in the England area'.[51] This was supported by the decryption of a message from General Ōshima on 6 January reporting a conversation with German Foreign Minister Joachim von Ribbentrop, who stated that an invasion was likely across the narrows of the Channel, timed to coincide with a large Russian attack on the Eastern Front.[52]

By late March, *Generalfeldmarschall* von Rundstedt was expecting an invasion imminently. He issued an appreciation on 21 March, which was communicated to Kesselring in Italy via the BREAM teleprinter link and read by Bletchley Park on 6 April. In it, he commented that:

> According to all information invasion preparations in the English motherland are as good as complete. The jumping off point of the invasion base points clearly to the occupied west coast [of France].[53]

This opinion was supported by FHW in a message decrypted by Bletchley on 12 April, predicting an invasion on the coast of France between the

Pas-de-Calais and the river Loire.[54] A message was also intercepted on 17 April from *Großadmiral* Dönitz to all ranks of the German navy, many of whom, it should be remembered, formed the garrisons of gun batteries in the Atlantic Wall. His message to 'all ranks and ratings' read:

> The Allies' invasion preparations have been completed. A large scale landing in western Europe may be expected at any time. The success or failure of this invasion will be decisive for the issue of the war and for the existence of the German people.[55]

In April, leave was cancelled among the German forces in the west and increased efforts were made to bomb the southern ports of the UK. German E-boats also intercepted the invasion rehearsal at Slapton Sands on 28 April (Exercise TIGER), giving the Germans a pretty good idea of what was to come.[56]

The character of German expectations was confirmed at Bletchley by the interception of a further appreciation by von Rundstedt from 8 May (deciphered by 14 May). In it, he commented on the poor performance of the *Abwehr*, remarking that he had received 'no special information from agents apart from a plethora of landing dates, mainly pointing to the first half of May'. However, he went on to give a remarkably perceptive analysis of the likely invasion:

> Anglo-American invasion preparations in England completed. Although photo and visual recce had not yet been able to include whole English south coast, it was clear from the observed concentrations of landing shipping space, especially in the area north of Isle of Wight, (Portsmouth and Southampton), that a special *schwerpunkt* [a critical focus of military effort] was being formed in that area ... Normandy and perhaps also Brittany were suitable for operations on a large scale with the object of forming a bridgehead. The *schwerpunkt* within the whole threatened channel front stretching from Scheldt to northern tip of Brittany, appeared to be roughly from

Boulogne as far as Normandy inclusive. For this it was essential for the Allies to capture large harbours with good performance. Of primary importance as such: Le Havre and Cherbourg. Of secondary importance (also in performance): Boulogne and Brest.[57]

The focus on Normandy, Le Havre and Cherbourg in this analysis must have caused a certain amount of nervousness in Allied headquarters. This would not have been helped by a German air force message intercepted on 9 May from *Luftflotte* (Air Fleet) 3, based in Paris. This 'Confirmed once more the view of *Luftflotte Three* already often expressed that landing is planned in the area Le Havre–Cherbourg.'[58] From these and other messages it seems clear that as the month of May progressed, the German high command had an ever-clearer idea of the likely point of attack.

However, while it may not have proved possible to bluff the Germans as to the point of initial invasion, there remained the possibility that they would interpret this as only the first in a series of attacks – and potentially also as a smaller-scale diversionary operation prior to a main attack elsewhere. As we saw above, crucial to this latter possibility was the German overestimation of the Allied strength and amphibious landing capability. In his appreciation of 8 May, von Rundstedt revealed his misunderstanding of Allied potential:

> Observed tonnage of landing shipping could be taken as sufficient for 12 or 13 divisions (less heavy equipment and rear elements) for fairly short sea routes. In all, (estimating the capacity of the other English ports not so far covered by visual and photo recce) probable employment of at least 20 and probably more divisions in first wave must be expected. To these must certainly be added strong air-landing forces.[59]

The idea that twenty Allied divisions could be transported across the Channel at the same time was wide of the mark, to say the least.

When the FORTITUDE deception plan was approved in February 1944, a key plank of the deception was to focus this German overestimation of Allied potential onto a specific idea: the creation of a second invasion force in south-east England aimed at invasion of the Pas-de-Calais. This was achieved through the now famous use of First US Army Group (FUSAG) as the foundation for this fictional army. In fact, FUSAG began life as a real formation: a skeleton Army Group headquarters had been created with the idea that, in due course, it would take over command of US armies in France once they had reached a sufficient size. This (real) task was transferred to General Omar Bradley's Twelfth US Army Group, while FUSAG was installed in Berkshire with, at its head, General George Patton, freshly returned from the Mediterranean. Patton was allocated real troops, in the form of First Canadian Army (which was, in fact, part of 21st Army Group) and Third US Army (which was actually in Cheshire, training as a follow-up force for the Normandy invasion, but which was to be portrayed as based in Essex, ready to invade at Calais). As mentioned above, there was relatively little need to create visual deceptions around this force, as German air reconnaissance was virtually non-existent, and so FUSAG operated largely on the basis of dummy wireless traffic – in particular, the use of false order of battle information channelled through Double Cross agents.

Examination of the *Abwehr* reports collated by the Western Front Committee and other intercepted material shows that a steady stream of false information was passed on to FHW and to OKW. FUSAG first appeared in a German assessment based on W/T evidence, sent on 9 January and deciphered by 26 January.[60] Patton was identified in the UK (albeit from open source information from Reuters) in a message on 29 March,[61] and both he and FUSAG also appeared in an FHW appreciation deciphered on 12 April.[62] The consequence of these deceptions (as well as German long-term overestimations) was to keep alive in the minds of German commanders the idea that, even if evidence pointed to a landing in Normandy, this could still be followed by an equivalent (or even larger) operation in the Pas-de-Calais.

Perhaps the most striking example of the pervasiveness of this concept of a two-pronged Allied attack was contained in a message transmitted by General Ōshima on 30 May, after a meeting with Hitler on the 27th. In it he reported that the Allies had completed their preparations to invade and that they had 80 divisions at their disposal. He went on to report the Führer's opinion that Germany would not be deceived by 'diversionary actions' and that:

> After they have established bridgeheads in the Norman and Brittany peninsulas and seen how the prospect appears, they will come forward with the establishment of an all-out Second Front in the area of the Straits of Dover.[63]

The Allied commanders took great comfort from this revelation. The Joint Intelligence Committee (JIC) drew what Hinsley described as a 'relaxed' conclusion:

> There has been no intelligence during the last week to suggest that the enemy has accurately assessed the area in which our main assault is to be made. He appears to expect several landings between the Pas de Calais and Cherbourg.[64]

This was perhaps a little too relaxed on the part of the JIC. Allied intelligence suggested that the Germans *had* accurately assessed the area in which the assault was to be made. But their misunderstanding of the Allied order of battle had caused them to misinterpret it.

The FUSAG deception formed only FORTITUDE SOUTH, or half of the overall FORTITUDE deception plan. FORTITUDE NORTH aimed at persuading the Germans that an amphibious operation against Norway was imminent, to be launched from the ports of Scotland and Northern Ireland. Given the distance between the ports of departure of this operation and German-held territory, this deception did not require physical decoys and again focused largely on creating a false SIGINT picture of an

Allied build-up in the north, along with double-agent material. This deception involved the creation of a fictional force of eight divisions (including a false US division in Iceland) and the incorporation of real units forming in Scotland and Northern Ireland, but which were actually bound for France.[65]

It is clear that the Germans did become aware of these forces and considered their use in a northern operation. A signal intercepted from Naval High Command (OKM) on 5 March gave a summary of their views:

> Consequently there could be expected to be four to six English divisions in Scotland ready for employment, in addition to one or two American divisions in Iceland, which might be used for possible operations in Northern area. Concentrations of shipping reported in harbours of east Scotland would suffice to transport this number of troops. Therefore prerequisites as regards forces and shipping space were satisfied for an operation of limited scope which might be directed against central or south Norway with object of tying down German forces in northern area.[66]

However, the references to 'limited scope' and 'tying down German forces' show that there was never a perception that this would be the Allies' main effort, or that it would replace a main effort in the Channel area. German high command was never sufficiently concerned to move forces into Norway at the expense of France and the Low Countries (or, for that matter, in the other direction) and the garrison there remained steady at twelve divisions. As late as 25 May, FHW reported that 'no noticeable movement from these areas [the Scottish ports] to Norway is planned'.[67] This suggests that FORTITUDE NORTH was not successful in convincing the Germans to redeploy their forces. As Michael Howard has pointed out:

> They had never altered their perfectly correct belief that the main Allied concentrations were in south and south-eastern England and that the main attack would be launched across the Channel.[68]

If one were to be charitable about the deception effort against Norway, it could be pointed out that no German troops were moved *from* Norway into France. The same argument has been deployed with regard to FORTITUDE SOUTH, insofar as no German units were moved from *15. Armee* in the Pas-de-Calais to Normandy. But both these arguments are based on the *absence* of evidence of manifest failure, rather than on any tangible evidence of success. German opinion remained as it always had been: when it came, the Allied attack would be across the narrows of the Channel.

One might go further and suggest that the Germans were also correctly expecting an attack in Normandy, but they relegated it to the status of a feint or supporting operation. Michael Howard was scathing: 'In fact the attempt to deceive the Germans as to the fact and the timing of Operation Overlord was a predictable failure.'[69] He went on to highlight the scepticism with which some of the Double Cross agents' material was greeted at FHW, where a report on 20 March suggested that agent reports were 'to be treated as intentional disguise of enemy intentions...and are contradicted by troop movements observed in England'.[70] This suspicion also appears in the Western Front Committee 'Records'. A note included in the 'Record' of 30 April 1944 observed:

> ABW [*Abwehr*] HQ is casting more and more doubt on the authenticity of agent reports received from LISBON and has voiced opinion that any or all of these agents may be bogus.[71]

It cannot be claimed, therefore, that deception material was consumed uncritically by either the *Abwehr* Headquarters or by FHW. But both organisations were potentially guilty of a high degree of *confirmation bias*: material that conformed to their preconceptions of an attack across the Channel was accepted wholeheartedly, while ostensibly equally compelling information about an attack on Norway or elsewhere was disregarded.

So, how important was Bletchley Park in the deception effort? It would appear that its direct role in deception operations has perhaps previously been overemphasised. Much of the material obtained from ISOS was essentially random noise, and a good deal of it internally contradictory. It is hard to see how even those directing the deception operations can have gained much useful feedback from it. On the other hand, Bletchley was clearly far more successful in its more conventional intelligence role of monitoring the communications of the German high command and deducing its ongoing strategic expectations. Whether or not the FHW and OKW were actually deceived, Bletchley was able to follow their thinking from January 1944 onwards, and OVERLORD could be launched with reasonable confidence among Allied commanders of German expectations.

Ralph Bennett argued that German expectations throughout the build-up to OVERLORD simply reflected the idea that 'They will do what we would do in like circumstances', and an invasion across the narrows of the Channel made the same sense in 1944 to Allied planners as it had to German planners in 1940.[72]

Some accounts of the events of 1944, not least that provided by Tommy Flowers described in Chapter 2, have sought to suggest that confirmation of the success of FORTITUDE was a vital part of Eisenhower's decision-making process in launching the invasion. But this is to overstate the case. The idea that he would (or could) have called off the attack had the success of deception operations not been 'confirmed' by the Ōshima message on 30 May is patently an exercise in hindsight. His principal concern in the first week of June 1944 was not German expectations, but the weather.

DISCERNING THE GERMAN STRATEGIC RESPONSE

The final aspect of the Germans' high-level thinking that could be revealed by SIGINT was their defensive planning for after an invasion. How would the German forces respond tactically and strategically to an attack in Normandy? In the spring of 1944, German opinion on this was divided. A concise summary of the two opposing positions was provided in a report written in captivity in 1946 by *Vizeadmiral* Friedrich Ruge, who was naval liaison officer at the headquarters of *Generalfeldmarschall* Rommel's German *Heeresgruppe B*, and thus party to Rommel's thinking:

> Field Marshal von Rundstedt, C-in-C in the west, and General Geyr von Schweppenburg, who was in command of the panzer-type divisions, did not see any possibility of preventing the Allies from landing considerable forces. As a large-scale landing seemed inevitable to them, they prepared to counterattack somewhere inland. By rapid operations with their concentrated reserves they hoped to push the Allied forces back or even to encircle them.
>
> Rommel's ideas were fundamentally influenced by the vast superiority of the Allied air arm. He was deeply impressed by the fact that in North Africa a numerically inferior air force had kept him, with 80,000 men, 'nailed to the ground', as he expressed it, for two or three days. In view of this and other experiences, he was of the decided opinion that the operations planned by Rundstedt and von Schweppenburg would either be nipped in the bud or at least so much delayed that they were bound to fail. To Rommel, the only hope of repelling the invasion seemed to lie in offering the strongest possible resistance to the actual landing. The first 24 hours would be decisive. Once the Allies established a large beachhead it would be impossible to drive them back into the sea because of their superiority of material. He expressed this opinion to the Führer both verbally and in writing. He repeatedly told us that the Führer had agreed with him.[73]

This argument would continue until the actual invasion. Rommel wanted all the available mobile units to be under his command and positioned near the coast, ready to intervene as soon as the Allies hit the beach. Von Rundstedt wanted a powerful reserve which he could deploy towards a landing wherever it might occur along his, admittedly very long, defensive front. A compromise solution was reached in March 1944. Rommel was provided with three panzer divisions under his command in

Heeresgruppe B (one of which would be able to intervene against the invasion around Caen at an early stage). Four panzer and panzer-grenadier divisions were placed as the central reserve under von Schweppenburg in *Panzergruppe West*. And the remaining three were in the south of France under *Heeresgruppe G*.[74]

Initially the Allied planners at COSSAC had assumed that the length of vulnerable coast would force the Germans to follow Rundstedt's strategy of counterattacking once the Allies were ashore. This was supported by telegrams from Ōshima in February, reporting that even Hitler believed that it would be impossible to defeat any landing entirely at the water's edge.[75] However, a degree of uncertainty and contradiction could be discerned in German thinking. The contrasting 'coastal' strategy was spelled out in a telegram sent from the Japanese military attaché in Vichy on 17 February and read at Bletchley. He claimed to have been briefed by von Rundstedt's chief of staff as follows:

> Primary objective of German defences in Holland Belgium and France is 'to hold firmly on the coast'. Strategic aim therefore is to destroy the Allies on the sea and on the beaches, if that be impossible to destroy them in areas as near the coast as possible. No policy of luring Allies inland for subsequent destruction is being adopted.[76]

Rommel's assignment to command *Heeresgruppe B* was also suggestive of a possible shift in approach. His appointment was followed at Bletchley Park, and its possible strategic implications inferred from further Japanese messages. As the Western Front Committee 'Record' for the week ending 17 March commented:

> The eventual set-up in the West has been cleared to some extent by JMA reports. It seems probable that operational forces directly employed against invasion will be grouped under Army Group B, commanded by ROMMEL, while RUNDSTEDT (although an abler general) with Army

Group D will take second place. The principal Panzer commander is to be Gen. d. Pz. GEYR von SCHWEPPENBURG.[77]

The existence of *Heeresgruppe B* under Rommel and of *Panzergruppe West* under von Schweppenburg was also confirmed by Enigma decrypts during March, which also revealed the locations of their respective head-quarters in St Quentin and west of Paris.[78] What was not clear was the exact chain of command. Von Rundstedt remained C-in-C West, but it was not certain how much control he had over Rommel. Meanwhile, von Schweppenburg and the panzer reserve were under the direct control of OKW – and, in theory, of Hitler himself.

Even after the Rommel–Rundstedt compromise, the debate continued. Reports from the Japanese continued to emphasise Rommel and the coastal strategy. A lengthy message from the Japanese naval attaché in Berlin (intercepted on 4 May and circulated by Bletchley's Naval Section on 7 May) stated:

> Since Marshal ROMMEL took over his command and made a detailed inspection on the spot in the autumn of 1943, his policy has been, on the assumption that the beaches form the main battle zone (HKL; HAUPT KAMPF LINIE), to destroy the enemy near the coast (most of all on the beaches) without allowing them to penetrate [?any considerable distance] inland.[79]

This matched Rommel's mantra ever since taking over *Heeresgruppe B*, as reported by Admiral Ruge: '*Die HKL is der Strand*' – 'The main line of resistance is the beach.'[80]

The detail of the discussions over command in France were never fully available to Bletchley Park or to the Allied commanders; however, enough conflicting information was obtained to see that there were tensions within the German high command over how to react to an invasion. This was reflected in a briefing given by General Montgomery on 7 April, when he commented that Rommel is a determined Commander and will hurl his armour into the battle. But according to what we know of the chain of command the armoured divisions are being kept directly under Rundstedt, and delay may be caused before they are released to Rommel . . . quarrels may arise between the two of them.[81]

In this assessment, Montgomery was substantially correct.

*

Overall, the Allied commanders were provided with a thorough understanding of what the Germans were expecting by way of invasion, and how they were planning to respond to it. They could also take comfort from the level of misunderstanding of both Allied intentions and capabilities that was visible in the German strategic appreciations. Bletchley played a large part in providing this insight, and thus its contribution to the success of the operation is undeniable. However, it is harder to determine how far the Germans' misunderstanding of Allied plans was rooted in their own incorrect strategic preconceptions, and how far it was really influenced by deception operations. Interception of *Abwehr* traffic by Bletchley certainly facilitated management of the Double Cross operation; but it is harder to prove that Double Cross influenced German thinking beyond the *Abwehr*, in OKW and in the mind of the Führer.

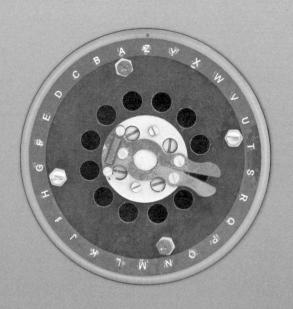

PART III

INVASION AND AFTER

CHAPTER SEVEN

GETTING ASHORE

OPERATION NEPTUNE AND THE LANDINGS

By June 1944 HMS *Warspite* was an old ship. A veteran of the Battle of Jutland in the First World War, it had also participated in nearly all the significant naval campaigns of the current conflict. The old battleship was present at Narvik in 1940, and served as Admiral Cunningham's flagship in the victory over the Italians at Cape Matapan in 1941, as well as in the evacuation of Crete later that year. It had even served in the Far East against the Japanese. So by 1944, it was something of a relic: much repaired, and without many of the guns it had originally been equipped with. Indeed, battleships of this class and size were increasingly an anachronism: air power, both from land-based airfields and, more and more, from seaborne aircraft carriers had made these great ships obsolete – and, worse, hopelessly vulnerable to bomb and torpedo attack.

Nonetheless, there was one thing at which these vessels were unmatched: shore bombardment. Such a task fell to *Warspite* on D-Day, 6 June 1944. Its 15-inch guns dwarfed anything in the arsenals of land-based artillery, and off the coast of the invasion beaches its fire-power would be devastating. At 05.30 local time (03.30 GMT) on D-Day, *Warspite* was in position off Sword Beach; it opened fire on the German shore batteries and defences. A little later, at 06.04 (04.04 GMT), Warspite's log records that it 'Engaged twelve enemy destroyers in mouth of the

Seine. 06.12 hit and sank one enemy destroyer.' This incident was described by one of the participants on board *Warspite*, Ordinary Seaman Ronald Martin:

> We arrived just as dawn was breaking and at 05.30, or just before, we sighted what we thought were torpedo E-boats coming out from Le Havre to attack us. I opened fire with the port armament. Almost at the same time the 15-inch guns opened up against our first shore battery. So the Warspite lays the claim to firing the first shots of the invasion. We sank one of the E-boats and the rest retired to Le Havre and didn't come out again.[1]

This German attack was launched by the *5. Torpedobootsflottille* (torpedo boat flotilla), under *Kapitänleutnant* Heinrich Hoffmann, which sailed from Le Havre to challenge the invaders. Hoffmann had three ships under his command: the torpedo boats[2] *T28*, *Moewe* and *Jaguar*. He was accompanied by a force of six smaller vessels of the *15. Vorpostenflotille* (patrol boat flotilla) under *Kapitänleutnant* Rall.[3] Initially the German force profited from a smokescreen laid by Allied aircraft to blind the coastal batteries around Le Havre; however, on passing through the smoke they were in for a rude surprise. By coincidence, they had approached the eastern flank of the landing fleet, consisting of not only *Warspite*, but also the battleship HMS *Ramillies*, as well as the monitor HMS *Roberts* and various smaller vessels. The three large British vessels were equipped with a total of sixteen 15-inch guns between them, some of which now turned to bear on the German flotilla.[4] Hoffmann's force weaved frantically and managed to fire eighteen torpedoes at the British ships, before diving back into the smoke bank. Only one found its target, hitting the Norwegian destroyer *Svenner*, which sank rapidly.[5]

While this battle was taking place in the Channel, Bletchley Park was following events closely via decrypts of German naval traffic. A message was intercepted at 01.54 (UK) on 6 June ordering Hoffmann's torpedo boat flotilla to 'Attack landing boats off Port En Bessin and Grandcamp.'[6]

This, incidentally, shows that the Germans thought they would only encounter enemy forces much further west, as Port en Bessin was near Omaha Beach in the American sector. The message was deciphered and teleprinted to the Admiralty from Bletchley Park at 04.17 GMT. The Admiralty then forwarded it to naval commanders, including Admiral Ramsay, in the form of an Admiralty Ultra Message timed at 04.20.[7] Thus the information would have reached naval commanders at about the time the German ships broke cover out of the smokescreen.

Further messages followed from both German commanders Rall and Hoffmann, describing the loss of one of the patrol boats, possibly to a mine (rather than a shot from *Warspite*), and a message from Hoffmann describing his situation: '6 battleships, about 20 destroyers, torpedoes expended in attacking, heavy consumption of ammunition, am off Le Havre'. This message was intercepted at 04.25 and was in the hands of the Admiralty at 06.51.[8] This is some time after the engagement itself had finished, but again shows a turnaround at Bletchley Park from interception to teleprinting of just 2 hours 36 minutes. Analysis of other messages intercepted during the early hours of 6 June shows that a processing time of around two and a half hours was typical for naval traffic. Thus, though not quite receiving German communications in real time, the Admiralty was nonetheless getting them in a time-frame that allowed them to be operationally significant.

*

So far, we have looked almost entirely at intelligence concerning land forces. But it should not be forgotten that OVERLORD was an amphibious operation. Before any fighting could take place in France, the invading forces had to be safely transported across the Channel, a process planned under the subordinate codename Operation NEPTUNE. Should the Germans be able to interfere in this to any extent – by air, with surface warships or, worst of all, with submarines – the results could be catastrophic; the attacking force would be at its most vulnerable while cooped up in ships sailing for France. Exhaustive preparations were therefore made for the protection of the force while it was at sea. In addition to physical protection in the form of naval escort vessels, and control of the skies above the fleet, it was vital to be able to detect any German naval response to the sailings, ideally before the German ships or submarines had the chance to attack. This would be a job for Bletchley Park's Naval Section, responsible for listening in on German naval communications.

THE GERMAN DEFENCES

In addition to active defence from naval vessels, the Atlantic Wall was protected by large passive defences, in the form of sea minefields. Naval Section at GC&CS and the Operational Intelligence Centre (OIC) at the Admiralty had been studying these minefields over several years before NEPTUNE, and their accumulated knowledge would be vital to the safe passage of the invasion fleet through these waters. In some cases, decrypts revealed sorties by minelaying vessels; but more often information was circulated by the Germans about the locations of new swept channels through existing fields, or alterations to navigation around them. This information was only useful against a background of painstakingly developed knowledge of the existing minefields; but once this had been gained, with the help of air photography, a good picture of the mine defences of the Seine Bay could be built up.

In the spring of 1944, further minefields were created, and Bletchley was able to monitor these developments. Between the end of February and late May, twenty-two minelaying sorties by torpedo boats, E-boats and minesweepers were detected.[9] On some occasions, the intelligence was sufficient not only to record the laying of mines, but also to actively disrupt the process. A signal decrypted on 20 May revealed that a mixed force of German vessels had been ordered from Cherbourg to Le Havre to lay additional minefields. The force was attacked both from the air and by British motor torpedo boats. Two German vessels were sunk and three damaged, putting an end to German minelaying in the area prior to the invasion.[10] Patrick Beesly, who worked in the Admiralty OIC, summed up this effort:

> In the initial assault stage of operation Neptune, 1,213 warships from battleships down to midget submarines, and 4,126 landing ships and small craft . . . had to follow the British swept channels to a point eight miles south of the Isle of Wight and then steam down the so-called Spout, across the enemy's minefields to Seine Bay and the assault area. The fact that only one destroyer out of the whole of the assault force was lost to mining was a tribute not only to the superb efficiency of the minesweepers, but also to the patient and laborious efforts of [head of OIC] Denning's staff in piecing together the many scraps of information which provided such a complete and detailed picture of these German defences.[11]

Bletchley was also able to read German U-boat communications more or less daily throughout 1944. The four-rotor Enigma key used by German submarines (known at Bletchley as SHARK) had been broken into in late 1942 and, with the help of US Navy bombe machines, which came into operation in summer 1943, these keys were broken daily, allowing Bletchley Park and the OIC to read traffic to and from U-boats almost as fast as the Germans themselves.[12] This allowed the potential underwater threat to the invasion fleet to be monitored in detail both before and during the invasion. From the beginning of April 1944, it became clear that Admiral Dönitz was concerned about the possibility of invasion, and over the next two months increasing numbers of submarines were held in French Biscay ports to provide a striking force against such an eventuality. This was revealed in decrypts, which had the double effect of informing the Allied naval command about the potential threat in the Channel and at the same time allowing them to reorganise transatlantic convoys on the basis that there were fewer U-boats available to attack them. This freed up escort vessels from the Atlantic to be redeployed to the invasion fleet.[13]

Once the invasion began, the German navy responded by launching a significant U-boat counterattack. The precise missions or patrol areas of these vessels were not revealed in SIGINT, but this was less important in the narrows of the Channel than in the wide spaces of the Atlantic. A dense barrage of air and surface anti-submarine patrols was placed across the passages from the Bay of Biscay to the Channel, and German submarines found it almost impossible to progress against this. On the night of 6–7 June, two U-boats were sunk in the Channel and six more were sufficiently damaged to have to return to port. Three more were sunk on the night of 7–8 June, and more damaged. SIGINT revealed the return to port of many of these damaged boats. In the two weeks following the landings, only one submarine reached its patrol position off the Isle of Wight, but retreated after only three days, having sunk one landing ship. Another was able to torpedo the British frigate HMS *Blackwood* on 15 June, but this was an isolated success. No U-boats were present in the Channel for much of the rest of June, and in July no more than four were ever present at any one time.[14] That it was possible to shut down these operations so completely was, in large part, due to the massive naval and air anti-submarine effort; but Naval Section at Bletchley was able to make a significant contribution to this, not least by keeping a tally of those U-boats at sea and those under repair, allowing the effectiveness of the Allied effort to be determined.

The German surface fleet also posed a threat to the invasion; however, the *Kriegsmarine* chose not to risk any of its major surface vessels in the Channel, and the few remaining large warships remained passive in Norway and the Baltic, either damaged or under refit. There were still small forces of destroyers and torpedo boats in the Channel and Biscay ports, as well as larger forces of E-boats and patrol vessels. Bomb damage to German naval landline communications meant that wireless intercepts revealed German operational planning of these vessels. As a result, the moves of the few remaining German destroyers from their bases in the Gironde towards Cherbourg were detected in advance, and a combination of air and surface attack between 6 and 8 June left one sunk, one driven ashore and a third badly damaged, neutralising the threat from these ships.[15] Little direct information about E-boat operations was revealed from intercepts, and in any case these operations were targeted rather predictably against the flanks of the invasion corridor. However, it was possible to identify in which ports these ships were concentrated when not at sea. This allowed Bomber Command to launch its largest daylight raid of the war on Le Havre, in the early evening of 13 June, before the German ships had put to sea for the night. The results of this raid were described in intercepted German Naval Command traffic as 'a catastrophe'. A similar raid was carried out on Boulogne on 15 June.[16] Again SIGINT played a role in identifying the number of vessels available to the Germans, how many were at sea, and the effectiveness of Allied countermeasures.

As well as its role at sea, the German navy was traditionally responsible for coastal defence, having been assigned that role by Kaiser Wilhelm in the 1880s.[17] As a result, in 1944 the *Kriegsmarine* remained responsible for most of the larger coastal defence gun positions in the Atlantic Wall and for the overall defence of key points, including ports. The stretches of coast in between fell under the responsibility of the local army garrison divisions. There was also a division in tactics. The navy intended to fight the invasion at sea with a mixture of coastal artillery engaging visible targets at sea (in the manner of land-based ships) and actual naval operations out at sea. The army, meanwhile, deployed most of its heavy guns inland, out of sight of the coast, but in positions capable of firing indirectly on invading forces as they landed on the beach.[18] Thus, in addition to any attack by ships at sea, the first land-based forces the Allies would encounter were likely to be under German naval command. The enemy's first realisation that an invasion was under way – and its initial reactions – were therefore likely to be detectable from German naval communications networks. Thus, it was imperative that GC&CS had as efficient a system as possible for intercepting and deciphering any message traffic from the *Kriegsmarine Admiral Kanalküste* (Admiral Channel Coast) and his staff, and the local *Seekommandant* ('Seeko') *Normandie*, the naval commander for the invasion area, based in Cherbourg.

INTERCEPTING ENEMY COMMUNICATIONS DIRECTLY

By 1944, the Royal Navy was engaged in the interception of German naval wireless traffic using two principal means. First, there were the 'coastal' stations (roughly eighteen in operation at any time) spread around the coast and listening on high frequency (HF) and very high frequency (VHF), mainly for voice communications between enemy ships in UK coastal waters. And then there were the larger high-frequency Y stations, chief among them Scarborough and Flowerdown (near Winchester), which listened for longer-range traffic, principally Morse, much of it encrypted using the Enigma system. These stations would intercept traffic, often from far out in the Atlantic (as well as elsewhere), and feed the encrypted messages back to Bletchley Park via teleprinter, for decryption and analysis. There it was the job of Naval Section V to manage all these listening assets. This department was officially entitled 'Enemy Communications', and its functions included 'Coverage of wireless traffic. Investigation of enemy communications. Traffic Analysis. Crypto-Intelligence. Liaison.'[19] What this meant in practice was that it had to analyse all the messages (both German and Japanese) intercepted by the naval Y stations and sort out the enemy's networks, frequencies and patterns of communication. This information was in turn fed back to the Y stations to tell them which frequencies to listen to, when and how to prioritise their listening resources.

In charge of W/T traffic in Naval Section V in 1944 was Lieutenant E.R. Dugmore, a Royal Naval Volunteer Reserve officer who had joined Bletchley Park and received a temporary commission in the Royal Navy in May 1941. He had previously worked on the analysis of French and Japanese naval traffic, but by 1944 was also responsible for the German navy.[20] With invasion looming, Dugmore applied himself to how the process for interception and decryption of German naval messages from the Channel could be speeded up. He realised that if these could be intercepted directly at Bletchley, the potential time delay in the transfer of messages to Hut 8 and decryption could be reduced. On 4 April 1944, he produced a report on how he had experimented with the reception at Bletchley Park itself of certain important German naval wireless networks originating in the Channel and Biscay areas. He followed this up a month later by putting more detailed proposals before Harry Hinsley (who, as 'intelligence staff officer' for Naval Section, was in charge of W/T intelligence). By this time, further reception tests had been carried out and a reasonable level of reception was achieved. A file note from Hinsley, dated 7 May 1944, reveals that after some discussion with Commander Bradshaw (head of administration) the project was endorsed as a good idea and efforts were put in train to implement it.[21] It is a salient demonstration of how Bletchley Park had the dexterity to make temporary adaptations to accommodate special circumstances.

Dugmore initially suggested a set-up of four receivers, manned by a team of fourteen operators, working on three watches, with personnel consisting either of naval signallers or of Wrens. These, he said, could be accommodated in Room 7, the training room at the end of Hut 18 (former Hut 8), from which Naval Section V already operated. In order to receive the signals, 30ft telescopic aerial masts could easily be erected outside.[22] While approving of the operation, Commander Bradshaw ruled that the use of Wrens was 'out of the question': the sets would be operated by male signallers.[23]

The aerials and receiver sets were installed in and around Hut 18 in mid-May, and a group of eighteen naval ratings arrived from the Y station at Scarborough on 20 May. As invasion approached, the team was expanded by a further six ratings.

Formal watchkeeping began on 22 May 1944, though the first week of operations was described as 'experimental'. The aim of the station, christened NSV(X), was to try to obtain messages that could be used as 'cribs' to break the daily settings of the German naval Enigma network (code-named DOLPHIN) used by *Kriegsmarine* surface vessels and by U-boats in the Channel and the North Sea. Attention was concentrated on specific frequencies used by German stations in the Channel, Biscay, Bight and South Norway areas which – it was thought – would provide suitable messages. A list of these (known as 'Cover A') was drawn up for monitoring from 10.00 GMT every day (equivalent to midday on the continent), when new Enigma keys came into operation, until those keys had been successfully broken. After that a lower-priority series of 'Cover B' frequencies would be monitored. There was also an arrangement with the coastal Y stations that, if they picked up any non-Enigma traffic, the frequencies were to be telephoned through to NSV(X), so that it could take over and investigate. This was particularly important, as these stations monitored activity in the occupied Channel and North Sea harbours from which a German attack might originate.[24]

The messages intercepted and decrypted by Hut 8 and Naval Section at Bletchley Park during the period of the Normandy invasion were passed on via two channels. Throughout the previous few years, GC&CS had been sending intercepted naval traffic direct by teleprinter to the OIC at the Admiralty. When these were forwarded by the OIC to local naval commands – and in particular to Admiral Ramsay and his Allied Naval Commander-in-Chief Expeditionary Force (ANCXF) headquarters in Portsmouth – this was in the form of Admiralty Ultra Messages.[25] In addition, from January 1944 ANCXF had its own SCU/SLU, which meant that it could also receive material direct from Bletchley Park without it going through the Admiralty. Both channels were used during the night of 5–6 June.

THE FIRST TWENTY-FOUR HOURS

Looking at the copies of the original teleprinted messages issued by Hut 8 and Naval Section, it is possible to build up a picture of the work of the naval codebreakers during the first critical twenty-four hours of the invasion, and more specifically to pick out messages on the frequencies being monitored by NSV(X). As described above, the German DOLPHIN key settings changed at midday German time (10.00 GMT) on 5 June 1944. Examination of the preserved intercepts does not reveal any messages transmitted on the 'Cover A' frequencies prescribed for Hut 18.

Messages teleprinted from Bletchley during the afternoon of 5 June consist of backlog traffic from the previous few days. However, the search for a 'crib' was clearly successful during the late afternoon, as from around 19.40 GMT a rush of decrypted traffic on the new key appeared, starting with a message intercepted at 16.49 GMT and teleprinted at 19.41 GMT.[26] Thus the message was intercepted, decrypted, translated and teleprinted to the Admiralty in under three hours. The message was intercepted on one of the frequencies listed for monitoring by Hut 18 under the 'Cover B' arrangements, and so it is possible that the intercept originated with the listeners at Bletchley. The original German message was sent by minesweeper *M83*, part of the 6. *Minensuchflottille* (minesweeper flotilla),[27] announcing its departure later that evening from the Channel Islands for Cherbourg, in company with another vessel. In fact, as the ship was due to sail at 22.00 (20.00 GMT) its departure was known to the Admiralty nineteen minutes before it even happened. As it would be sailing in the vicinity of the Allied invasion fleet, this type of real-time intelligence was of vital importance. A further five decrypted messages were sent to the Admiralty before 20.00 GMT, and eighteen more before 21.00 GMT. This flow was to continue throughout the night and into the early hours of the invasion on the following morning, 6 June.[28]

A small but particularly evocative collection of documents gives a vivid sense of sense of the unfolding drama as it was viewed by the codebreakers at Bletchley Park – along with a sense of the confusion and uncertainty which reigned on the German side of the Channel on that night. Donated to Bletchley by the son of a veteran of Naval Section, these 239 messages consist of a series of small slips of paper, each bearing the English translation of a single German naval message, handwritten in fountain pen, almost certainly the fair copy of messages produced by the watch officers in Naval Section, ready for transmission either to OIC or to Portsmouth. Most of the messages were transmitted either by *Seeko Normandie* or by *Admiral Kanalküste*, the first being intercepted at 23.58 GMT on 5 June, and the last at 20.14 GMT on 8 June.

The first indications that something unusual was afoot came at 00.18 GMT on the 6th, when a report was received of parachutists; but these were identified as straw dummies. Shortly after, however, real parachutists were identified; a message at 00.24 GMT stated 'Some parachutists captured, [airborne] Landings continue.' These landings were confirmed within the hour, in a message from the *Admiral Kanalküste*: 'Airborne landing at south end of east side of COTENIN peninsula' (00.58). At 02.03 there was the suggestion of a seaborne landing, but the situation was described as 'still confused'; by 04.30, however, the situation was clearer. At that time, the commander of *11. Unterseebootsflottille* (U-boat flotilla) issued the order 'Immediate readiness. There are indications that the invasion has begun.' This was countermanded at 05.37 by a message from *Seeko Normandie* that the '0700 [05.00 GMT] report about landings was premature.' By 07.00, however, there could be no doubting that a major seaborne landing was in progress. *Seeko Normandie* relayed a message at 07.11 from its coastal battery commander at Saint Marcouf of 'A great many landing craft approaching, protected by battleships and cruisers.' He went on to report:

MARCOUF area under heavy artillery fire. Between VIRE and ORNE, principally at VIERVILLE and COLLEVILLE, enemy tanks on land. Steep coast near PONT DU HOC ascended with scaling ladders, fighting in progress. (07.17)

One narrative which can be traced in these messages (and which offers an insight into the German experience of the day) describes the increasingly desperate position of the naval shore battery at Saint Marcouf. Having exchanged shots with what was thought to be a light cruiser out to sea, the garrison had the pleasure of seeing its target explode and sink. This was the USS *Corry*, a destroyer, which may in fact have struck a mine.[29] Subsequently, however, the battery came under increasingly heavy bombardment from ships at sea, was bombed and watched as seemingly endless numbers of paratroopers and gliders appeared in the sky overhead. By the evening of 6 June, several of the battery's guns had

1. The German commander in the west, Gerd von Rundstedt (left), meets Erwin Rommel in Paris shortly after the latter's transfer to France, December 1943. Their disagreements over defensive strategy would be closely followed by Bletchley Park.

2. The Japanese ambassador in Berlin, General Ōshima (centre), touring the Atlantic Wall with other Japanese and German officials in September 1943. Bletchley Park would read Ōshima's detailed reports of these visits.

3. Eric Jones, head of Hut 3. Under his enlightened management Hut 3 would lie at the heart of Bletchley Park's contribution to OVERLORD. Here he is photographed in 1957 when he was the director of GCHQ.

4. Brigadier John Tiltman, head of Military Section at Bletchley Park. One of the finest cryptanalytical minds at Bletchley, Tiltman was instrumental in breaking the German Lorenz cipher machine as well as several Japanese codes.

5. William 'Bill' Tutte, member of Bletchley Park Research Section. Tutte, along with John Tiltman, was responsible for first understanding, and then breaking, the German Lorenz cipher machine.

6. A 'Morrison Wall' at Bletchley Park, used to represent diagrammatically the structure of German wireless networks. They were compiled using data developed by the Traffic Analysis Section, SIXTA.

7. A Robinson machine in the Newmanry at Bletchley Park. These machines were used to perform statistical analysis of Lorenz-enciphered messages as part of the codebreaking process.

8. Bombe machines in 'Greece' bay at Eastcote outstation. Each machine is named after a Greek city. These machines were used in finding daily keys for Enigma traffic. By D-Day more than 100 of these machines were in operation in the UK.

9. Block D at Bletchley Park. From early 1943 this building housed the Enigma-breaking sections formerly in Hut 6 and Hut 8, as well as the Hut 3 reporting section. Much of the intelligence provided by Bletchley Park for D-Day was produced in this building.

10. An Enigma I cipher machine as used by the German army and air force. The three encryption rotors, lamp board, keyboard and the plugboard on the front of the machine are all visible.

11. A Lorenz SZ42 cipher machine with its protective cover removed. This machine created the encryption for German teleprinter messages known as FISH at Bletchley Park.

12. A US-built analogue of the Japanese PURPLE diplomatic cipher machine. Messages encrypted on the Japanese version of this machine were broken regularly by the Allies from 1940 until 1945.

13. The teleprinter copy of an intercepted German Enigma message. The message was transmitted in Morse code in uniform five-letter groups. The various annotations and stamps were applied as the message was processed at Bletchley Park.

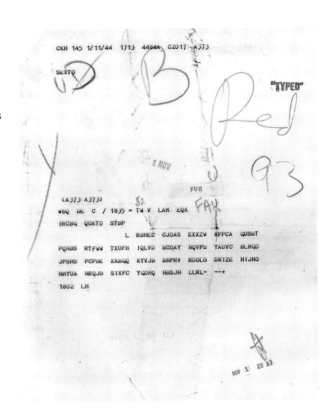

14. The deciphered German plaintext of the message in Plate 13. This was produced on a paper strip using an adapted Typex machine, which was then gummed to the back of the original teleprint.

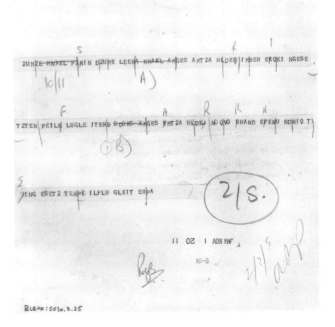

15. The deciphered version of an intercepted FISH message. This message was sent in February 1945 from German forces encircled by the Soviets in Kurland, now Latvia.

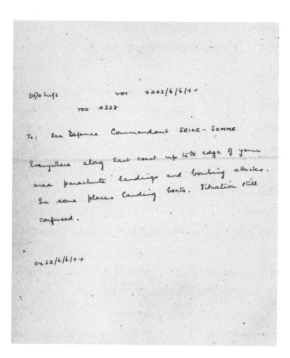

16. The handwritten transcript of a German naval Enigma message transmitted on 6 June 1944. This message, intercepted at 02.03, had been broken by Bletchley Park and was ready for forwarding to commands by 04.32 – less than two and a half hours later.

i.   Abwehr.   All paragraphs from ISOS. Dr. Palmer PAX 300.

ii.. Navy.   1. Plaice.   Lieut. E.J. Talbot Ponsonby, PAX 218
                        2. Dolphin.   "   "
                        3. Plaice   "   "

iii. Army.   1 - 10. Captain Pryce Jones. PAX 262.
                        1. CX/MSS (Quince)
                        3 - 4. Martian report
                        6. Martian report
                        7. Bream
                        8 - 9. Martian report
                        10. Dolphin
                        11 - 16. Captain Manson. PAX 382
                        15 - 16. Log information comes from 21 Army Group
                                   logs. Major Brown. PAX 344.

iv. Police.   Solo. Captain Baker. PAX 342.

17. A list of 'Sources and Contributors' from the 'Record of the Western Front', 10 March 1944. This lists exactly which sources – Enigma or FISH networks, or elsewhere – provided each item of intelligence.

18. *Generalfeldmarschall* Rommel inspects the Atlantic Wall defences, April 1944. Here, timber beach obstacles have been installed to obstruct Allied landing craft. Despite German efforts, many of these defences were incomplete on D-Day.

19. Rommel inspects a self-propelled artillery unit of *21. Panzer-Division*, Normandy, May 1944. The poor equipment of this division is illustrated here: the vehicles are hybrids built on obsolete French tank chassis.

20. A German propaganda photo of a paratrooper from *Fallschirmjäger-Regiment 6*, Cotentin peninsula, June 1944. Bletchley Park's identification of this unit led to the rearrangement of US parachute drops in the area on D-Day.

21. Canadian infantrymen in a Landing Craft Assault (LCA) going ashore on Juno Beach, 6 June 1944. Thanks to Bletchley Park these men had a good idea of the German forces they would be facing on landing.

22. Troops of the 9th Canadian Infantry Brigade going ashore after the successful capture of Juno Beach, 6 June 1944. By the end of 6 June the Allies had a firm foothold on all five invasion beaches and over 156,000 men had landed.

23. US troops of Company A, 16th Infantry, 1st Infantry Division (the 'Big Red One') wading onto Omaha Beach on the morning of 6 June, 1944. The fighting here was particularly intense, against stronger-than-expected German defences.

been destroyed, one embrasure was on fire, and the outlying infantry positions had been occupied by US troops. Perhaps rather unhelpfully in the circumstances, that evening *Seeko Normandie* signalled: 'Suggest IRON CROSS (1st Class) be awarded to S.O. [Senior Officer] MARCOUF for his outstanding achievements' (21.10).

What is notable in all these messages is just how much the Allies managed to maintain the level of tactical surprise. A fleet of 6,500 vessels had put to sea, including 4,250 landing craft, in 75 convoys each 5 miles long. And yet this had escaped the notice of the Germans. The Allied mine-sweeping fleets off the French coast in the last hours of daylight on 5 June observed only five German aircraft, none of which apparently noticed anything unusual; and overnight there was no air activity over the fleet. Allied planners had assumed that the departure of the force would be known to the enemy by at least H-12 hours (twelve hours before the first scheduled landing) and its destination clear to them by H-4; but this was not the case. At least in part, this was due to the weather: German forecasts had predicted unsuitable conditions for several days, and in fact the German navy had cancelled its usual patrol and minelaying operations for the night of 5–6 June.[30] Furthermore, as we saw in the Introduction, on 6 June General Marcks spent his birthday at an anti-invasion exercise in Rennes. He and a number of other key commanders from Rommel down-wards were absent from their headquarters that night. This allowed the invading forces a critical window of time in which to consolidate on shore before the German defenders fully understood the scale of what they were facing and organised their counterattacks. The Germans' own preconcep-tions also hampered their defensive efforts, as the idea persisted that the attack might be diversionary and only a prelude to a larger attack in the Pas-de-Calais. All of this provided the invaders with a vital advantage.

CLEAR SUCCESSES AND CONTROVERSIES

During May 1944, as the invasion drew ever closer, Hut 3 and Bletchley Park as a whole had two concerns. First, had they got their assessment of the German dispositions and defensive plans right? And, second, would the enemy make any last-minute changes to his deployment which Bletchley might not be able to spot? Historical accounts of D-Day have focused on two such episodes – one widely deemed a success; the other a failure. These were the successful identification of German troop movements in the Cotentin peninsula in the days before the invasion; and the counter-balancing failure to properly identify the location of the German *352. Infanterie-Division*, which would play a part in the fighting at Omaha Beach in particular. Just how much was known about *21. Panzer-Division* around Caen has also been the subject of debate. Through looking at these events we can determine exactly what Bletchley did or did not know, how complete the intelligence picture for commanders was, and how far this influenced the subsequent battle.

COTENTIN

In the first few months of 1944, the Cotentin peninsula was defended by two German infantry formations: the *709. Infanterie-Division* on the east and north coasts; and *243. Infanterie-Division* on the west and across the base of the peninsula. Both of these formations were known to Bletchley Park and were listed in the order of battle for 25 March produced by Section 3M in Hut 3. The *243. Division* is listed as 'possibly in the Cherbourg Peninsula' since February, and is described as formed of *Grenadier-Regimenter 920, 921* and *922*. Meanwhile, *709. Division* was listed as in 'Cherbourg' since December 1943.[31] However, this picture changed on 24 May, when a series of JELLYFISH messages were intercepted, revealing that *91. Luftlande-Infanterie-Division* (air-landing division) was moving into the Cotentin.[32] This information was relayed in the Western Front Committee 'Record' (No. 38) of 26 May:

> Bringing up of 91 Air Landing Division into the CHERBOURG peninsula is being carried out. Its battle HQ is at Chateau HAUT North of CARENTAN; this formation was previously in the VANNES area.[33]

The *91. Luftlande-Infanterie-Division* had been formed in January 1944 to take part in Operation TANNE, an operation scheduled for March 1944 to capture islands in the Gulf of Finland. However, this had never gone ahead and the division was re-posted west. The unit was 'airborne' in name only, consisting of two ordinary infantry regiments – the *Grenadier-Regimenter 1057* and *1058* – and only one parachute unit, *Fallschirmjäger-Regiment 6*. By this point in the war, even parachute units received little or no jump training and consisted simply of slightly better-quality infantry. Nonetheless, while under strength, the division still represented a respectable fighting force incorporating a number of Eastern Front veterans. It was supported by an armoured unit, *Panzer-Abteilung 100*, equipped with a motley assortment of captured French tanks.[34] Bletchley had tracked *91. Luftlande-Division* since its arrival in France in April, first identifying it in Strasbourg before its move west. Now it was moving to occupy a position in the centre of the base of the Cherbourg peninsula, with its two grenadier regiments around Pont l'Abbé, and *Fallschirmjäger-Regiment 6* south of Carentan.

This had an immediate effect on Allied planning. Up to that point, the US planners had intended to drop 101st Airborne Division on the eastern side of the Cotentin peninsula, immediately behind Utah Beach, in order to secure the causeways off the beach for the amphibious landing. Meanwhile, General Bradley had argued for the 82nd Airborne Division to be dropped further west, around La Haye-du-Puits (only 9.5 miles (15km) from the west coast). Thus it was intended that the two airborne divisions would cut off the base of the peninsula and rapidly isolate Cherbourg to the north. Eisenhower had been sceptical, as he had been less than impressed by the ability of paratroopers to land on target during the invasion of Sicily a year earlier. However, he saw the strategic advantage and so approved the plan.[35] Now, it seemed, 82nd Airborne would be falling practically on the heads of *91. Luftlande-Division*. A hastily revised plan was created, reverting to Eisenhower's original concept of landing both divisions in the area immediately behind the beach, concentrated around the town of Sainte-Mère-Église, which would become famous for the fighting which later took place around it.

In the event, the landings of 82nd Airborne were widely scattered, in particular those on the west side of the Merderet river, which flowed from north to south on the west side of Sainte-Mère-Église. Equal confusion reigned in *91. Luftlande-Division*; the divisional commander *Generalleutnant* Wilhelm Falley was away at a command exercise when the landings began, and on his return he was killed in an ambush by US paratroopers. Nonetheless, both *Grenadier-Regimenter 1057* and *1058* were able to launch counterattacks which effectively bottled up the US paratroopers east of the Merderet river, leading to several days of fierce fighting. There is little doubt that had the 82nd landed further west, as originally intended, the additional German forces in the area would have been able to isolate them very quickly and cause significant casualties; thus the JELLYFISH intercepts of two weeks before played a significant part in the success of the US airborne operation – or at least prevented a potential catastrophe.

In the case of *91. Luftlande-Division*, therefore, Allied intelligence and the codebreakers at Bletchley could be congratulated on a job well done.

OMAHA

But their performance over a second German reinforcement has become more controversial among historians of D-Day. This was the move of *352. Infanterie-Division* into the area of the invasion beaches, in particular Omaha.

At the beginning of 1944, the whole of the coast from Carentan, at the base of the Cotentin peninsula in the west, as far as Caen and the Orne river to the east – a distance of some 50 miles (80km) – was defended by only the *716. Infanterie-Division*. This was one of the so-called 'static' divisions: it was both under strength (consisting of older soldiers and those in lower medical categories) and almost completely lacking in transport. The division was formed of two grenadier regiments – *726* and *736* – each comprising three battalions. To each of these regiments had been added a fourth, so-called *Ost* battalion of Eastern European volunteers, ex-POWs, etc., of dubious fighting quality. The three battalions of *Grenadier-Regiment 726* were spread out along the coastal defences on the western side of the divisional area; *Grenadier-Regiment 736* occupied the area north of Caen in the east of the sector, with its battalions similarly strung out along the coast.[36] The two *Ost* battalions were placed at either end of the line: at Isigny in the west, and on the east bank of the Orne at Breville.

The *716. Infanterie-Division* had been in this position since June 1942, and was well known to Allied intelligence. Bennett has pointed out that the division did not appear in any ULTRA traffic prior to the invasion; but this is not due to any omission on the part of Bletchley Park – rather it resulted from the fact that the division stayed in place and did little that was worth reporting as ULTRA.[37] Nonetheless, it had been identified by Hut 3 in the order of battle produced by 3M in March: the division was listed in the 'Geographical List of Divisions On or Near the Coast', placing it at Caen.[38] In the order of battle produced at the end of May, it was listed again, this time based around Bayeux.[39] Either of these locations was reasonable, as the division was strung along the coast near both of these towns, with one of its regiments based roughly north of each place. The divisional headquarters was actually in La Folie-Couvrechef, a north-western suburb of Caen.

This situation would change at the end of March 1944. As mentioned in the previous chapter, in March Rommel reached a defensive compromise with von Rundstedt which allowed him to position three panzer divisions nearer to the coast, as part of his preferred strategy of meeting the Allies in as much strength as possible on the beaches. A second tier of this strategy was to reinforce the coastal defences by supporting the static divisions currently in position with additional, more capable, mobile infantry divisions. One such was *352. Infanterie-Division*.

This division had been formed in December 1943 around St-Lô. It was made up from remnants of the battered *321. Infanterie-Division*, which had been withdrawn from the Eastern Front for rebuilding. Around these cadres of Eastern Front veterans, the division was built up to full strength with new eighteen- and nineteen-year-old conscripts, but its overall standard of training was quite high. It was in almost all respects a much more battle-worthy outfit than the static divisions in place along the coast. On 15 March, the division was ordered forward from St-Lô to take up positions on the coast in the Bayeux sector alongside *716. Infanterie-Division*.[40]

Three areas of historical debate have emerged in relation to this reinforcement: first, how much this augmented the German defences, especially around Omaha Beach; second, how much Allied intelligence knew about this and how much information was passed to local commanders leading the US attack; and, finally, how much effect it had on the fighting that ensued.

It has been argued that the move of *352. Division* to the coast 'doubled'[41] or even 'tripled'[42] the strength of the German defences at Omaha. Max Hastings calculated that 'At Omaha the Americans found themselves facing Germans of the 352nd Division as well as the 716th – eight battalions instead of four.'[43] In fact the situation was more complex than a simple multiplication of the number of Germans behind the beach, and *352. Division* was much more scattered in its deployment than these accounts suggest.

Unlike *716. Division* (which comprised two regiments each of three battalions), *352. Division* was made up of three regiments each of two battalions: *Grenadier-Regimenter 914, 915* and *916*, along with divisional artillery, anti-tank and reconnaissance elements. The division had its headquarters at Littry, approximately 9.5 miles (15km) due south of St Laurent-sur-Mer and Omaha. The three infantry regiments were distributed across the sector. In the west, *Grenadier-Regiment 914* was based near Isigny-sur-Mer, 6.25 miles (10km) east of Carentan (and 12.5 miles (20km) from Omaha). *Grenadier-Regiment 915* had its two battalions south and east of Bayeux.

This left *Grenadier-Regiment 916* as potential reinforcements for Omaha. But in fact the first battalion of this regiment was positioned 12.5 miles (20km) to the east, at Ryes. Thus, only the second battalion was actually in the Omaha area. Even then, however, the divisional commander, *Generalleutnant* Kraiss, broke with Rommel's doctrine and placed only two of the battalion's four companies overlooking the beach; the other two he placed in reserve, several kilometres behind.[44] The divisional anti-tank battalion (*Panzerjäger-Abteilung 352*) was placed 6.25 miles (10km) further back around Bricqueville in support, with what little armour was possessed by the division.[45]

This all goes to show that the immediate defences of Omaha Beach had been enhanced from perhaps four companies, formed of garrison troops from *716. Division*, to six companies, with a further two in reserve. This is hardly the jump from four to eight battalions previously quoted – though it could be argued that the force was 'doubled' and that the additional companies were of better quality.

The move of *352. Division* as a whole undoubtedly significantly reinforced the defences of the Calvados coast, and did indeed double the coastal garrison from eight infantry battalions to sixteen, as well as additional anti-tank and artillery units. However, these forces were distributed along the whole front between Carentan and Caen, and were by no means exclusively facing the American forces landing at Omaha. As a result, claims that 'The reconfiguration of the defences along the Bayeux coast in late March 1944 more than tripled their strength',[46] or that 'The German forces on Omaha Beach were more than three times the strength of those anticipated',[47] seem a little exaggerated.

Nonetheless, the German order of battle had changed. To what extent did Allied intelligence (and Bletchley Park) identify this? In its March order of battle (25 March), Hut 3 identified *352. Division* as based around St-Lô.[48] By that time, of course, the information was obsolete, as the division had moved north on 15 March. This error was repeated in the later order of battle, issued on 21 May, when the division was still described as 'S of St Lô';[49] so it would seem that no solid information confirming a move by the unit had been identified. However, suggestions of changes to the German defensive arrangements were filtering through. The Western Front Committee 'Record' (No. 34) of 30 April observed:

It is fairly clear that redispositions of the coastal sectors have taken place. There may be unidentified divisions South of DIEPPE and East of CAEN, and the coastal sectors in general can no longer be assumed to contain exactly one infantry division, but the extent of the overlap between divisional areas and coastal sectors cannot yet be assessed.[50]

This inference was drawn from information in a Martian report, rather than direct from SIGINT. Because it was probably based on reporting from the Resistance, it was given less credence than a more definitive piece of information might have been. The division was also identified again at the end of May via traffic analysis of a wireless exercise, and again this was shown in the 'Record of Western Front' (No. 38) on 25 May:

M 175 (CAEN sector)
This serial has thrown up a large and miscellaneous batch of unit numbers and a reference to Inf. Div. 352. In the subordinate units there was only one possible tie-up and this was the inclusion of G.R. 914 and G.R. 915 which according to MIRS/OB/EB/17/44 probably belong to 352 Inf. Division. CX/MSS places 352 Inf. Division in ST. LO, which would not be too badly placed for this network.[51]

However, the last line implies that those trying to identify these units fell back on the previous known location of the division (i.e. St-Lô) rather than trying to make any new interpretation.

Photographic reconnaissance of the coast in May also identified a build-up of troops in the coastal defences; however, it was not possible to identify directly the units concerned. The frustration at this lack of detail was expressed in a 21st Army Group intelligence report on 14 May, which pointed out that it was

a most unsatisfactory state of affairs that we cannot specifically identify all the elements which go to make up the sector ... This much is evident – that we shall on D-Day make contact immediately with

716th, 709th, 243rd, the fringe of 711th and, within a very short time, 352nd Infantry and 21st Panzer.[52]

This assessment was refined on 4 June to something which came close to describing the reality of the situation:

> For some time now in other areas coastal divisions have been narrowing their sectors, while divisions the role of which has hitherto been read as lay-back have nosed forward into the gaps provided by the reduced responsibility of the coastal divisions ... the evidence that the same has happened on the left in the case of 716th Division is slender indeed ... yet it should not be surprising if we discovered that it has two regiments in the line and one in reserve, while on its left 352nd has one regiment up and two to play.[53]

Unfortunately, this assessment by 21st Army Group came too late to be communicated to the attacking formations, which thus went ashore expecting only *716. Division* to resist them. Some sources have reported a claim by Brigadier 'Bill' Williams, the 21st Army Group intelligence chief, that he received correct information about *352. Division* prior to the attack, but that he was unable to pass it on to the forward commanders.[54] No firm evidence of this has been identified, beyond the 4 June assessment. In any case, it is hard to see what could have been done with the ships already loaded and much of the invasion force already at sea.

The defences of Omaha Beach and its environs were stronger than had been predicted. Nonetheless, the above review of the exact dispositions of the division shows that the reinforcement did not provide the defenders with an overwhelming boost of strength. Despite this, the attack on Omaha was one of the most costly in casualties of all the landings on 6 June, and the two facts are often linked as cause and effect: US troops were killed in large numbers, it is argued, because they faced an enemy they did not expect to meet. At the same time, it is clear that significant elements of *352. Division* were present further east, at Gold Beach, where Allied casualties were not nearly as severe. Indeed, up to a third of the divisional strength was engaged in fighting there, organised into an informal battlegroup – *Kampfgruppe Meyer*. This was heavily defeated when it attempted a probe towards Villiers-le-Sec late on the afternoon of 6 June.

This is not the place to give a detailed account of the fighting at Omaha; but if the problems faced by US V Corps on that beach were not the result of overwhelming unexpected opposition, then what went wrong? The first difficulty was geographical: the beach was not ideal as a landing spot. It was overlooked by high bluffs and had only a few restricted exits; however, it was the only viable landing spot on the otherwise almost continuous 25 miles (40km) of coastal cliffs between Arromanches and the Cotentin. This, incidentally, had not been lost on the German defenders, who could predict pretty closely where a landing along that stretch of coast would be practicable. There were also flaws in the attack plan, which meant that the preliminary bombardments were shorter than initially desired, and air support both before and during landing was inadequate.[55] Finally, the operation was severely hampered by a combination of weather and bad luck, which meant that much of the supporting armour (both amphibious tanks and conventional vehicles) failed to reach the beach, or was destroyed very quickly after landing. These and other factors conspired to make what was already a tough task almost impossible. In these circumstances, even a modest unexpected addition to the strength of the defenders would have been very unwelcome. It was, however, not the only factor in the losses suffered at Omaha.

21. PANZER-DIVISION

The other German formation that (it has been suggested) was misplaced or misunderstood by Allied intelligence prior to D-Day was *21. Panzer-Division*. Again, the question revolves around the closeness of the division to the beaches, and its ability to intervene in the first hours of the landing. It has been argued, for example, that 'The British feared the possible arrival of the German *352 Division* within eight hours, *12 SS* possibly in twelve; they did not realise that the *21 Panzer Division* was virtually in-situ.'[56] Invading Allied forces would encounter elements of *21. Panzer* very early on in the battle, and the degree to which this came as a surprise has been much debated. The unit was one of the three panzer divisions under Rommel's immediate command in *Heeresgruppe B* – and the only one of the three in the Normandy area. The other two (*2.* and *116.*) were north of the Seine as part of *15. Armee*. The other armoured units within striking distance of the invasion area (i.e. within a day or two's march) fell under the remit of von Schweppenburg's *Panzergruppe West* and would not be in a position to respond immediately to an attack; *21. Panzer*, on the other hand, formed part of Rommel's plan for an immediate armoured response to the invasion.

The division had been re-formed in France in July 1943, after being virtually destroyed at the end of the North African campaign in May of that year. Initially it was based at Rennes, but in accordance with Rommel's forward strategy it moved to Caen in May 1944. The division appeared a number of times in Western Front Committee 'Records': it was identified at Rennes on the basis of a Martian report in mid-April,[57] and this was confirmed in early May by Guderian's tour of panzer units revealed in a JELLYFISH decrypt from 20 April.[58] The division was subsequently identified on the move to Caen during the week of 13–19 May, and in the same week medium-grade traffic analysis of a wireless exercise held in the Caen area suggested that the units involved were from *21. Panzer-Division*.[59] After this date, little or no information about the division was forthcoming. Huge amounts of air reconnaissance of the Caen area were carried out, but, apart from a few tantalising tank-track marks in the fields, very little additional information was revealed. As a result, 21st Army Group concluded that the tank strength of the division was concentrated south of Caen, and that, while elements may be contacted earlier, the bulk of the division could not be expected to intervene in the battle before the evening of D-Day. In addition, it is clear from reports produced after the event by local commanders that British I Corps, landing on Sword Beach, assumed that the division lay around 19 miles (30km) south-east of Caen, and would not be encountered until after Caen itself had fallen.[60]

In this assessment both 21st Army Group and I Corps were partially correct. The *21. Panzer-Division* was formed of one tank-equipped panzer regiment (*Panzer-Regiment 22*) of two battalions, and two panzergrenadier regiments (*125* and *192*). Each of the latter also had two infantry battalions: one transported in trucks, and the other in armoured carriers. The panzer regiment was located, with most of the division's armour, at Aubigny, nearly 19 miles (30km) south-east of Caen, and this matched the Allied estimate. These troops were also constrained from making any move in response to an attack, unless authorised by the divisional commander, *Generalmajor* Feuchtinger, or directly by Rommel at *Heeresgruppe B*. By chance, both of these men would be absent from their headquarters on the night of 5–6 June, and as a result the division remained immobile. *Major* Hans von Luck, who was in temporary command of *Panzergrenadier-Regiment 125* described the frustration of enduring a developing attack without orders to respond:

> The hours passed. We had set up a defensive front where we had been condemned to inactivity. The rest of the division with the panzer regiment and Panzer Grenadier Regiment 192 was equally immobilised, though in the highest state of alert.[61]

This meant that the bulk of the division's tanks would remain south of Caen until later in the day on 6 June, out of the battle and awaiting movement orders.

However, what the Allied planners had not appreciated was that the two panzergrenadier regiments in the division, and much of its artillery, had actually been positioned much closer to the coast. *Panzergrenadier-Regiment 192* was deployed on the west bank of the river Orne, with its more mobile first battalion (the one with armoured transport) in reserve to the south-west of Caen, and its truck-borne second battalion in defensive positions north-west of Caen, within 6.25 miles (10km) of Sword Beach.

While the immediate opposition from elements of *Grenadier-Regiment 736* on Sword Beach was overcome relatively quickly, the push inland by the British 3rd Division then ran up against elements of *Panzergrenadier-Regiment 192*, as well as *21. Panzer* divisional artillery. This would slow its advance towards Caen at a critical stage. On the east bank of the Orne, *Panzergrenadier-Regiment 125* occupied similar positions, with its first battalion in reserve and its second battalion further north in the area of Ranville, Troarn and Colombelles.[62] This placed the companies of the second battalion more or less directly at the landing zones of the British 6th Airborne Division. Thus, even without definitive movement orders from divisional HQ, these troops were forced into combat with the Allied airborne troops almost immediately, in a fashion that neither side was expecting.

Although British 6th Airborne Division was able to hang on to Pegasus Bridge (the principal crossing of the river Orne north of Caen), it faced a much harder fight than had been planned, and the bridgehead it had established on the eastern bank of the river was, by the end of the day, much smaller than had been hoped.[63] This resistance on both sides of the Orne was one of the factors which led to the failure to capture Caen as planned on the first day of the invasion. Continuing German occupation of the city would present a serious obstacle to Montgomery's plans for the remainder of the campaign.

*

The fact that Allied intelligence did not provide a timely and detailed account of the locations of both *352. Infanterie-Division* and *21. Panzer-Division* has been characterised as an intelligence failure. However, to assess intelligence in this binary success/failure mode is to oversimplify the problem. John Ferris has analysed this question at some length. He has pointed out that the OVERLORD plan was based as much on what was achievable by the Allies, the size of the invading forces, the location and date of the landings, and so on, as it was on intelligence about the Germans. The landings represented what was achievable, not what was ideal. Also, the plans had to be finalised long in advance of 6 June, based on intelligence assessments which inevitably would be out of date by the time troops were on the beach. Any late changes of deployment by the Germans would just have to be absorbed by the existing plan, which was too large and complex to be nuanced at the last minute. He made this point specifically with regard to Omaha and Caen:

> The real problem was that the Germans held Caen, not the fact this surprised the allies. These failures in the intelligence cost lives, but not the battle. Even had they known the truth, the allies would have had to try to take Caen on 6–7 June, and largely in the same way – otherwise they would have been condemned for passivity. In any case, they crushed the only German counterattacks launched during the landing, and ensured ultimate victory. So too, certain knowledge of the location of 352 Division could have done nothing to stem the slaughter at Omaha beach. These intelligence failures were indicative, but not influential.[64]

The concluding remarks of his assessment also put these 'failures' or otherwise into perspective: 'On 6 June 1944, the problem was the enemy, not intelligence about it. Intelligence had done well enough, as much as could be expected. The rest was up to the men.'[65]

What the stories of both *352. Infanterie-Division* and *21. Panzer-Division* do indicate, however, is that the sources available to Bletchley Park were essentially strategic in character. The high-level nature of the communications mostly intercepted by GC&CS made them very useful in positioning whole divisions on a map of France, but were less helpful in placing battalions and companies on a map of Normandy. This lack of granularity in the intelligence picture created presented a problem for local commanders once the attack had begun, even if the strategic infor-mation had been of vital importance for the higher-level planners in advance of the operation. Once the Allies had 'troops in contact' (in modern parlance), the value of this strategic-level information decreased in favour of tactical information gained by battlefield intelligence sources. Also, as the tempo of the battle increased, even the fast turnaround times achieved by Bletchley's codebreakers were only sufficient to provide information on events as they unfolded, as opposed to predictive intelligence. Both these aspects – the organisation's continuing strategic effectiveness and the increasing difficulty it had in keeping up with a fast-paced battle – would be apparent in the remainder of the land campaign.

CHAPTER EIGHT

STAYING ASHORE

THE NORMANDY CAMPAIGN

Nineteen-year-old Wilf Neal landed on Omaha Beach in Normandy on 7 July 1944. Wilf was a British signaller in SCU 8, the wireless unit tasked with providing ULTRA intelligence direct to the headquarters of Third US Army and General Patton. After an unpleasant channel crossing in a 'Liberty' cargo ship, he described his unit's arrival in the theatre of war:

> On the evening of 7 July, we disembarked down a rope ladder over the side, and onto a flat Rhino landing barge which deposited us in our vehicles, in the water, a little way from the beach. All made it safely ashore except for our Dodge 6x6 which had to be towed in by a tractor. We moved a short distance inland and spent the night sleeping out in the open, after going through the task of removing the water-proofing material from the vehicles.

Wilf's journey that ultimately led to Normandy had started eight months earlier, in October 1943. One Tuesday evening he had returned home from his factory job in Birmingham. After giving him his tea, his mother reluctantly produced the post. Wilf's call-up papers had arrived. He was instructed to present himself at 'Royal Corps of Signals, S.C.U. 1, Bletchley' for training as a signalman. At his National Service interview, Wilf had specifically asked *not* to be put in the Royal Signals: while he had been an amateur radio enthusiast at school, his interest in wireless had waned in favour of driving and mechanics. Clearly the army thought differently, and he soon found himself at the signals training school at Little Horwood near Bletchley.

Signals training continued through the winter of 1943–44, and conditions were bleak. Wilf was initially accommodated in the stables at Little Horwood, where there was no heating or hot water, and only primitive sanitation. The men were required to parade in the cold first thing in the morning, before being marched in formation to breakfast. In the spring, however, both the conditions and the weather improved, and Wilf was posted to SCU 8, a wireless unit attached to the American forces, at that time headquartered in Bushy Park, near London.

In June came D-Day, but SCU 8 was sent not to Normandy, but to Knutsford in Cheshire. This was where General Patton's Third US Army headquarters was based, pending its eventual move to France. Wilf and his colleagues remained there for three weeks, before being declared 'operational' on 25 June. In early July, they made their way to Southampton, and thence to France.

Wilf spent the next three months on rolling shifts, listening to coded transmissions from the UK intended for Patton's intelligence staff. The unit lived out of their vehicles and slept in two-man tents. Meals consisted of US ration packs, often eaten in the open air. What little leisure time the troops had was spent sleeping or sheltering in the trucks. However, life was more comfortable, as all the drills and inspections of their training days ceased; and, as long as the work got done, no one bothered SCU 8 about any of the more formal aspects of soldiering.

Wilf followed Third US Army headquarters across France and into Germany, finishing up in Regensburg at the time of the German surrender in May 1945 (by which time German signals traffic had withered away to leave the unit essentially idle). Such was the compartmentalisation of the organisation that, despite being part of Patton's headquarters for nearly a year, Wilf saw the general in person only twice, and that at a distance. Nor did he have any idea of what was in the enciphered messages he was taking down from his wireless set. It was only in the 1970s, when the wider story of Bletchley Park was revealed, that he learned what his part in OVERLORD had really been.[1]

*

By the end of 6 June 1944, Allied commanders had reason to be satisfied. On that first day, 75,215 British and Canadian and 57,500 US troops had landed by sea on the beaches of Normandy. They were supported by a further 23,000 airborne soldiers. This landing had been achieved at the cost of roughly 10,000 Allied casualties.[2] Not only were these casualties lower than the Allied planners had feared, but Rommel's defensive plan – to defeat an invasion while it was still at sea or on the beach – had failed. Much remained to be done – and indeed very few of the Allied first-day objectives had been attained (notably, the cities of Caen and Bayeux still lay in German hands); but the invasion force was ashore, and there it would stay. Montgomery had initially devised a 90-day campaign that would drive the German forces back to the line of the river Seine.[3] In the event, progress was faster than planned; German resistance in Normandy collapsed after the closure of the Falaise pocket in mid-August, and Paris was liberated on 25 August, only 80 days after the first landings.

Throughout the campaign, Bletchley Park would continue to supply intelligence to commanders in the fashion that had evolved over the previous year and a half, assisted – now that battle had been joined – by the SCU/SLU teams attached to each of the Allied headquarters on the continent. Rather than simply cataloguing the many intelligence items passed daily to Allied commanders in this period,[4] we should take a slightly wider view and examine the flow of intelligence and the extent to which it altered from before the invasion, as well as the impact that the material provided had on the battle.

ULTRA'S USES

As the invasion approached, Hut 6 (responsible for German army and air force Enigma) braced itself for the arrival of a vastly larger volume of traffic. In particular, German army keys that had been mostly silent during the spring of 1944 were expected to burst into life. It was also expected that there would be a corresponding increase in German air force traffic. In the event, the latter proved more productive. Traffic on Luftwaffe keys increased from 729 messages intercepted on 5 June to 1,297 on 6 June and a peak of 2,936 on 9 June.[5] A total of fifteen different keys were broken. Of these the general Luftwaffe key RED remained a staple: it alone provided 809 of the 2,936 messages on 9 June.[6] A further key, OCELOT, was identified on 31 May and was broken within twenty-four hours each day from 8 June until the end of August. This was an army–air liaison key – a so-called 'Flivo' key, after the *Fliegerverbindungsoffizier* (air liaison officer) responsible for the traffic. These messages provided briefings to German air commanders on the ground situation and order of battle, and arranged air support for military operations. As such, they were a goldmine for Bletchley. Other keys that were regularly read included PLATYPUS (used by the Luftwaffe anti-aircraft *III. Flak-Korps*) and FIREFLY (used by *Fallschirmjäger* (parachute) units). Both of these formations were involved in ground fighting and so provided useful battlefield information.[7]

German army keys proved more recalcitrant. Much of the success in breaking Enigma relied on the use of cribs. Unfortunately, the identification of these predictable phrases or patterns depended on the enemy developing a set routine. In the initial chaos of the invasion, these cribs were hard to spot. As the 'History of Hut 6' put it: 'Thus when D-Day finally came bringing with it floods of traffic, we had a very good idea what keys to expect, but very little notion of what they would be saying.' However, the German procedural error of re-encoding messages from one key to another allowed Hut 6 to make progress on army links by 10 June. The *Heeresgruppe B* key, BANTAM, was broken on 8 June, and this in turn led to breaks into the *7. Armee* key, DUCK I, and its staff key,

DUCK II, on 10 June. These keys would continue to be broken with varying degrees of frequency through late June and July.[8] These were supported by continuing success in breaking the SS keys ORANGE and QUINCE.

After the landings, FISH traffic continued to flow into Bletchley from Knockholt, and a new intercept station was created at Kedleston Hall in Derbyshire. Unfortunately, problems were not far away. From 1 to 17 June 1944, the JELLYFISH link used by *O.B. West* employed the same wheel patterns each day, but thereafter it started to change the wheel patterns every twenty-four hours (see Chapter 2). This habit spread to other links on the FISH network during July and August. Now, instead of having to 'break' the wheels only once per month, the process had to be repeated daily. Fortunately, as was described above, a method of wheel-breaking using Colossus had been identified in the first half of 1944, and this had been incorporated into the design of Colossus II.

Nonetheless, after 17 June only one JELLYFISH daily key was broken that month. In July, three daily breaks were achieved on JELLYFISH and another five in August; meanwhile, on the Italian BREAM link, only six breaks were achieved in July and another six in August. An additional link was identified at Bletchley in June (codenamed GRILSE, a type of young salmon), linking *Heeresgruppe B* in France with Berlin; but only sporadic, single-day breaks were achieved on this link. As a result, the overall proportion of FISH traffic that could be read successfully fell from its 1944 peak of 3.1 per cent of messages intercepted in June to 1.9 per cent in July and 1.8 per cent in August. However, this was offset by an increase in the overall number of messages being intercepted. Consequently, the volume of material decrypted grew slightly from just under 2 million characters in June to 2.1 million in July and August.[9] As with all FISH traffic, the actual decryptions continued to take at least several days to achieve, and so little of this material was of immediate operational relevance. This view was supported by the writers of the 'History of Hut Three', who commented on the usefulness of the FISH intercepts being provided:

The intelligence provided by Army Fish was complimentary to that provided by Army E [Enigma], and there was little overlap. Compared with Army E, Fish was *strikingly non-operational and carried practically no tactical information*; the only operational messages normally passed in Fish were routine or morning situation reports. The bulk of the traffic consisted of routine reports on supplies, strength-returns, tank returns, and traffic-situation reports, together with occasional general appreciations.[10]

The type of intelligence that was being provided by Bletchley Park after 6 June continued to have broadly the same character as that delivered before the invasion. Enigma traffic between German units at corps and army level constituted much of the 'high-grade' material, and FISH continued to provide both strategic appreciations by senior commanders, and logistical and unit-composition information. Thus, a steady flow of enemy divisional headquarters locations and other order of battle information was delivered, as well as occasional items revealing enemy appreciations of the situation. As we have seen, this material was of vital importance to the planning process prior to the start of the battle; however, once the fighting was under way in some respects its usefulness diminished. When ULTRA provided the only means of locating a German division in France, this was crucial to the planning process; but once Allied troops were actually in contact with that formation on the ground, being informed of its location clearly became less important.

Once the Allied forces were in contact with the enemy, they were also provided with a range of intelligence streams not previously available. These included local reconnaissance and patrolling, POW interrogation and – particularly importantly – tactical wireless interception. Lower-level tactical signals interception was handled by Y units attached to army and corps headquarters in France. For the British and Commonwealth troops, this fell under the control of No. 1 Special Wireless Group (SWG), an army formation that accompanied 21st Army Group to France. Subordinate to No. 1 SWG was a series of special wireless sections, divided into two types: larger Type 'A' sections, which were attached to army headquarters (British Second and Canadian First Armies), and smaller Type 'B' sections formed of both British and Canadian signallers, which were attached to individual corps headquarters.[11] The US forces similarly had US Army Signal Service companies attached at corps level.[12] These units handled 'medium-grade' and 'low-grade' signals intelligence, including transmissions using hand ciphers, as well as plain-language material. They were also engaged in traffic analysis and direction finding. They thus had a significant role in providing up-to-date SIGINT to the commanders with whom they were located. These units did report some material to GC&CS and were supported in cryptanalytical methodology by the research teams at Bletchley Park, but they were not part of the Bletchley organisation and functioned largely autonomously. They were in operation in France not only after the invasion, but also in the weeks beforehand, as many of them were moved to locations on the south coast of the UK, where they could already intercept German tactical traffic from across the Channel.[13]

Thanks to all these additional intelligence resources, commanders in France were well supplied with intelligence about their immediate enemies and the tactical battlefield. Often there was little that ULTRA could add to this picture. In a 1945 paper on 'The Use of ULTRA by the Army', Edgar 'Bill' Williams, Montgomery's intelligence chief at 21st Army Group, described how he regarded ULTRA largely as a back-stop to his own local intelligence. He pointed out that local 'Y' was often of supreme importance:

> This note is devoted mainly to Ultra, but the time ought not to pass without reference to the part Yorker [tactical Y] played in making the rounder pattern which Ultra could not achieve; frequently, and in battle usually, replacing it, and in general building up a day-to-day knowledge of the enemy which allowed us to handle Ultra with more confidence, and to be prepared to say that Ultra was not true (a very important psychological step in dealing with such material).[14]

Williams was suspicious of those intelligence officers who relied too heavily on ULTRA, as he considered it the lazy man's substitute for detailed local intelligence work. The inevitable delay in breaking each daily key and decrypting, analysing and disseminating the messages also meant that the ULTRA received in the field was, as he put it, 'of course usually out of date'.[15] Nonetheless, even if he had (in his own words) 'beaten Ultra' by compiling an equivalent intelligence picture from his own local sources, Williams still liked the reassurance of a second supply of information:

> At an Army HQ we maintained, however, that during battle we had not done our day's work properly unless we had beaten Ultra, unless we knew what was happening and could appreciate what would happen before it could arrive. This did not mean that we were not glad of its arrival, for at best it showed that we were wrong, usually it enabled us to tidy up loose ends, and at worst we tumbled into bed with a smug confirmation.[16]

This attitude applied during periods of active combat. However, Williams admitted that 'In a planning period between battles its [ULTRA's] value was more obvious.'[17] The movements of German units and their locations prior to an operation, or where they were out of contact with Allied forces, was information that could still be provided most effectively from Bletchley Park. It was in this role that GC&CS would prove most useful during the Normandy campaign.

Bletchley's role in monitoring the progress of German units towards the battlefield in Normandy became crucial from the first moments of the campaign. Prior to the landings, the planners at COSSAC had made a prediction of how large and fast the German build-up in the Normandy area might be, and what the tolerable limits would be for a successful invasion. Their last estimate was produced on 23 May, when they predicted a slightly larger German force than they had initially deemed acceptable – an additional three divisions on D-Day itself; six or seven (rather than the hoped-for five) by D+2; and eleven to fourteen (rather than nine) by D+8. However, their report offered the counter-balancing suggestion that, while this initial build-up might be quicker, overall forces available to the Germans over the whole length of the campaign remained within acceptable limits.[18]

The most important German units in any build-up of forces to oppose the invasion would of course be the panzer divisions, many of which were also elite SS formations. As we saw above, only three of these were near the coast: *21. Panzer-Division*, which would be encountered by the invading forces in Normandy from the outset, and *2.* and *116. Panzer-Divisionen*. Further inland were the four panzer and panzergrenadier divisions placed as the central reserve under von Schweppenburg in *Panzergruppe West*. Of these, two (*12. SS-Panzer* and *Panzer-Lehr*) were within 95 miles (150km) of the landing beaches in the triangle Caen–Paris–Le Mans; *17. SS-Panzergrenadier* was further away to the south of the river Loire; and *1. SS-Panzer* was re-forming north of Brussels. The remaining three armoured divisions in France (*9.*, *11.* and *2. SS*) were in the south of France, at Avignon, Bordeaux and Toulouse, respectively, under *Heeresgruppe G.*[19] Of these nine divisions (in addition to *21. Panzer*) as many as five might be expected to join the fighting within a few days of landing. Only the three divisions in the south of France and *1. SS-Panzer* in Belgium could be considered to be excluded from the initial fight.

On the night of 5–6 June, senior German commanders were relatively slow to react. While both *7.* and *15. Armeen* were brought to their highest state of alert, senior figures in all three services – including, in Rommel's absence, his chief-of-staff at *Heeresgruppe B, General* Speidel – initially believed that the landings in Normandy were a feint before a larger attack in Calais (of which more later). At around 04.00, von Rundstedt intervened to order *12. SS-Panzer-Division* forward to the invasion area, and *Panzer-Lehr* was advised to stand by to move; but at 07.30, after this order had been sent to OKW for confirmation, *Generaloberst* Jodl countermanded it; he wanted to check with the Führer before committing so many troops. Unfortunately, Hitler would be in bed until lunchtime and did not like to be disturbed, and so these movement orders could not be reinstated until the afternoon of 6 June.[20] As a result, Allied troops only started to encounter elements of these two divisions on D+1 (7 June). The presence of these formations in the battle area was no surprise – their pre-invasion positions were known and it had been predicted that they would be encountered early in the battle. Both divisions were identified and located on 7 and 8 June.[21]

However, no information was forthcoming from ULTRA about these movements. Though a significant amount of naval material was (as mentioned above) intercepted between *Seeko Normandie* and *Admiral Kanalküste*, it mostly concerned the immediate coastal defences. Little army traffic of any significance was obtained in the first two days. As Hinsley bluntly put it: 'High grade sigint provided no intelligence of value to *Juno* or *Gold* forces before 9 June.'[22] The first useful decrypts relating to army and SS activity only started to be available on 8 June. A 'Flivo' message (presumably obtained from OCELOT, the Enigma key described earlier) intercepted at 08.00 on 7 June was circulated twenty-four hours later on the morning of the 8th, describing a proposed attack by *12. SS-Panzer-Division* and *Panzer-Lehr* in support of *352. Division*.[23] However, this attack did not materialise.

At around this time more detail of the internal composition of the divisions became available, as the FISH messages intercepted in May (see above, Chapter 5) were finally deciphered, revealing detailed personnel and tank strengths for *12. SS-Panzer-Division* among others.[24] A subsequent message in the early hours of 9 June also described the subordination of both *12. SS-Panzer-Division* and *21. Panzer-Division* to local command by *I. SS-Panzer-Korps* headquarters in Falaise.[25] Again, it is interesting that the source of this information was provided in the ULTRA message text 'according FLIVO'; this shows both the importance of breaking OCELOT, and also the apparent relaxation of the non-SIGINT cover story for the source of ULTRA.

Soon after the landings, ULTRA helped deliver a blow against the Germans: the destruction of the headquarters of *Panzergruppe West* on

10 June. This headquarters had been established in Paris under *General* Geyr von Schweppenburg, with the express task of managing armoured forces in response to an invasion. On 8 June, von Schweppenburg moved his headquarters forward to the chateau at La Caine, 12.5 miles (20km) south-west of Caen, with a view to being able to control directly an armoured riposte to the invasion. Transmissions from the new HQ were rapidly identified by Bletchley, and direction finding (possibly carried out by local 21st Army Group Y operators) helped determine its location. An ULTRA message sent at 04.39 on 10 June stated 'Battle Headquarters Panzer Gruppe West evening ninth at La Caine.'[26] In response, the Allied Tactical Air Force mounted a devastating raid, involving over forty rocket-firing Typhoon aircraft and sixty bombers. The chateau itself suffered relatively little damage, but the complex of command and communications vehicles in the adjacent orchard were totally destroyed. Eighteen members of the HQ staff were killed outright, including the chief of staff, and even more wounded, including von Schweppenburg himself (a fact revealed by a subsequent intercept on 12 June).[27]

As a result, *Panzergruppe West* headquarters withdrew to Paris and would not be ready to resume its command function until 28 June.[28] This caused serious disruption to the planning of organised German counter-attacks, and command had to be passed in the interim to *I. SS-Panzer-Korps* headquarters in Falaise. The first act of *I. SS-Panzer-Korps* that evening was to cancel the large-scale armoured attack planned for the following day, 11 June, a decision (also reported by ULTRA)[29] that would have a significant impact on German prospects for the remainder of the campaign.[30]

Despite the German ambitions for a substantial decisive thrust against the Allied invasion area, this proved difficult to coordinate: whenever new units arrived at the front, they found themselves responding piece-meal to different attacks. However, one organised attack against the American lodgement in the west of the front was launched on 13 June. This involved the commitment of *17. SS-Panzergrenadier-Division*, which had previously been based south of the river Loire. The advance of this division from the Loire was first noted by Bletchley Park on 7 June and signalled on 8 June.[31] The message described the transfer of the division from *1.* to *7. Armee* and mentioned its ultimate destination as Villedieu, 19 miles (30km) south of St-Lô. This was confirmed in a message later in the evening of 8 June, which also described the division's subordination to *Panzergruppe West.*[32] By late on 9 June, *17. SS* had arrived in St-Lô and had been joined by elements *of II. Fallschirm-Korps* and *3. Fallschirmjäger-Division.* This was reported by ULTRA on 10 June.[33]

The first indications that an attack might be developing came in traffic intercepted at lunchtime on 11 June (and distributed at midnight 11/12 June) placing *3. Fallschirmjäger-Division* alongside the remains of *352. Infanterie-Division* along the St-Lô to Bayeux road, with *17. SS-Panzergrenadier* behind to the south for 'mobile operations depending on situation.'[34] This was followed by a message circulated at 11.01 GMT on the morning of 12 June, indicating a counterattack by *17. SS* towards Carentan.[35] Perhaps unhelpfully, this message described the attack as commencing that very morning. Had the Germans kept to their schedule, the information would have been somewhat redundant, as the attack would already have been in progress. However, a subsequent message intercepted at 07.45 and forwarded at 13.16 suggested that *17. SS* was demanding urgent air support for an operation and the attack would not be launched until 15.00 that afternoon.[36] A further message, intercepted at 11.00 and passed on as ULTRA at 15.04, reported that the attack had again been postponed – this time until the morning of 13 June.[37] This was followed by a further intercept from 15.30 (passed on at 21.59) which provided the German objectives and axis of attack for the following day.[38]

The attack by *17. SS* had been put back from the 11th to the 13th on account of Allied air attacks, which had made the move forward to St-Lô extremely difficult. The divisional StuG assault guns, in particular, had been badly delayed. This was important, because the division had received no tanks for its panzer battalion, and so its only armoured force consisted of the 42 StuG of its assault-gun battalion. (This information was known to the Allies from the FISH divisional tank states decrypted back in May.) The attack was finally delivered towards Carentan from the south-west at around 06.00 local time on the 13th. The defending US paratroopers of 101st Airborne Division were initially pushed back; but, having been previously alerted to the possibility of attack, General Bradley had formed an armoured task force based around the tanks of the US 2nd Battalion, 66th Armored Regiment. This unit reinforced the paratroopers later in the morning and the German attack was repulsed, leaving Carentan in US hands.[39]

Hinsley argued that 'There can be little doubt that these decrypts helped the US forces to repulse this counter attack',[40] and clearly Bradley had enough warning to put together a counter-force to defeat the German thrust. However, it should be borne in mind that the ULTRA messages giving warning of the attack only arrived at (or after) the times the Germans originally intended to begin the operation. Had the Germans not been delayed, the messages would have been too late to help the Americans. On a fast-moving battlefield, where enemy operations were being planned and executed on a command cycle lasting only hours (or at most a day or two), it was difficult for Bletchley Park to turn around intelligence from intercepts fast enough to contribute. The speed with which some of the intercepts of 10–13 June were processed into ULTRA is impressive – as little as four hours, in some cases. However, other messages were taking up to twelve hours, and that was not always quick enough.

In addition to the *12.* and *17. SS* divisions already discussed, the Allied forces would encounter four other Waffen SS divisions during the Normandy campaign: the *1.* and *2. SS-Panzer-Divisionen* (in Belgium and the south of France, respectively) and the *9.* and *10. SS-Panzer-Divisionen*, recalled from the Russian front shortly after the invasion. Bletchley Park was able to monitor the progress of all four units as they made their way to the Normandy front during the remainder of June, providing Montgomery and 21st Army Group with both reassurance of their initial absence and warning of their imminent arrival. Again, ULTRA would prove most useful when the enemy units concerned were not yet engaged in combat with Allied troops.

The decision to bring *1.* and *2. SS-Panzer-Divisionen* to Normandy was taken by von Rundstedt on 8 June.[41] The *1. SS-Panzer-Division* formed part of OKW reserve and so von Rundstedt had to seek permission from Berlin. Permission was granted and the unit was transferred to control of *7. Armee*. This fact was picked up by Bletchley and appeared in an ULTRA message the same day.[42] This was not unexpected news for 21st Army Group, which had planned for the appearance of these two formations on the battlefield from about D+6 (12 June). Activity in both divisional areas had also been detected via air reconnaissance and agent reports, and it was concluded that *1. SS-Panzer-Division* would probably arrive first.[43] Shortly after, however, on 10 June, its move was countermanded, after the Führer and OKW became concerned about a second landing in the Calais area. This will be discussed in more detail later, but it effectively halted *1. SS-Panzer-Division* until 16 June.[44] The following day, in part influenced by the shock of the attack on *Panzergruppe West* headquarters, Rommel and von Rundstedt met. They submitted similar, but separate, reports to Hitler describing the seriousness of the situation. This led to the decision on 11 June to bring *9.* and *10. SS-Panzer-Divisionen* back from Russia.[45]

Meanwhile *2. SS-Panzer-Division* had begun what would become an infamous march from the south of France to Normandy, harassed along the way by air attack and local French Resistance forces, against whom the SS would exact fierce reprisals. Its progress was followed by Bletchley Park in intercepts over the coming days. The division appeared in traffic on 11 June at Périgueux, halfway between Toulouse and Poitiers.[46] The following day it was reported at Poitiers.[47] A further intercept included the rather chilling statement that the division was waiting for additional motor transport and that 'until then short term operations by part units against increasing guerrilla unrest could not be avoided'.[48] The grim truth behind this bland observation would later be revealed: 48 hours earlier, elements of the division had murdered 642 French civilians at Oradour-sur-Glane, in one of the most notorious war crimes of the campaign.[49] On the 13th, the division was reported heading for Tours;[50] and on the 14th it was reported demanding fuel supplies from *1. Armee* at Châtellerault, on the road from Poitiers to Tours.[51] By 18 June, *2. SS-Panzer-Division* had arrived in Normandy, reported on that day around St-Sever-Calvados (25 miles (40km) south of St-Lô).[52] By the 21st it had arrived at its new base at Torigni-sur-Vire, only 9 miles (14km) from St-Lô, and was preparing to enter the battle.[53] Thus, throughout this eleven-day journey, the progress of the division was followed via SIGINT, meaning that Allied commanders had nearly two weeks' notice of the appearance of its soldiers in Normandy. This strategic-level intelligence is what ULTRA did best.

The ability to follow these out-of-contact units was not only important from the point of view of planning the immediate battle in Normandy. It also allowed the units to be attacked from the air. Phillips O'Brien has examined the effect of Allied air power on the strategic mobility of German forces during the battle. He concludes that the interdiction of the movement of reinforcements into the Normandy area was fundamental to the outcome of the campaign:

> Instead of the German army unleashing one hammer-blow to try to drive the Allies back into the sea, its units were slowly fed into a meat-grinder from which they could not withdraw. The 2nd SS Panzer division, which was sent from Toulouse was originally expected to be able to attack the landing areas by June 9 or 10, but was not able to assemble in the battle area until June 23, seventeen days after departing ... Even divisions being sent from as close as Holland had bizarre circuitous journeys before they could reach the fighting.[54]

If the journeys of these units could be followed in detail via SIGINT, it made it easier to disrupt their movements and use air attack to degrade the formations before they were committed to battle. Bletchley's ability to track the movements of these formations thus made a significant contribution to their defeat.

TRACKING GERMAN SUSPICIONS

Just as important as information on German units that were making their way to the Normandy front was information on those that weren't. We saw in Chapter 6 how German opinion among the most senior commanders, including the Führer, favoured the idea of an Allied invasion in the Pas-de-Calais, even if this was preceded by a 'feint' or diversionary attack elsewhere. This suspicion about the true scale of the Allied landing in Normandy hampered German defensive efforts on the night of 5–6 June, and the shadow of a possible second landing would hang over German planning decisions for several weeks after the campaign began. This has led commentators to focus once again on the role of Double Cross operations and their influence on German thinking once the fighting had begun. However, it remained the role of Bletchley Park not so much to alter what the Germans *might* think as to discern what they *were* thinking, and what plans they were drawing up on that basis.

Suspicion that another attack might be imminent continued in German thinking in the days that followed the invasion. This was picked up in signals traffic. *Kriegsmarine Gruppe West* cautioned on 6 June that attacks in other areas should be expected,[55] and on 9 June von Rundstedt issued a general State of Emergency in case of 'further landings outside current bridgehead'. This latter message was recirculated by *Luftflotte 3* on a key that Bletchley Park had broken, and was forwarded as ULTRA on the afternoon of 10 June.[56] Nonetheless, as we have seen, the decision to bring *1. SS-Panzer-Division* down from Belgium and *2. SS-Panzer-Division* from the south to Normandy had already been taken by von Rundstedt on 8 June. In addition, the two remaining army panzer divisions – *2.* and *116.* – which remained north of the Seine in *15. Armee* were both ordered to send elements south to Normandy on 9 June. As Hinsley put it:

All the armour that had been kept back behind Fifteenth Army was being sent to the Normandy battle on D+3, much as the allies had predicted, notwithstanding the German fear of a second landing.[57]

225

On 10 June, something changed. The movement of *1. SS-Panzer* was halted, and no units from *116. Panzer-Division* were sent south of the Seine. The subordination of these two divisions to local commanders in their existing locations in Belgium and east of Calais, respectively, was confirmed by Bletchley in a decrypt of an *O.B. West* report issued on 10 June and read on 14 June.[58] The question that arises from this is what prompted the change? On the same day that Rommel and von Rundstedt met to emphasise to OKW the urgency of their plight in Normandy, key reinforcements were halted.

When Roger Hesketh wrote his original classified account of Operation FORTITUDE, he placed the credit for a return of the German focus to Calais on the double agent 'Garbo', and in particular on one message sent by 'Garbo' on 9 June to his handlers in Madrid. In this message, the Spanish spy claimed that the current landings were a 'diversionary manoeuvre' to draw off reserves prior to a 'decisive attack in another place'. That other place he named as Pas-de-Calais.[59] Of course, at the time exactly how much influence this message had on German thinking was completely unknown; however, after the war's end a document was made available from German archives which had annotations showing that a summary of the message had reached *Generaloberst* Jodl at OKW, and that he in turn had shown it to the Führer. Hesketh was keen to find out how successful his deception work had been. He wrote that his initial efforts to establish this were hampered because Keitel and Jodl 'could not clearly remember the individual reports they received at that busy time'; but later, when Keitel was shown a copy of the 'Garbo' message, he allegedly expressed 'ninety-nine percent certainty' that it was this message which had prompted the change of plan at OKW.[60]

This conclusion by Hesketh has led to significant hyperbole among other historians. Max Hastings described FORTITUDE as the operation 'which imprisoned almost the entire Fifteenth Army in the Pas-de-Calais until late July'.[61] Ronald Lewin suggested that 'the whole of the Fifteenth Army was neutralised'.[62] And Peter Calvocoressi claimed that 'a false report sent in the name of an agent still trusted by the Abwehr caused the cancellation of an order to move a whole German Army (15 Army) to Normandy'.[63] There are a number of problems with this interpretation.

The first has to do with the evidence: too little weight is given to the fact that Jodl and Keitel were reading a large volume of material, and to confront them with one document and ask whether that item in particular made all the difference is – more often than not – likely to produce the answer 'yes', even if it is by no means certain. It should also be noted that both men were prisoners facing indictment for war crimes (and would in due course both be executed), and so their testimony can hardly be considered to be wholly disinterested. We have seen that OKW was bombarded by the *Abwehr* with conflicting information concerning the invasion before the landings, and there is no reason to believe that this diminished after the battle started. In the week of 6–13 June, the ISK Section at Bletchley intercepted nearly 1,500 individual *Abwehr* Enigma messages;[64] it is unlikely that the situation at OKW was any different. Thus, to single out one item and identify it as *the* crucial item is difficult to sustain without a good deal more supporting evidence. In his secret account of Double Cross, Masterman also mentioned the possible influence of messages from 'Garbo'. He recorded that 'Secret Sources' (i.e. ISOS traffic) revealed that von Rundstedt had requested more information on the contents of a 'Garbo' message concerning Guards Armoured Division, which was at that time still in the UK. However, Masterman associates this with a message sent by 'Garbo' on D+8 (14 June), several days after the decision to halt the movements of the panzer divisions in *15. Armee*.[65] It should also be remembered that Hitler was *already* convinced of a larger follow-up operation in the Pas-de-Calais. This was a view that he had held since late 1943 and had not deviated from since. As we have seen, this was based in part on strategic probability and Germany's own previous cross-Channel attack plans, and in part on a fundamental overestimation of the Allied order of battle. This latter factor was at least as important an influence on FHW and German high command thinking as the opinions of any single double agent, however well regarded by the *Abwehr*. A final factor worthy of consideration is the question of why the

9 June message was shown to the Führer in the first place. One of the problems facing all German intelligence agencies was that Hitler was notoriously impatient of information that contradicted his own previously held views and 'inspirations'. It is thus quite possible that the 'Garbo' message reached him not in order to change his mind, but precisely because it accorded with a view he held already.

The second problem is that far from 'a whole German Army', the forces available for redeployment to Normandy – even had OKW or von Rundstedt wished it – were only a fraction of the whole strength of *15. Armee.* Of the twelve infantry divisions and three Luftwaffe field divisions in *15. Armee*, eleven were occupying coastal defence positions; and, while only two were officially 'static' divisions, the remainder were static in all but name – entirely without motorised transport and reliant on horses and bicycles for their mobility. This left only the three panzer divisions (*1. SS, 2.* and *116.*) and possibly one or two Luftwaffe divisions available to be transferred to the battle in the south. As we have seen, all three panzer units were initially instructed to prepare to move, although this did not actually take place for several weeks.[66]

Bletchley Park was able to monitor the ongoing indecision on the part of OKW about what to do with these mobile units. As we have seen, on 10 June the moves of *1. SS-Panzer* and *116. Panzer* were postponed. Multiple intercepts over the next few days showed a continuing preoccupation with the coast north of the Seine, in Belgium and Holland.[67] There was even a demand for air reconnaissance of the ports around Hull, in the light of a possible attack on the coast of Denmark.[68] Hitler responded by ordering that the panzer divisions in the line facing the Allies in Normandy should be withdrawn and replaced by infantry; reinforced by the (as yet) unengaged panzer units north of the Seine, they should then launch a devastating counterattack. However, he stressed that all fronts should be weakened, *except* that of *15. Armee*. If units were to be removed from Calais, they would be replaced by formations transferred in from Norway, Denmark or the Reich itself.[69] An assessment produced by FHW on 11 June, almost certainly read by Bletchley Park as a FISH decrypt, became available on 16 June, and this also emphasised expectations of a second landing by the mythical FUSAG, and for this:

> The sector between the Seine and the Somme comes first into question, because, in the first place it corresponds to the deployment of the Anglo-Saxon [*sic*] air force, and in the second place, it allows the expectation of early strategic co-operation between the two Anglo-Saxon Army Groups against the line Paris–St Quentin.[70]

This concept of an Allied landing north of the Seine, followed by the capture of Le Havre and a push on Paris coordinated on both banks of the river, was repeated in an appreciation by von Rundstedt prepared on 26 June and transmitted to Italy via BREAM (and broken at Bletchley Park by 7 July).[71] German anxieties were also reported in Japanese diplomatic traffic, which continued to be intercepted throughout June and July. The embassy in Vichy reported fears of possible landings in the Boulogne–Calais area on 7, 11 and 13 June, and similar messages were read from Berlin on 7, 12 and 15 June.[72]

In addition to following the overall strategic concerns of the enemy during this period, Bletchley Park was able to monitor the locations of the specific units that formed the subject of these debates. Thus: *1. SS-Panzer-Division* was confirmed to be still in Belgium on 16 June, when the '*Flivo*' of the division reported on Allied bombing raids in the Dunkirk–Ostend area;[73] the start of a move south (on 19 June) was reported in an ULTRA message of 20 June, which also mentioned the subordination of the division to *I. SS-Panzer-Korps*; and the same ULTRA message passed on the tank strength of the division, obtained in a FISH intercept from 25 May, as 45 *Panzer IV* tanks and 41 Panthers (well below establishment strength).[74] The division reached the Normandy area on 23 June, when 21st Army Group intelligence located it at Thury-Harcourt, 19 miles (30km) south of Caen, two weeks after von Rundstedt had initially requested it. Ultimately *116. Panzer* would not become involved in the fighting for another month: not until the Allied attacks east of the Orne on 18 July did the division finally cross the Seine into the battle area.[75]

In summary, it would appear that of the three armoured formations north of the Seine on D-Day, and potentially available to reinforce the Normandy front, two did not move for several weeks. The broad reason for this was continuing German apprehension about a second landing north of the Seine, a result of a continuing overestimation of Allied capabilities. However, it should be borne in mind that, even if they knew that Normandy was the only landing they would face (in northern France at least), the Germans simply did not have the flexibility to redeploy large portions of *15. Armee* southwards. Whatever the case, the significant point for us is that GC&CS was able to report accurately both on the high command appreciations produced by von Rundstedt and FHW (which reflected those fears) and on the resulting movements (or lack thereof) of the divisions concerned.

The other formation that would play a significant part in the ongoing campaign through to the end of August was *II. SS-Panzer-Korps* from Russia. This formation and its constituent *9.* and *10. SS-Panzer-Divisionen* started to arrive at Nancy by rail on 18 June, and their build-up continued for the next few days. This was reported by Bletchley Park on 24 June.[76] Generally, ULTRA was able to give a complete picture of German defensive arrangements in the last week of June, but the exact location of *II. SS-Panzer-Korps* remained uncertain, along with how and when it would be committed to battle. This question would be answered when, on 29 June, the corps launched a counterattack against the salient on the river Odon created by the Allied Operation EPSOM, begun a few days earlier.

BLETCHLEY PARK'S ROLE CHANGES

By the first weeks of July, almost all the major German armoured units which would be committed to the battle had arrived in Normandy. Other reinforcements would be brought up in the form of additional infantry, but the German order of battle stabilised.[77] These weeks in early July have also been identified as a period of attritional fighting, with little movement in the front lines of the opposing forces, despite fierce combat.[78] This was matched by a decline in the volume of useful ULTRA being produced. German units were able to re-establish landline communications and, as we saw earlier, FISH interceptions became increasingly difficult to decipher. Ralph Bennett described this as 'one of the few lean periods for ULTRA in the west. The volume of traffic dropped when the front became temporarily stabilised soon after the fall of Cherbourg [29 June] and was slow to pick up again.'[79]

However, despite the lack of immediately important tactical intelligence, Bletchley did continue during this period, and indeed throughout the campaign, to provide background information on the wider state of German forces in Normandy. Shortages of fuel, transport and equipment of all kinds were widespread, and significant signal traffic was devoted to requests for (and equally often denials of) additional supplies. For example, detailed fuel and ammunition states for *7. Armee* for the period up to 3 July were reported on 11 July. This included the fact that three army fuel dumps, including an *O.B. West* dump as far away as Dijon, were 'out of stock'.[80] Casualties were also mounting: an *LXXXIV. Armeekorps* report from 10 July reported nearly 600 killed, wounded and missing from its constituent divisions on that one day.[81] All of this information must have given comfort to Allied commanders that, while major territorial gains might not be forthcoming, the German forces were being progressively worn down in a battle of attrition they were doomed to lose. Bletchley would continue to provide a regular commentary on this aspect of the enemy situation – information which, because it was not as time sensitive as reports on tactical activity, remained extremely useful whatever the delay in the interception and delivery cycle.

One significant development at the start of July not revealed by ULTRA was a meeting of Rommel, von Rundstedt and Hitler to discuss the strategic situation in the west. Von Rundstedt recognised that a static defence was ultimately doomed on account of Allied superiority in resources; he wanted to pull back and regroup. The Führer disagreed. This resulted on 2 July in the sacking of von Rundstedt as *O.B. West*, to be replaced by *Generalfeldmarschall* von Kluge, and two days later the replacement of Geyr von Schweppenburg at *Panzergruppe West* by *General* Eberbach.[82] Hitler rejected any suggestion of retreat or flexible defence, and promulgated another of his notorious orders that no ground should be yielded. He demanded that the 'keynote of fighting on all fronts [should] be to gain time' and that his troops should 'defend every square kilometre tenaciously'. This latter message was intercepted, and was circulated by Bletchley on 11 July.[83] As Ellis described it in the British official history of the campaign, 'while fighting was being conducted with skill by local commanders and stubborn bravery by their troops, the battle as a whole was directed by Hitler ... not even a division could be moved without his concurrence'.[84] As we shall see, the necessity for him to confirm even tactical decisions opened up channels of communication between Berlin and the battlefield, as well as command delays, which GC&CS could potentially exploit.

Both the volume of traffic and its importance would pick up again in late July and August. But, once again, ULTRA was only directly helpful to Allied battlefield commanders if it was able to provide intelligence on enemy movements or intentions with sufficient advance notice for those commanders to be able to act on it, or react to it, before it went out of date.

A good example of the benefit of advanced warning from ULTRA came in the case of the German counterattack at Mortain in the first half of August. At the beginning of that month, von Kluge received a boost to his order of battle in the form of *9. Panzer-Division*, previously part of *19. Armee* in the south of France at Avignon, and a further six infantry divisions. These troops were badly needed simply to maintain the status quo on the existing German defence line; but Hitler had more ambitious ideas. Following Operation COBRA, US forces had reached Avranches and broken out into Brittany. There were few German forces to oppose them as they advanced south and east. On 3 August, Hitler ordered von

Kluge to use the additional infantry to relieve the panzer units currently in the line, and to mass the accumulated armour on the left (west) end of the front to launch an attack towards Avranches. This would reconnect the German front with the west coast of the Cotentin peninsula and cut off the US forces to the south.[85] Kluge was not keen on this ambitious and unrealistic plan, and was supported by both *General* Eberbach of *Panzergruppe West* and Josef 'Sepp' Dietrich, commander of *I. SS-Panzer-Korps*; but their objections were overruled.[86]

As Hinsley described it, 'intelligence gave accurate and timely warning of all the decisions and movements made by the Germans in the first week of August.' Bletchley would break more army Enigma in August than in any other month in 1944, and tactical Y in Normandy proved equally fruitful, as German radio nets sprang once again to life.[87] As each of the panzer divisions along the front withdrew, this was identified: *10. SS-Panzer* and *12. SS-Panzer* on 4 August,[88] and *1. SS-Panzer* on the 5th.[89] This was followed on the evening of 6 August by a series of messages which outlined the locations: 'From right to left: 116 Panzer division, 2 Panzer division, First SS Panzer Division, and Second SS Panzer Division' subordinated to *XLVII. Panzer-Korps* for an attack directed westwards;[90] there was also a request for a preliminary bombardment of Mortain and St Hilaire, timed to start at 20.30 local time that evening.[91]

Even as the attack was gearing up on 6 August, Hitler changed his mind again and ordered von Kluge to revise his attack to incorporate not only the four panzer divisions already involved, supported by the remnants of *17. SS-Panzergrenadier* and *Panzer-Lehr* divisions, but all the available armour in Normandy, including the divisions of *II. SS-Panzer-Korps*. Such a move would potentially fatally delay the attack as the additional units were brought up, and so von Kluge won the right to go ahead with his attack, as planned, on the night of 6/7 August. By the end of the following day, little progress had been made against determined US opposition. Not only were the German units under strength, but as soon as daylight came and the mist lifted on 7 August, Allied air attacks made movement almost impossible and the attack faltered as units sought cover from the relentless attention of Allied fighter-bombers.[92] This, too, was followed by Bletchley as the German air force reported its efforts to protect the ground assault with a 'very strong fighter effort', which 'did not get through to target area owing to continuous air battles'.[93] Ralph Bennett, who was in the thick of this fight in Hut 3, commented that 'The sustained, violent and (thanks to Ultra) well-prepared attacks by 83 Group RAF and IX US air force were in fact one of the turning points of the battle'.[94]

Despite this lack of success, the Führer persisted with his plan, moving *General* Eberbach west from his command at *Panzergruppe West* (recently renamed *5. Panzerarmee*) to lead *Angriffsgruppe* (counterattack group) *Eberbach*, which would be formed as soon as the additional panzer units could extricate themselves from the fighting around Caen and Falaise, and make their painful way west to Mortain. This attack was initially scheduled for 9 August, but movement difficulties led to its postponement until the 11th, and then until the 20th. Orders for the attack on 11 August were issued on the evening of 9 August and were in the hands of Allied commanders in the early hours of the following morning: Eberbach's force was tasked with an assault, the 'Objective of attack: the sea at Avranches'.[95] In the event, the attack was cancelled on 11 August, as von Kluge attempted to fend off the envelopment of his forces by the Third US Army, by then pushing eastwards towards Le Mans; but the knowledge the day before that the bulk of Eberbach's panzer forces were persisting with a move west in spite of this risk of envelopment was of great assistance to Bradley and the planners at Twelfth US Army Group.

These and subsequent movements were followed by Bletchley Park. Hinsley observed that 'the intelligence obtained from Sigint was prompt and copious between 8 and 21 August'. However, he placed a caveat on this, pointing out that

there may be some danger of over-rating its value to the commanders who received it piecemeal while the battle was being fought. Even when allowance has been made for this, however, the fact remains that all the enemy's major decisions were disclosed with little delay.[96]

For the remainder of the campaign, as the Germans attempted to extract their forces from what would become known as the Falaise 'pocket', Bletchley Park continued to provide a commentary on German activity, rather than predictions of it. Bennett described the flow of ULTRA during this final campaign as 'bewildering riches poured out by the source',[97] but also remarked:

> Most of the fifty or sixty pieces of tactical information derived from Ultra during these hectic days were probably out of date by the time they reached Allied headquarters in France, although they were often only a few hours old when dispatched with high priority.[98]

ULTRA was ultimately best used as a planning tool. Its ability to keep pace with a fast-moving tactical battle was mostly found wanting during the campaign of June–August 1944. Only on rare occasions was intelligence of enemy plans provided sufficiently far in advance for Allied commanders to make anything but last-minute preparations for a German attack. Nonetheless, intelligence from Bletchley was of vital importance in monitoring the wider strategic picture, as enemy units made their way around the hinterland behind the front line, preparing to join the battle or staying away in expectation of Allied attacks elsewhere. It was in following these movements that ULTRA proved its worth.

CHAPTER NINE

THE IMPORTANCE OF BLETCHLEY PARK TO OVERLORD

Two central questions lie at the heart of the previous chapters. What part did GC&CS at Bletchley Park play in the planning and execution of Operation OVERLORD and the subsequent campaign in Normandy? And how useful to that campaign was the strategic signals intelligence produced by Bletchley?

The year of OVERLORD, 1944, coincided with the period when GC&CS was approaching its peak of personnel and organisation, and the preparations for D-Day can be used as a lens through which to examine the character of Bletchley Park not only in that year, but throughout the latter phase of the Second World War. The picture that emerges is one of industrial efficiency, somewhat at odds with the popular vision of Bletchley as a place of intellectual eccentricity and individualism.

Bletchley Park in 1944 was not the hutted, collegiate, informal organisation of popular myth. After 1942–43, much of the significant codebreaking work, in terms of the development of decryption techniques, had been done. The task was not to provide a fertile habitat for individual genius, but rather to scale up and industrialise the techniques developed by the master codebreakers, and to create systems allowing their methods to be applied to thousands of items of data, at speed, by staff without an Oxbridge level of education. This is not to argue that there were no significant intellectual breakthroughs after 1943: the work of Donald Michie and Jack Good on using Colossus for the 'wheel breaking' of Lorenz was a major theoretical achievement, and the changes made to Enigma in 1944 and 1945 continued to tax the greatest brains in Hut 6. However, the greater part of the work done was to exploit existing techniques with ever greater efficiency, rather than to break into wholly new codes and ciphers.

It has also been emphasised that the actual process of cryptanalysis – the 'codebreaking' – occupied only a small part of a much longer data-processing chain. Without all the prior traffic analysis, key identification and crib finding, any attempt to break a day's Enigma traffic would have been doomed to failure. Moreover, that preliminary work was in itself capable of producing useful intelligence, even if the content of the messages was never read. The steps that followed decryption were equally important. We have to challenge the previous impression, created by Bennett and others, that Bletchley Park's involvement with a message finished when it was deciphered and transmitted to a customer: it is clear that both the indexes (especially those of Hut 3) and the 'backroom' research teams which collated intelligence were vital in the production of longer-term synthetic intelligence studies, and also that the day-to-day process of codebreaking would have been, if not impossible, then a good deal harder if the opportunity had not existed to contextualise a day's traffic with information previously received and painstakingly catalogued.

The work of the Western Front Committee offers a clear example of how long-term intelligence can be developed and in consequence can be extremely detailed and comprehensive. The committee shows Bletchley looking forward – a year or more into the future – and preparing analysis that would support future operations. This contrasts with the image of Bletchley Park as a 'news agency', simply deciphering messages each twenty-four hours and distributing them, without any longer-term 'memory' of the past, analytical capacity or capability for producing predictive intelligence.

The change in the character of Bletchley Park from the hutted 'cottage-industry' institution of 1939–42 to the later 'factory' was reflected in the physical structure of the site. Although the earlier numbered huts still stood, by 1944 many of these had been turned over to minor administrative functions. The heart of the intelligence effort had moved north of the mansion and the lake, to the complex of massive lettered blocks clustered around the communications centre in Block E, and connected by conveyors and vacuum tubes. Work here was carried out on production-line principles. As a result, while mostly it was very dull for those engaged in it, it was highly efficient. Much of the credit for this should go to Edward Travis, who was elevated from deputy director (but de facto head of Bletchley Park) to director in March 1944, his subordinate Nigel de Grey and (further down the chain of command) Gordon Welchman, who, as assistant director responsible for 'machines and mechanical devices', was tireless in his development of the technical processes that allowed codebreaking to take place efficiently.[1]

Despite this apparent regulation and efficiency, the GC&CS organisation was not static during 1944: the workforce grew from just under 7,000 in January 1944 to nearly 9,000 by January 1945 – an increase of more than 40 people a week. Bletchley Park also remained a building site throughout, as ever-more blocks were built to house the steady influx of staff. Delivery of bombe machines also continued throughout 1944, at the rate of approximately one a week; and additional Robinson and Colossus machines were delivered, albeit at rarer intervals. Directing this rapid expansion appropriately, while maintaining the smooth running of the existing organisation, required significant skill and foresight from the senior management. In any large organisation, managing change is always challenging, and the ability of Bletchley Park to adapt and evolve while continuing to function at a high level of efficiency was a significant achievement.

The other aspect of Bletchley's work to emerge here is the level of liaison with outside organisations. It has been widely thought that GC&CS worked in a peaceful vacuum, divorced from the hurly-burly of the war taking place outside, and that its staff did not allow external knowledge to cloud the purity of their analysis of the code-groups in front of them. While this is an attractive idea for those who admire the codebreakers' intellectual achievements, it does not stand up to scrutiny. In the first place, those codebreakers needed as much information as possible about what the messages they were examining *might* say, in order to work out what they *did* say; and this could only come from a thorough understanding of the battles in which the traffic was generated. Secondly, there was never a time when Bletchley Park had enough intercept sets in the Y stations, bombes, Colossus machines or personnel to cover all the demands on its attention. It was necessary, therefore, to prioritise its limited resources on a daily, and sometimes hourly, basis. This could only be done with a good knowledge of what the enemy was doing, and of what Bletchley's customers at Allied headquarters were planning to do. This was achieved by regular liaison with government departments and commanders in the field. We have seen how weekly visits were made to the ministries in London to discuss intelligence needs and to forge the friendly human relationships that oil the wheels of these arrangements. The same was to continue once the campaign in France began, albeit at arm's length via wireless and teleprinter links. Bill Williams' remark, quoted in Chapter 3, that 'One felt one was talking to friends',[2] is significant in this respect and reflects the deep collaboration and understanding achieved between Bletchley Park and its customers.

Bletchley also relied heavily on its suppliers – not just the Y stations, but other intelligence-gathering bodies. We have seen the close relationship with the Combined Intelligence Section of Home Forces and with MI14, and the detailed source notes on the orders of battle produced by Bletchley and the appendices to the Western Front Committee 'Record' both show that the analysts in Hut 3 were as happy to deal with 'human intelligence' derived via Martian reports, or aerial photo or POW data, as they were with pure SIGINT. GC&CS's all-source analysis has not been fully appreciated before. It provided an essential complement to the information derived from interception alone, which was by nature partial and incomplete. Only by contextualising the decrypts with external information on Allied activity, and external intelligence on the Germans, could Bletchley Park develop a complete picture.

The other collaboration that was fundamental to the success of the intelligence effort for Normandy was that between the UK and the US. Once US forces had become engaged in the European war at the end of 1942, they would have been able to make a case for developing their own European SIGINT operation. But this did not happen: instead (as described in Chapter 1), US personnel were incorporated into the various departments of GC&CS, ran their own Y station and undertook bombe operations at Eastcote. Moreover, although they were mostly used for naval tasks, Bletchley also had operational control of US-built bombe machines in Washington DC, which could be individually tasked by the control room at Bletchley. This integration allowed intelligence not only to flow seamlessly to the joint Allied planning staffs at COSSAC and SHAEF before the invasion, but also after the landings intelligence was provided to both British and US commanders without distinction of nationality, solely on the basis of the usefulness of the product to the particular recipient.

This level of intelligence sharing was unprecedented and stood in stark contrast to German intelligence efforts, which were divided across a large number of sometimes competing agencies. There were no fewer than six bodies within the German war machine tasked with SIGINT and codebreaking alone: individual units within the army, navy and air force, as well as an OKW unit, a unit for the foreign office and one within the Nazi party apparatus.[3] The tensions within the wider German intelligence system and the *Abwehr* in particular have also been described. As the campaign in Europe developed and more forces were moved to the continent, the British, US and Canadian forces diverged structurally, each becoming more autonomous. But during the campaign in Normandy they remained fully integrated: where a senior commander was American, his subordinate was often British (or vice versa). This was reflected in the freedom with which it was possible to pass intelligence to all parties. Given the extreme secrecy of the ULTRA project, the level of trust displayed by all sides in this process is remarkable.

Some consideration should also be given to the nature of the product worked on at Bletchley Park. Widely famous for its work on Enigma,

Bletchley handled a much broader range of intelligence intercepts. In fact, we have revealed that prior to D-Day, the German army in the west provided little or no Enigma traffic containing useful intelligence: its fixed positions and extensive landline network made such communications largely unnecessary. The Luftwaffe and SS, on the other hand, provided a significant haul of Enigma decrypts to feed Hut 3 and its analysts. This was assisted by a very significant haul of FISH decrypts. While this material was not as profuse as the Enigma material, its usefulness was often out of all proportion to its volume. Both high-level command appreciations and nuts-and-bolts descriptions of divisional tank states were derived from FISH traffic in a way that was not possible from Enigma messages. It might therefore be suggested that at least as much credit for the successes of SIGINT on D-Day should go to the teams in the Newmanry and the Testery as to Hut 6. Any credit for non-Enigma codebreaking that has been apportioned in the past has tended to flow towards Tommy Flowers and the creators of Colossus; indeed, both the machine and the man seem at times to have developed a cult status. It should be remembered, however, that right up to the end of the campaign Robinsons outnumbered Colossus machines by some margin: the second Colossus was only delivered a few days before the Normandy invasion began. Thus, while Colossus Mark II was a remarkable innovation, eighteen months of work in preparation for the invasion had been carried out without it, using older techniques.

We have also described the substantial contribution of Japanese diplomatic traffic to the intelligence picture before and during the campaign. Again, this resulted from remarkable feats of codebreaking both separately and in collaboration, on both sides of the Atlantic. Add to this the results obtained from traffic analysis and from the many lower-level codes and ciphers attacked by GC&CS and a highly diverse picture emerges. The intelligence product derived from all these sources was also delivered to customers in a range of different ways, from urgent ULTRA signals to daily teleprints, 'Headlines' and longer-form analyses. The idea that Bletchley Park's job was only to turn Enigma into ULTRA obscures the true picture of GC&CS as a fully developed, multi-source intelligence agency, drawing on a much wider range of sources and delivering a much wider range of products.

BLETCHLEY PARK'S CONTRIBUTION TO THE PREPARATION FOR OVERLORD

The intelligence advantage that the Allied forces had on 6 June 1944 is summed up in the words of one private soldier who landed that day on Juno Beach – Rifleman Les Wagar of the Queen's Own Rifles of Canada:

> Each man's job had been set and memorized days before and there was really nothing to say. We knew the width of the beach we had to cross, the mines we had to avoid, the bunkers, the gun positions, the wall we had to get over or through, the streets and the buildings of the town we had to take, the minefields, the possible enemy strength, the perimeter we had to establish for the next wave to go forward.[4]

Although much of the local intelligence that Wagar describes would have been gained from Martian reports, derived from local resistance (HUMINT) and air photography, rather than SIGINT, the point remains that the landing forces were extremely well informed about the enemy they were about to face.

At the strategic level, much of this information was obtained by Bletchley Park. We have seen how Hut 3 was able to identify and locate (more or less approximately) all fifty-eight German divisions in France and the Low Countries, and to develop detailed orders of battle for each of them, listing subordinate units, commanders and, in some cases, individual numbers of tanks, guns and personnel. Previous analysis of the completeness of this picture by Ralph Bennett, based as it was only on the ULTRA messages available to him at the time, suggested a variety of errors or omissions in Bletchley's understanding of the Germans in

France. However, access to more recently declassified material – including GC&CS's own internal orders of battle, as well as other non-ULTRA material – has shown that in fact Bletchley's understanding of the enemy's dispositions was much more detailed and complete than was hitherto appreciated. There is no doubt that this depth of knowledge was vital to the Allied planners. The value of the work of Bletchley Park to the wider Allied intelligence effort was summed up in a report produced in 1945 by MI14, the body tasked with assessing the German armed forces:

> It may fairly be said that practically all M.I.14 appreciations of a general nature, including any on order of battle or directly bearing on operations, contained ULTRA, and most were based primarily on ULTRA information.[5]

This intelligence was equally important to the politicians burdened with the decision on whether or when the invasion should take place. The confidence that Allied leaders could place in the picture of the enemy provided to them was fundamental to their decision-making, and again stands in marked contrast to the significant misunderstanding of the Allied position offered to German decisionmakers by their intelligence agencies. Thus, during the planning stages of OVERLORD, the importance of Bletchley-derived SIGINT is undeniable. It was a key tool in developing the operation.

Reference to the German misunderstanding of the Allied order of battle brings us to Double Cross and Bletchley Park's role in it. It is clear that Allied deception efforts were substantially successful in misleading FHW and OKW over the strength and capabilities of the Allied invasion forces. This led to a significant strategic miscalculation by the Germans over whether the Normandy landings were the main effort, or merely a diversion prior to a larger landing in Pas-de-Calais. However, this deception operation was led by MI5 and the Double Cross Committee, and was not the responsibility of GC&CS.

It has been argued that Bletchley was key to deception operations because intercepts of *Abwehr* traffic between local *Abwehr Abwehrstellungen* and Berlin were read and were used to fine-tune the deception effort. An examination of the wildly varying assessments provided by the *Abwehr* of potential invasion threats simultaneously against Greece or the Balkans, and Norway or Denmark, quite apart from France, suggests that such a process would have been fraught with difficulty, since even the *Abwehr* itself had no fixed idea of what was likely to happen. Unlike Bletchley, which went to great lengths to filter and rationalise its intelligence product, the *Abwehr* took the opposite approach and bombarded its customers with a deluge of unfiltered material – proof that too much intelligence is as unhelpful as too little. Also, the question arises of how much of this information actually changed German perceptions outside the ranks of the *Abwehr* itself. Much of the evidence presented for the success of deception operations was only available post-war, via interviews with captured German leaders; there is little to suggest that those running the Double Cross operation were aware in any detail of their success or otherwise at the time in 1944. It is likely, therefore, that this aspect of Bletchley Park's work in 1944 has previously been overemphasised, or that it needs to be nuanced by a deeper analysis of how deception information was processed by German commanders.

Nonetheless, GC&CS can be credited with successfully following the development of German strategic thinking and anti-invasion planning. This was not done via the conversations of Double Cross agents and their handlers, or by *Abwehr* intercepts, but came straight from the 'horse's mouth' via high-grade SIGINT – in particular, FISH intercepts. Appreciations by von Rundstedt, and even strategic opinions expressed by Hitler himself, were successfully intercepted by Bletchley Park, both from German and Japanese sources. These showed a remarkably consistent picture, with both the Führer and OKW holding on to the conviction that a major attack would come across the narrows of the Channel, even after the Normandy battles had begun. Even had no deception operations been undertaken, it is probable that Bletchley Park would have collected this high-level intelligence and revealed the thinking of the German generals – information that again was crucial to the confidence with which the invasion could be launched, and to its ultimate success.

BLETCHLEY PARK'S CONTRIBUTION AFTER THE INVASION

After the invasion began, GC&CS was able to continue to supply strategic-level information, particularly about German formations not yet engaged by the Allied forces. In this way, Eisenhower and Montgomery were given prior knowledge of likely reinforcements to their enemy's forces. It was also possible to bring the Allies' devastating air power to bear on these targets, slowing their progress towards the front line. Information about the higher-level order of battle also continued to flow in, and so Bletchley Park was able to maintain a current picture of which forces were engaged. This was coloured periodically by more detailed information (derived typically from FISH) about the equipment states of these units. The value of this is supported by a further remark in the MI14 report:

> By far the greater part of ULTRA intelligence was concerned with strategy, intentions, tactics, the strength and condition of the forces in the forward areas, and order of battle. In this sphere its values can hardly be rated too high.[6]

It would appear, then, that Bletchley was very good at identifying where German units were at any time, and in some cases at determining their detailed strength. This was of crucial importance before the invasion began, and continued to be relevant to the ongoing campaign after 6 June. However, once Allied units were 'in contact' with German forces, this high-level picture was overtaken by locally derived tactical intelligence, gained by army Y units and by traditional reconnaissance methods. ULTRA continued to be valued, but as *confirmation* of information already gathered, rather than as a primary source. Also, once the tactical battle had begun in France, the planning cycle for German operations was often very short, as the enemy scrambled to mount counterattacks against advancing Allied forces. This cycle – which was often as little as twelve to twenty-four hours – was mostly too short for the (albeit highly efficient) intelligence cycle at GC&CS to keep up. Often ULTRA would warn of German attacks only as they were in progress, and it was only when Allied air power was able to force delays and postponements that ULTRA became useful as a warning tool. There were a few occasions when German operations were developed sufficiently far in advance for high-level SIGINT to detect them with adequate warning. This was particularly the case after the beginning of July, when Hitler became more personally involved in directing the battle and thus more planning was discussed on high-level links. However, such occasions were the exception rather than the rule. More generally, in the later stages of the campaign ULTRA provided a wide survey of the current picture, rather than predictive intelligence of what was likely in the future. It was more useful for planning than for immediate war-fighting. The account of this provided by the 'History of Hut Three', quoted earlier, bears repeating:

> Indeed, one may say without serious error that much of the red-hot tactical Intelligence could have been jettisoned without irreparable harm: but the long-term things, nearly always less spectacular, often individually very trivial, were yet indispensable and unique in the history of Intelligence.[7]

It may seem odd that a work devoted to the Normandy campaign has devoted only its final chapters to operations after the invasion had begun. This reflects two factors: first, the chronological scope of the invasion as a project, which began at Bletchley Park with the formation of the Western Front Committee in late 1942, eighteen months before the invasion; and second, the relative importance of the work carried out by GC&CS. Bletchley Park played its biggest part in OVERLORD before any troops landed on the beaches and landing grounds, as a tool for Allied planners and politicians. In this regard, its importance is hard to overestimate. After the battle had begun, ULTRA was still highly valued by its recipients, but it had become only one of a number of contributors to the intelligence picture, more strategic than tactical, and more general than specific.

THE FINAL VERDICT

All this brings us to the final question – the question most frequently asked of historians of intelligence and by visitors to Bletchley Park, and yet perhaps the most unanswerable: how important was GC&CS in the successful outcome of the Normandy invasion, and more widely of the Second World War? It is easy to assume with the benefit of hindsight that because they were a success, the Normandy landings were fated to succeed. But that is not how things appeared at the time. Indeed, Eisenhower was moved to draft his famous statement on June 5:

> Our landings in the Cherbourg-Havre area have failed to gain a satis-factory foothold and I have withdrawn the troops. My decision to attack at this time and place was based upon the best information available. The troops, the air and the navy did all that bravery and devotion to duty could do. If any blame or fault attaches to the attempt it is mine alone.[8]

History records that it was not necessary for him to release those fateful words. However, the fact that he wrote them shows how uncertain he and his staff were of getting ashore. Any number of factors contributed to that success, and to claim that one of them was the most important would be invidious. Besides which, the bravery and sacrifice of the men (and women) involved in the landings cannot be overlooked: good intelligence can provide an advantage in war, but someone still has to fight the battle.

It is possible to argue that if one (or more) of the numerous different advantages possessed by the Allies had been absent, the invasion might have failed. Certainly, OVERLORD without ULTRA would have been a much riskier undertaking. Indeed, without the ability to predict the nature of the opposition and the likelihood of success, it may never even have been attempted.

Harry Hinsley addressed the wider question of whether the war was shortened by Allied codebreaking in a lecture entitled 'The Counterfactual History of no ULTRA', delivered in Cambridge in October 1993.[9] He argued that the war was shortened by at least two years thanks to ULTRA (using the definition in its broadest terms). His calculation was based on the idea that from 1942, ULTRA speeded up victory in the North African campaign, and in 1943 contributed to the defeat of the U-boats in the Atlantic. All this allowed D-Day to take place in June 1944, rather than be postponed to 1945 or 1946.

Hinsley has been widely criticised. His predictions take no account either of the use of nuclear weapons in the west or of success by the Soviet Union, unsupported by a second front. Either of these scenarios might have led to a very different outcome. However, one point that he makes seems undeniable: without victory in the Atlantic in 1943, the build-up for Normandy in 1944 would have been much harder. Thus, the contribution of Bletchley Park SIGINT to D-Day extends far back beyond 6 June 1944. Frederick Winterbotham also picked up the argument about the shape of post-war Europe had the western Allies not been able to compete in the race to Berlin: 'Without Ultra we might have had to meet the Russians on the Rhine instead of the Elbe, and they would have stayed put.'[10] All of this, however, is speculation. The last word should go to Montgomery's chief of intelligence, Bill Williams, who pointed out that 'very few armies ever went to battle better informed of their enemy', and that ultimately

What we should have done without it is idle to linger over, yet it must be made clear that Ultra and Ultra only put Intelligence on the map.[11]

A NOTE ON SOURCES AND FURTHER READING

T wo works provided a vital starting point for this book. The first is Ralph Bennett's *Ultra in the West: The Normandy Campaign 1944–45*, which was first published in 1979. This was followed by F.H. ('Harry') Hinsley's magisterial five-volume official history, *British Intelligence in the Second World War*. The first volume was published in 1979 and the fourth (the last of the volumes produced by Hinsley himself) came out in 1990; Volume 5 was also published in 1990, but under the authorship of Michael Howard. Given the importance of these two studies, a few words on the authors is relevant.

RALPH BENNETT

Ralph Bennett worked at Bletchley Park from 1941 to 1945. Prior to the war, he had first studied and then taught history at Magdalene College, Cambridge, specialising in medieval and religious history. He was a German speaker, having spent a year at Munich University in 1935.[1] Commissioned into the Intelligence Corps, Bennett was posted to Hut 3 in February 1941. He became 'duty officer' in that hut in early 1942 and, apart from a few months at the end of 1942 when he was in Cairo, would remain in that position for the rest of the hostilities.[2] After the war,

Bennett returned to Magdalene, where he rose to be president of the college. In 1977, when copies of many of the messages decrypted at Bletchley Park and sent to field commanders (many of them drafted by Bennett himself) were declassified and deposited in the National Archives (then the Public Record Office), he set himself to read and analyse the messages, comparing them with the more widely recorded history of the events of the western campaign. Bennett would go on to publish three further works on Second World War intelligence: *Ultra and Mediterranean Strategy* (1989); *Behind the Battle: Intelligence in the war with Germany 1939–45* (1994); and finally, *Intelligence Investigations: How Ultra changed history* (1996), this last being a collection of his lectures.

By his own calculations, Bennett read many thousands of outgoing messages from Bletchley Park. Historians owe him a great debt for this work, and *Ultra in the West* provides a very useful catalogue of the most significant of the messages, where they are associated with command decisions or events in the field. Unfortunately, Bennett's assessments were hampered by his lack of access to other material and by his own recollections of the highly compartmentalised world of Bletchley Park. His role as a duty officer in the Watch Room of Hut 3 was to receive raw decryptions of German messages, translate them, prioritise them in order of urgency and importance, and then draft signals based upon them. These would form the corpus of signals (codenamed ULTRA) to which he would return as an historian. In his own account, he makes much of the objectivity of this process, describing Hut 3 as simply a conduit through which information from German messages flowed:

> Hut 3's job was to process with meticulous care a stream of intelli-
> gence items as they came in, and to publish them. Our function was
> to elucidate each item, not to assess the broad significance of them all
> or to issue periodical commentaries upon the intelligence as a whole.
> It was not for us to write position papers or propose action, scarcely
> even to suggest that a certain interpretation might be placed upon a

number of apparently unrelated items if they were viewed together in a particular light, unless the reason for doing so derived from our specialized technical knowledge. These things were the province of command staffs and service ministries; we were neither an operational headquarters nor an aloof body of strategists. But since we did not issue appreciations or forecasts, we could hardly make mistakes on the grand scale, although we might err in translating or interpreting single items.[3]

This image of Hut 3 – and more widely of Bletchley Park – as an objective and indeed perhaps aloof organisation which simply distributed the information acquired from wireless intercepts fails to do justice to the full range of its activities. Documents declassified after the publication of Bennett's work show that Hut 3 was involved much more deeply in what would now be described as the *intelligence fusion* process, assembling intelligence information not only from the decrypts themselves, but from reports from other Allied intelligence agencies and inputs of other non-SIGINT intelligence. This work informed the process of analysis of the decrypted messages. Indeed, it is probable that without this wider flow of information it would have been difficult for Bletchley Park to produce meaningful interpretations of the messages received and in turn to produce useful output to ULTRA. This book goes beyond Bennett's narrow interpretation of events and examines the wider signals intelligence process.

The corpus of material available to Bennett for his later historical analysis was also quite incomplete. By his own admission, he examined around 45,000 ULTRA messages for the period January 1944 to May 1945.[4] By contrast, the 'History of Hut 6' suggests that in the summer of 1944, Hut 6 alone was producing over 2,000 decrypted messages *per day*.[5] Of course those that contained the most important intelligence information often became the subject of ULTRA messages: indeed, this selection process formed part of Bennett's job. However, those messages that became ULTRA signals represent only a fraction (less than

5 per cent) of the intelligence material collected. In addition, often it was the urgency of the content, rather than the longer-term significance, that dictated whether a decrypt made it into an ULTRA message. Less time-sensitive intelligence, while often important, could be left to be delivered via bag to the service ministries and their intelligence departments. This material was not available to Bennett. Subsequent declassifications have made more of it obliquely accessible, but much of it is still missing. It was one of the purposes of this book to examine the evidence available for this additional material and assess its importance.

In addition to the messages themselves, GC&CS also produced a significant body of more complete, longer reports and documents, including many produced by Hut 3, such as thematic intelligence assess-ments and orders of battle. Bennett was himself only involved in the drafting of ULTRA signals. Possibly as a consequence of his own limited role, his account also overlooks much of this more analytical product. Many of these documents have now also been declassified, and it is possible to gain a fuller picture of the output of the hut and thus its influ-ence on the course of events on the battlefield. These documents also shed further light on what Hut 3 'knew' about German activity. Limited as he was in his later research to ULTRA messages alone, Bennett could only infer the state of knowledge of the enemy in Hut 3 at any point from the information included in ULTRA. Hut 3's understanding of the battle was often much deeper than that revealed in the messages it sent out in this form. It is risky to conclude – as Bennett does on occasion – that, simply because a German army formation was not mentioned in an ULTRA message, Bletchley Park was ignorant of its whereabouts.

Another consequence of the limited material available to Bennett in his research in the 1970s is that he does not distinguish in his analysis between intelligence garnered from Enigma decrypts and that gained from other SIGINT sources. In particular these included messages sent via teleprinter, encrypted using the German Lorenz cipher machine (codenamed FISH), and hand Morse messages encrypted using Enigma. As a member of the watch in Hut 3, Bennett would have received not only Enigma decrypts from Hut 6, but also FISH material from the so-called 'Testery' in Block F. The ULTRA signals sent out to field commanders deliberately masked the origin of the information they contained, so it is not possible to separate information in these messages that was sourced from 'E' (Enigma) or 'F' (FISH) (although in some cases the length and nature of certain messages would suggest a FISH derivation). It is hard to determine whether Bennett was aware of FISH while he was at Bletchley Park; a number of members of Hut 3 certainly were, but he does not allude to it in his book. Instead he uses an oblique form of words to describe such traffic – for example, when talking about traffic in the summer of 1944 he refers to 'a number of isolated days' traffic in hitherto impregnable army keys'.[6] It is now clear that these were FISH messages.

An analysis of Bennett's apparent overlooking of FISH has been carried out by Paul Gannon in his book *Colossus: Bletchley Park's greatest secret* (2006). Gannon showed that Bennett 'consistently downplayed the role of Fish' – not only in *Ultra in the West* (where it is possible that he was being deliberately discreet about an aspect of Bletchley Park's work that in the 1970s had yet to be declassified), but also in his later works, after the secrets of FISH and Colossus were in the public domain.[7] Gannon offers this perhaps surprising suggestion:

> The conclusion can only be that Bennett, an intelligence officer during the war in Hut 3, never knew of the wireless teleprinter/ Geheimschreiber/Fish/Colossus operation. This is an indication of just how strong were the rules about not sharing any information outside one's immediate job at Bletchley Park. At least some – and probably most – of the intelligence officers in Hut 3 who did know about Enigma were not allowed to know about Fish, although they may well have been privy to the intelligence revealed by Fish decodes.[8]

Arguably the exact source of each intelligence item was not crucial to Bennett's narrative: it was enough to state what Bletchley knew, rather than exactly *how* it knew. Nonetheless, the fact that recently declassified information enables these various sources to be distinguished from each other (at least partially) allows a far more nuanced and granular view of the intelligence picture than could be derived from the ULTRA messages alone. Bennett's work, therefore, while it represents a significant piece of historical research, still leaves gaps in our understanding of the role of GC&CS, which this work hopes to fill, at least in part.

HARRY HINSLEY

The second (and much longer) work which forms a 'jumping-off point' for the present book is Hinsley's *British Intelligence in the Second World War*. Francis Henry 'Harry' Hinsley was of humble origin, but in 1937 he went up to St John's College, Cambridge, where he achieved some academic distinction. In the winter of 1939–40 he was recruited to GC&CS.[9] From November 1939, Hinsley worked in Naval Section at Bletchley. Despite his youth (he turned twenty-one that November), he was instrumental in persuading an initially sceptical Admiralty of the power of GC&CS SIGINT. He continued his rise through Naval Section, reaching the senior (if slightly nebulous) grade of 'intelligence staff officer' by 1943. In 1945, he became chairman of the Target Intelligence Committee (TICOM), which was responsible for collecting German communications and SIGINT equipment, as well as information about codes and ciphers, behind the advancing Allied forces in Germany. This gave him a detailed insight into 'the other side of the hill' and German intelligence activity. After the war, Hinsley returned to St John's College and continued his career as an academic historian, becoming a professor of international relations and serving a term as vice chancellor of the University of Cambridge. In 1971, he embarked on the production of the first volume of *British Intelligence in the Second World War*, which was published in 1979; he continued with subsequent volumes for another eleven years, publishing Volume 4 in 1990. He died of cancer in 1998.[10]

Hinsley had the advantage over Bennett in that his was an 'official' history. The difficulties of access to classified information were largely removed. As he describes in his preface to Volume 1:

> No considered account of the relationship between intelligence and strategic and operational decisions has hitherto been possible, for no such account could be drawn up except by authors having unrestricted access to intelligence records as well as to other archives. In relation to the British records for the Second World War and the inter-war years we have been granted this freedom as a special measure. No restriction has been placed on us while carrying out our research ... we set out to see all [the records], and if any have escaped our scrutiny we are satisfied that over-sight on our part is the sole explanation.[11]

On that basis, it might be thought that Hinsley would be able to tell the complete story and that would be an end to the matter. However, this is not the case – for several reasons. The first is simply that *British Intelligence* is of necessity a very long and dense work; as such, it is not particularly accessible to the general reader. In addition, the very scope of the project meant that Hinsley had to be selective about what he included. He was also, despite his assertions above, still subject to security restrictions: his ability to quote from and to reference what he describes as 'the domestic records of the intelligence collecting bodies' was limited by official secrecy, which remained in place.[12] His focus was also on the broad strategic intelligence picture and the decisions based on it, rather than on the precise processes by which that intelligence was obtained. In this, he differs from so many Bletchley Park researchers who focus very heavily on 'process'; Hinsley dealt with that aspect hardly at all, referencing only the finished intelligence product. He himself acknowledged this omission:

> As for the contribution of the many men and women who carried out essential routine work at the establishments in the United Kingdom

and overseas – who undertook the continuous manning of intercept stations or of cryptanalytic machinery ... and the endless indexing, typing, teleprinting, ciphering, and transmitting of the intelligence output – only occasional references to it have been possible in an account which sets out to reconstruct the influence of intelligence on the major decisions, the chief operations and the general course of the war.[13]

It has been the aim of this present work to straddle these two approaches and – for Bletchley at least – to show the complete picture: both the activities of the 'many men and women' in the production of intelligence and its overall 'influence'.

Hinsley went on to observe, with typical academic modesty:

That room remains for further research is something that goes without saying. Even on issues and episodes for which we have set out to supply the fullest possible accounts, the public records will yield interpretations that differ from those we have offered.[14]

CRYPTANALYSIS

A number of books on Bletchley followed Frederick Winterbotham's *The Ultra Secret* (1974) in the late 1970s and early 1980s, but, like that book, were based largely on personal recollection and made little use of historical documentation, much of which remained classified at the time and hence unavailable. See, for example, Peter Calvocoressi's *Top Secret Ultra* (1980) and Gordon Welchman's *The Hut Six Story* (1982).

Once established, this pattern has since been followed by a number of other writers, who, though they had access to increasing amounts of primary source documentation, have made cryptanalysis rather than intelligence the focus of their work. The breaking of Enigma is perhaps the most famous of Bletchley's achievements, and this has been well covered, with an emphasis on the naval side of the story, in works such as

David Kahn's *Seizing the Enigma* (1991) and Hugh Sebag-Montefiore's *Enigma: The battle for the code* (2000). However, while both books provide a detailed account of the various intellectual breakthroughs, as well as 'pinches' of vital documents and equipment that went into the reading of German Enigma traffic, neither work seeks to provide a detailed account of the intelligence impact of this achievement on the war – or more specifically on the Battle of the Atlantic, with which both books are principally concerned. Other works have focused on particular cryptanalytic problems, such as those on 'Colossus', the electronic machine used in 'key finding', as part of the process of breaking the Lorenz cipher: Paul Gannon's *Colossus* and B. Jack Copeland's *Colossus: The secrets of Bletchley Park's codebreaking computers* (2006). While both books provide great detail on the story of the development of the relevant cryptanalysis, and assert the significant impact of this achievement on the outcome of the war, neither develops to any great depth an account of what kinds of intelligence were produced or what impact this information actually had.

My book is intended for the general reader, as well as for the academic or intelligence professional, and thus much of the more technical codebreaking material has been omitted, and only summary accounts of the various codes and ciphers attacked by Bletchley have been included. Readers keen to know the intimate workings of Enigma or the Lorenz SZ42 are directed to the many more detailed works available on the subject.

SOCIAL HISTORY

A second genre of literature has also developed around the story of Bletchley Park. This is the social history of the institution, based on the written and spoken testimony of veterans – for example, Sinclair McKay's *The Secret Life of Bletchley Park* (2010), Michael Smith's *The Debs of Bletchley Park* (2015) and Tessa Dunlop's *The Bletchley Girls* (2015). These works have proved highly popular and, along with several fictional or semi-fictional TV dramas and films, largely make up the public perception of the organisation. However, these do little to elucidate the significance of the work the staff were actually carrying out.

INTELLIGENCE OPERATIONS

Those intelligence operations that have been covered also tend to be examined in isolation. Studies concentrate on a particular intelligence-gathering methodology or subject area without necessarily placing the work within the wider operational intelligence context. An example of this would be the deception operations surrounding OVERLORD, in particular Operation FORTITUDE. Deception operations are described in this work, but it is emphasised that they formed just part of a much wider intelligence-gathering operation. Readers looking for more information about FORTITUDE have a choice of several popular books on the topic, for example Ben Macintyre's *Double Cross* (2012) or Joshua Levine's *Operation Fortitude: The greatest hoax of the Second World War* (2012), or, for a more academic study, Mary Barbier's *D-Day Deception: Operation Fortitude and the Normandy invasion* (2007).

MORE RECENT DEVELOPMENTS

In the forty years since the publication of Hinsley's and Bennett's books, the public records have indeed become much fuller, as more material has been declassified. However, some of this material has reached the public domain only very recently in historical terms. After the war, the archives of GC&CS were subsumed into those of its successor organisation, GCHQ, and the whole of the British SIGINT effort remained secret until the 1970s. The first major release of information occurred in 1977, with the deposit in the Public Record Office of the ULTRA message traffic, which formed the basis of Bennett's work. This was followed by more message traffic, in the form of the 'DIR C' files, released in 1993. These include the daily selection of important traffic passed via the director of the Secret Intelligence Service ('C') to the prime minister. Three sets of messages were passed on each day: the 'Hut 3 Headlines' (which dealt with army and air force matters); the 'Naval Headlines'; and the 'Blue Jackets' (BJs), which contained diplomatic and commercial decrypts. These form an important supplement to what was included in the messages to commands released previously. The 1990s also saw the release of some of the domestic records consulted by Hinsley, in the form of 'The History of Hut Three', compiled internally by GCHQ after the war and released in 1995; a number of administrative papers also became publicly available between 1998 and 2004.[15]

It was not until the early 2000s that more material became available, with the release of the 'History of the Fish Subsection', along with the papers of the Western Front Committee at Bletchley Park, in 2004. The latter documents have not previously been examined in detail in a published work, but they form a key resource for this study. The 'History of Hut 6', which provides details of the Enigma-breaking work done by that team, did not become available until 2006. Some parts of the story remain classified, and the equivalent history of SIXTA (the section responsible for traffic analysis) was released only in September 2018. At the time of writing (autumn 2018), GCHQ has given an informal undertaking that all remaining GC&CS files relating to the Second World War will be released by the end of 2019. It remains to be seen what revelations will result.

One other recent study has exploited the new evidence to paint a modern picture of Bletchley Park: Professor Christopher Grey's *Decoding Organization* (2012). This is one of the few scholarly works (as opposed to popular histories) to appear in recent years on the subject. However, as the title implies, the book has as its main focus the internal arrangement and functioning of Bletchley from a specifically organisational point of view. Thus the book, while a fine study of its chosen field, has little to say about the wider intelligence picture.

The official documentation examined for this study was supplemented by material in the archives of the Bletchley Park Trust itself. The Trust's holdings include material that was not retained by the National Archives, as well as personal material from veterans. There are also a number of samples of working documents and message traffic, the bulk of which was not retained by GCHQ after the war. These items were held unofficially in private hands and now offer a unique insight into the working processes of the organisation. Since 2011, the Trust has also engaged in an oral history recording project, and has captured the memories of over 400 employees of GC&CS as well as 'Y station' staff and others involved in the SIGINT process. This, too, provides an important window onto wartime events.

FURTHER READING

ARCHIVAL MATERIAL

Much of the surviving documentation concerning the work of GC&CS has now been declassified by GCHQ and passed to the National Archives (TNA) in Kew, London. This is mostly held in the HW document series. Copies of ULTRA messages are also contained in relevant DEFE and ADM series.

The Bletchley Park Trust also holds an archive of wartime materials. Some of these duplicate files held at TNA, while others are personal donations from veterans and their families. The Trust also maintains the Bletchley Park Roll of Honour, a list of all those individuals known to have worked in association with GC&CS during the war. A programme of oral history interviews is ongoing with veterans, and transcripts of these interviews are also available from the Bletchley Park Trust. The Roll of Honour and transcripts are accessible via the Trust website: www. bletchleypark.org.uk/

The personal papers of a number of senior figures in GC&CS – including 'Nobby' Clarke and Alastair Denniston – are held in the Churchill Archives Centre at Churchill College, Cambridge.

A collection of Alan Turing's papers is held at the Modern Archives Centre at King's College, Cambridge.

PUBLISHED SOURCES

Bletchley Park and D-Day

Bennett, Ralph, *Ultra in the West: The Normandy Campaign 1944–45*, Hutchinson, 1979.

Hinsley, F.H., *British Intelligence in the Second World War* (4 vols), HMSO/CUP, 1979–88.

General histories of Bletchley Park

Budiansky, Stephen, *Battle of Wits: The complete story of codebreaking in World War II*, Viking, 2000.

Grey, Christopher, *Decoding Organization: Bletchley Park, codebreaking and organization studies*, Cambridge University Press, 2012.

Hinsley, F.H. and A. Stripp (eds), *Codebreakers: The inside story of Bletchley Park*, Oxford University Press, 1993.

Smith, Christopher, *The Hidden History of Bletchley Park: A social and organisational history, 1939–1945*, Palgrave, 2015.

Smith, Michael, *The Secrets of Station X: How the Bletchley Park codebreakers helped win the war*, Biteback, 2011.

Smith, Michael and Ralph Erskine (eds), *Action This Day: Bletchley Park from the breaking of the Enigma code to the birth of the modern computer*, Bantam Press, 2001.

The breaking of Enigma and its effect on the Battle of the Atlantic

Beezly, Patrick, *Very Special Intelligence: The story of the Admiralty's operational intelligence centre 1939–1945*, Sphere, 1977.

Kahn, David, *Seizing the Enigma: The race to break the German U-boat codes 1939–1943*, Houghton Mifflin Harcourt, 1991.

Sebag-Montefiore, Hugh, *Enigma: The battle for the code*, Wiley, 2000.

The breaking of Lorenz

Copeland, B. Jack, *Colossus: The secrets of Bletchley Park's codebreaking computers*, Oxford University Press, 2006.

Gannon, Paul, *Colossus: Bletchley Park's greatest secret*, Atlantic, 2006.

Roberts, Jerry, *Lorenz: Breaking Hitler's top secret code at Bletchley Park*, History Press, 2017.

Japanese codes and ciphers

Boyd, Carl, *Hitler's Japanese Confidant: General Oshima Hiroshi and MAGIC intelligence, 1941–1945*, University Press of Kansas, 1993.

Clark, Ronald W., *The Man Who Broke 'Purple': Life of the world's greatest cryptologist, Colonel William F. Friedman*, Weidenfeld & Nicolson, 1977.

Smith, Michael, *The Emperor's Codes: Bletchley Park's role in breaking Japan's secret ciphers*, Biteback Press, 2010.

Individuals who wrote about Bletchley from their own experience

Calvocoressi, Peter, *Top Secret Ultra*, Pantheon, 1980.

Welchman, Gordon, *The Hut Six Story: Breaking the Enigma codes*, McGraw-Hill, 1982.

Winterbotham, F.W., *The Ultra Secret*, Dell, 1974.

Biographies of other significant individuals

Batey, Mavis, *Dilly: The man who broke Enigmas*, Biteback, 2017.

Greenberg, Joel, *Gordon Welchman: Bletchley Park's architect of Ultra intelligence*, Frontline, 2014.

Greenberg, Joel, *Alastair Denniston: Code-breaking from Room 40 to Berkeley Street and the birth of GCHQ*, Frontline, 2017.

Hodges, Andrew, *Alan Turing: The Enigma*, Hutchinson, 1983.

Researchers should also investigate relevant papers and articles in the journals *Cryptologia*, *Intelligence and National Security* and the *Journal of Intelligence History*.

ENDNOTES

INTRODUCTION

1. GCHQ historian, personal communication, 2017.
2. The reason for this is that – particularly from 1943 onwards – the Allies were engaged in a massive air offensive against Germany, with bombing raids almost nightly into occupied Europe. As a result, the air intelligence story is an extremely complex one. Moreover, it is impossible to draw a distinction between the different uses to which intelligence on the Luftwaffe could be put: understanding the German fighter defences in France and the Low Countries, their radar installations and their wider air defence network was, of course, vital to invasion planning; but it also supported the Allied bombers. It would not be possible to do justice to this complete effort in a work of this length; and to try and divide it into 'D-Day' and 'non-D-Day' narratives would lead to a partial and incomplete account.

1 THE INTELLIGENCE FACTORY

1. F. Birch, 'A History of British Sigint 1914–1945', unpublished GCHQ typescript, Vol. I, pp. 17–18.
2. S. Fox, 'To Burlington and Beyond: The story of the central government war headquarters': http://burlingtonandbeyond.co.uk/wp/part-1/ (accessed 22 January 2019).
3. A.G. Denniston, untitled typescript (1944) published as 'The Government Code and Cypher School between the Wars', *Intelligence and National Security*, 1:1 (1986), pp. 48–70.
4. Ibid., p. 50.
5. Ibid., p. 52.
6. A. Denniston, 'Notes on Senior Staff September 1939', TNA HW14/1.
7. K. Johnson and J. Gallehawk, *Figuring it out at Bletchley Park 1939–1945,* BookTower Publishing, 2007, p. 9.
8. Birch, 'A History of British Sigint 1914–1945', Vol. II, p. 471.
9. Ibid.
10. Mrs Peggy Huntington (née Munn), BPT oral history project, interview 8 December 2011.
11. R. Whelan, 'The Use of Hollerith Punched Card Equipment in Bletchley Park', TNA HW25/22, Section 26.

12. C. Grey, *Decoding Organization: Bletchley Park, codebreaking and organization studies*, Cambridge University Press, 2012, p. 197.
13. Denniston, 'Government Code and Cypher School', p. 49.
14. Ibid., p. 52.
15. Chiffriermaschinen Gesellschaft Heimsoeth & Rinke, Memorandum on sales, October 1935, copy supplied by Frode Weierud.
16. F.H. Hinsley, *British Intelligence in the Second World War*, Vol. 1, HMSO, 1979, p. 273.
17. For details of the construction and occupation of the huts and blocks, see GCHQ, *History of Bletchley Park Huts and Blocks 1939–45*, BPT Report No. 198 (2009).
18. Birch, 'A History of British Sigint 1914–1945', Vol. III, p. 830.
19. Ibid., Vol. II, p. 295.
20. D. Taunt, 'Hut 6 1941–1945', in F. Hinsley and A. Stripp, *Codebreakers: The inside story of Bletchley Park*, Oxford University Press, 1994 (first published 1993), pp. 100–12.
21. H. Fletcher, *Hut 6 Bombe Register*, Vols 1 and 2, TNA HW25/19 and HW25/20.
22. 'B.T.M. 3-Wheel bombes and B.T.M. and W.W. 4-Wheel Bombes', TNA HW25/17.
23. P. Gannon, *Colossus: Bletchley Park's greatest secret*, Atlantic, 2006, p. 126.
24. 'General Report on Tunny with Emphasis on Statistical Methods', unpublished GCHQ typescript, TNA HW25/4, p. 281.
25. Gannon, *Colossus*, pp. 88–9.
26. Ibid., p. 335.
27. L. Monckton et al., 'Historic Buildings Report: Bletchley Park, Wilton Avenue, Bletchley, Milton Keynes, MK3 6EB', English Heritage typescript report, 2004, Vol. 1, p. 124.
28. Ibid., p. 321.
29. Ibid., p. 223.
30. Ibid., Vol. 2, p. 444.
31. Birch, 'A History of British Sigint 1914–1945', Vol. II, table opposite p. 527.
32. Monckton et al., 'Historic Buildings Report: Bletchley Park', Vol. 2, p. 487.
33. Ibid., p. 479.
34. Mrs Joyce Bogoni (née Roberts), BPT oral history project, interview February 2015.
35. Memo from Capt. Melrose to Commander Bradshaw, 9 November 1943. Other detail in this paragraph taken from associated items in same file, TNA HW64/62.
36. Monckton et al., 'Historic Buildings Report: Bletchley Park', Vol. 2, pp. 405–06.
37. G. Pidgeon, *The Secret Wireless War: The story of MI6 communications 1939–1945*, UPSO, 2008, pp. 14ff.
38. Ibid., p. 78.
39. Birch, 'A History of British Sigint 1914–1945', Vol. II, pp. 211–12.
40. S. Budiansky, 'The Difficult Beginnings of US–British Codebreaking Cooperation', *Intelligence and National Security*, 15:2 (2000), pp. 52–54.
41. M. Smith, *The Emperor's Codes: Bletchley Park's role in breaking Japan's secret ciphers*, Biteback, 2010 (first published 2000), p. 74.
42. This meeting was recalled later by Barbara Abernethy, Denniston's personal assistant; see M. Smith, *The Secrets of Station X: How the Bletchley Park codebreakers helped win the war*, Biteback, 2011, pp. 148–49.
43. C. Currier, 'My "Purple" Trip to England in 1941', *Cryptologia*, 20:3 (1996), pp. 196–97.
44. Ibid., p. 198.
45. Budiansky, 'Difficult Beginnings', p. 55.
46. Denniston memorandum to 'C', quoted in ibid., p. 55.
47. R. Erskine, 'The Holden Agreement on Naval Sigint: The first BRUSA?', *Intelligence and National Security*, 14:2 (1999), p. 188.
48. Smith, *The Secrets of Station X*, p. 153.
49. Erskine, 'The Holden Agreement on Naval Sigint', p. 191.
50. Budiansky, 'Difficult Beginnings', p. 61.
51. https://www.nsa.gov/Portals/70/documents/news-features/declassified-documents/ukusa/spec_int_10jun43.pdf (accessed 14 January 2019).

52. Letter from Col. Bicher to E.W. Travis, 28 January 1944, TNA HW14/59.
53. L. Gladwin, 'Cautious Collaborators: The struggle for Anglo-American cryptanalytic co-operation 1940–43', *Intelligence and National Security*, 14:1 (1999), p. 140.
54. 'Technical History of the 6813th Signal Security Detachment', 20 October 1945, NSA typescript: https://www.codesandciphers.org.uk/documents/a6813his/us6813.pdf (accessed 22 January 2019).
55. Private First Class Hervie Haufler, 6811th Signal Security Detachment, US Army Signal Corps, oral history testimony: http://www.historynet.com/my-bit-of-history.htm (accessed 22 January 2019).
56. Ibid.
57. 'Personnel at BP', typescript, 14 January 1945, TNA HW14/154.
58. Budiansky, 'Difficult Beginnings', p. 69.

2 INCOMING INTERCEPTS AND CODEBREAKING

1. W. Tutte, 'At Bletchley Park', typescript memoir, 2002, p. 1. Thanks are due to Richard Youlden, Bill Tutte's great nephew. A slightly edited version of the text appears in B.J. Copeland, *Colossus: The secrets of Bletchley Park's codebreaking computers*, Oxford University Press, 2006, Appendix 4.
2. Tutte, 'At Bletchley Park', p. 1.
3. 'Research Section: First Meeting of Directing Sub-Committee', 8 April 1941, TNA HW78/1.
4. Tutte, 'At Bletchley Park', p. 6.
5. Ibid., p. 11.
6. D. Kahn, *Seizing the Enigma: The race to break the German U-boat codes 1939–1943*, Houghton Mifflin Harcourt, 1991, pp. 31–4.
7. http://cryptomuseum.com/crypto/enigma/i/index.htm (accessed 13 March 2018).
8. http://cryptomuseum.com/crypto/enigma/m3/index.htm (accessed 13 March 2018).
9. http://www.cryptomuseum.com/crypto/enigma/i/index.htm (accessed 13 March 2018).
10. Auguste Kerckhoffs, 'La cryptographie militaire', *Journal des sciences militaires*, vol. IX (January 1883), pp. 5–83; (February 1883), pp. 161–91; see Wikipedia, https://en.wikipedia.org/wiki/Kerckhoffs%27s_principle (accessed 20 January 2017).
11. D. Rijmenants, 'Enigma Message Procedures Used by the Heer, Luftwaffe and Kriegsmarine', *Cryptologia*, 34 (2010), pp. 329–39.
12. F.H. Hinsley, *British Intelligence in the Second World War*, Vol. 2, HMSO, 1981, Appendix 4, p. 658.
13. P. Calvocoressi, *Top Secret Ultra*, Pantheon, 1980, p. 82.
14. The figures are derived from Hinsley's *British Intelligence in the Second World War*.
15. 'History of Hut 6', unpublished GCHQ typescript, Vol. I, TNA HW43/70, p. 245.
16. 'History of Hut 6', Vol. III, p. 72, which includes a statistical table of 'Traffic Breaks and Decodes'.
17. https://www.feldgrau.com/WW2-Germany-Statistics-and-Numbers (accessed 25 January 2018).
18. C.H.O'D. Alexander, 'Cryptographic History of Work on the German Naval Enigma', unpublished GCHQ typescript, TNA HW25/1, Para 57.
19. A.P. Mahon, 'The History of Hut Eight 1939–1945', unpublished GCHQ typescript, TNA HW25/1, p. 115.
20. Birch, 'A History of British Sigint 1914–1945', Vol. III, p. 830.
21. Ibid., Vol. II, p. 527.
22. Johnson and Gallehawk, *Figuring it out at Bletchley Park*, p. 71.
23. F. Hinsley, 'An Introduction to Fish', in Hinsley and Stripp, *Codebreakers*, p. 141.
24. F. Hinsley, *British Intelligence in the Second World War*, Vol. 3, Part I, HMSO, 1984, p. 477.

25. Gannon, *Colossus*, p. 90.
26. Letter from Deniston to Mair, 11 July 1932, TNA HW 72/2.
27. Letter from Denniston to Peters, 14 December 1936, TNA HW72/9.
28. Smith, *The Secrets of Station X*, p. 223.
29. 'General Report on Tunny', TNA HW25/5 Section 41C.
30. Tutte, 'At Bletchley Park', p. 10.
31. Gannon, *Colossus*, p. 168.
32. S. Budiansky, 'Colossus, Codebreaking and the Digital Age', in Copeland, *Colossus*, p. 58.
33. This description of Robinson is largely drawn from Copeland, *Colossus*, pp. 65–71.
34. H. Cragon, *From Fish to Colossus: How the German Lorenz cipher was broken at Bletchley Park*, Cragon Books, 2003, p. 67.
35. This description of Colossus is largely drawn from Copeland, *Colossus*, pp. 71–7.
36. 'Thomas Flowers Biography', *Oxford Dictionary of National Biography*, Oxford University Press, 2008. doi:10.1093/ref:odnb/71253
37. T. Flowers 1944 diary entries, quoted in Copeland, *Colossus*, p. 75.
38. T. Flowers, 'D-Day and Bletchley Park', in ibid., p. 80.
39. Message serial BAY/KV 179, 1/6/44, quoted in Hinsley, *British Intelligence in the Second World War*, Vol. 3, Part II, HMSO, 1988, p. 61.
40. B.J. Copeland, 'Colossus and the Dawning of the Computer Age', in M. Smith and R. Erskine (eds), *Action This Day: Bletchley Park from the breaking of the Enigma code to the birth of the modern computer*, Bantam Press, 2001, p. 343.
41. Timeline in 'General Report on Tunny', TNA HW25/5.
42. Copeland, *Colossus*, p. 77.
43. D. Du Boisson, quoted in Copeland, *Colossus*, p. 160.
44. C. Caughey, quoted in ibid., p. 165.
45. In particular, from two key documents: the 'General Report on Tunny', TNA HW25/4, p. 281 (declassified in 2000), and the 'History of the Fish Subsection', p. 6 (declassified in 2004). The latter document in particular has detailed lists of FISH links broken by date, and tables of decryptions achieved.
46. 'General Report on Tunny', TNA HW25/4, p. 281.
47. 'History of the Fish Subsection', p. 6.
48. Hinsley, *British Intelligence in the Second World War*, Vol. 3, Part I, p. 482.
49. Smith, *The Emperor's Codes*, p. 223.
50. S. Budiansky, *Battle of Wits: The complete story of codebreaking in World War II*, Viking, 2000, p. 177.
51. The description of the functioning of the machine is drawn from W. Freeman, G. Sullivan and F. Weierud, 'PURPLE Revealed: Simulation and computer-aided cryptanalysis of Angooki Taipu B', *Cryptologia*, 27:1 (2003), p. 29.
52. Smith, *The Emperor's Codes*, p. 48.
53. C. Boyd, 'Significance of MAGIC and the Japanese Ambassador to Berlin: (I) The formative months before Pearl Harbor', *Intelligence and National Security*, 2:1 (1987), p. 151.
54. Smith, *The Emperor's Codes*, pp. 48, 73.
55. Letter from Gen. Marshall to Dewey, 25 September 1944; https://www.nsa.gov/news-features/declassified-documents/friedman-documents/assets/files/reports-research/FOLDER_513/41786189082519.pdf (accessed 23 November 2017).
56. Boyd, 'Significance of MAGIC and the Japanese Ambassador to Berlin: (I)', p. 164.
57. British military attaché report, TNA WO106/5530, quoted in Smith, *The Emperor's Codes*, p. 48.
58. Boyd, 'Significance of MAGIC and the Japanese Ambassador to Berlin: (I)', p. 150.
59. Smith, *The Emperor's Codes*, p. 220.
60. http://pwencycl.kgbudge.com/A/b/Abe_Katsuo.htm (accessed 20 December 2017).
61. https://www.nsa.gov/about/cryptologic-heritage/center-cryptologic-history/pearl-harbor-review/early-japanese.shtml (accessed 20 December 2017).

62. M. Smith, 'How the British Broke Japan's Codes', in Smith and Erskine, *Action this Day*, p. 143.
63. Ibid., p. 145.
64. C. Boyd, 'Significance of MAGIC and the Japanese Ambassador to Berlin: (V) News of Hitler's defence preparations for the allied invasion of Western Europe', *Intelligence and National Security*, 4:3 (1989), p. 461.
65. J. Thisk, 'Traffic Analysis: A log-reader's tale', in Smith and Erskine, *Action This Day*, pp. 264–77.
66. G. Welchman, quoted in Birch, 'A History of British Sigint 1914–1945', Vol. I, p. 207.
67. Birch, 'A History of British Sigint 1914–1945', Vol. II, p. 497.
68. Thisk, 'Traffic Analysis', p. 270.
69. Ibid., p. 273.
70. Ibid., p. 274.
71. Ibid., p. 270.
72. Birch, 'A History of British Sigint 1914–1945', Vol. III, p. 830.

3 OUTGOING INTELLIGENCE

1. Calvocoressi, *Top Secret Ultra*, p. 63.
2. https://www.gchq.gov.uk/features/gchq-christmas-carol (accessed 28 April 2018).
3. R. Bennett, *Ultra and Mediterranean Strategy*, Viking, 1989, p. 104.
4. 'The History of Hut Three', unpublished GCHQ typescript, Vol. I, TNA HW3/119, p. 4.
5. Mrs Doreen Nicolson (née Tabor), Hut 3, Air Index, BPT oral history project, interview May 2016.
6. 'The History of Hut Three', Vol. I, TNA HW3/119, p. 25.
7. Ibid., p. 9.
8. Ibid., p. 29.
9. Ibid., p. 50.
10. Ibid., p. 20. We are assisted in this by a sketch diagram in the Hut 'History' which not only shows the relative locations of the parts of the section in Block D, but also the routes of the traffic through the system.
11. Ibid., p. 189.
12. Ibid., p. 76.
13. Ibid., p. 14.
14. Ibid., p. 72.
15. Ibid., p. 118.
16. Mrs Doreen Nicolson (née Tabor), Hut 3, Air Index, BPT oral history project.
17. Ibid.
18. Hinsley, *British Intelligence in the Second World War*, Vol. 1, pp. 460–1.
19. 'The History of Hut Three', Vol. I, TNA HW3/119, p. 46.
20. Ibid., p. 46.
21. Ibid., p. 69.
22. Ibid., p. 45.
23. Oscar Adolph Oeser (1904–83), Australian Dictionary of Biography; http://adb.anu.edu.au/biography/oeser-oscar-adolph-15396 (accessed 28 April 2018).
24. 'The History of Hut Three', Vol. I, TNA HW3/119, p. 292.
25. Ibid., p. 316.
26. Hinsley, *British Intelligence in the Second World War*, Vol. 3, Part II, p. 780.
27. Budiansky, *Battle of Wits*, p. 48.
28. Letter D. Morton to 'C', 27 September 1940, TNA HW1/1, quoted in ibid., p. 149.
29. The contents of these daily briefs are held in the National Archives and cover most of the war. They include notes and annotations by the various readers, and associated correspondence. See http://discovery.nationalarchives.gov.uk/details/r/C9280 (accessed 17 April 2015).

30. 'The History of Hut Three', Vol. I, TNA HW3/119, p. 209.
31. K. Jeffery, *MI6: The history of the Secret Intelligence Service 1909–1949*, Bloomsbury, 2010 (paperback edition 2011), pp. 347–48.
32. Budiansky, *Battle of Wits*, p. 149.
33. A significant proportion of this material (or at least the teleprinted portions of it) survives in the National Archives at Kew, released by GCHQ from 1995 onward. TNA File Series HW5, 767 volumes.
34. 'The History of Hut Three', Vol. I, TNA HW3/119, p. 244.
35. C-in-C West Appreciation, 21 March 1944, TNA HW5/463.
36. C-in-C West Appreciation, 25 June 1944, TNA HW5/518.
37. 'The History of Hut Three', Vol. I, TNA HW3/119, p. 63.
38. F.W. Winterbotham, *The Ultra Secret*, Dell, 1974, pp. 22–5.
39. P. Beesly, *Very Special Intelligence: The story of the Admiralty's operational intelligence centre 1939–1945*, Sphere, 1977, p. 100.
40. Winterbotham, *The Ultra Secret*, p. 29.
41. Birch, 'A History of British Sigint 1914–1945', Chapter X: 'The Story of the SLUs', unpublished GCHQ typescript, TNA HW3/16, p. 1.
42. Ibid., p. 14.
43. Ibid., pp. 3–4.
44. Ibid., p. 33.
45. Pidgeon, *Secret Wireless War*, p. 79.
46. Birch, 'A History of British Sigint 1914–1945', Chapter X, pp. 34–5.
47. Ibid., p. 39.
48. Ibid., p. 6.
49. 'The History of Hut Three', Vol. 1, TNA HW3/119, p. 256.
50. Winterbotham, *The Ultra Secret*, p. 98.
51. Ibid., p. 78.
52. Ibid., p. 141.
53. F. Winterbotham, Imperial War Museum interview, reel 30; https://www.iwm.org.uk/collections/item/object/80007264 (accessed 5 February 2018). The reliability of Winterbotham's account of the work of Bletchley Park in his book *The Ultra Secret* has been called into question since its publication in 1974. He was working from memory and lacked much of the documentary material available to later scholars. He was also attempting to tell a wider story, in which he personally played only a supporting part, and his accounts of parts of the operation in which he was not personally involved – his memory of the bombes, for example – are demonstrably incorrect. However, where he described activities with which he was personally concerned, or scenes that he witnessed himself, his account potentially carries more authority.
54. B. Williams, 'The Use of ULTRA by the Army', typescript, 5 October 1945, TNA WO208/3575, p. 10.

4 INVASION PLANNING IN 1943

1. Details of this meeting are taken from '"Western Front" Committee, Minutes of First Meeting', 12 October 1942, TNA HW14/55.
2. GCHQ, 'Key Personalities at Bletchley Park 1939–45', unpublished, undated typescript, p. 18.
3. Ibid., p. 23.
4. Ibid., p. 118.
5. '"Western Front" Committee, Minutes of First Meeting', Para 5.
6. '"Western Front" Committee Minutes of Second Meeting', 17 October 1942, BLEPK 0080.1.2. In addition to the copies of these minutes held by TNA, a set of copies is held by Bletchley Park Trust. This and subsequent references are to the BPT copies.
7. GCHQ, 'Key Personalities', p. 51.

8. Zaloga, S, *The Devil's Garden: Rommel's desperate defense of Omaha Beach on D-Day*, Stackpole, 2013, p. 166.
9. Hinsley, *British Intelligence in the Second World War*, Vol. 3, Part II, p. 3.
10. F.C. Pogue, *US Army in World War II: European Theater of Operations: The Supreme Commander*, 1954, p. 24; http://www.ibiblio.org/hyperwar/USA/USA-E-Supreme/USA-E-Supreme-1.html (accessed 11 July 2017).
11. 'History of COSSAC (Chief of Staff to Supreme Allied Commander) 1943–1944', prepared by the Historical Sub-Section, Office of Secretary, General Staff, Supreme Headquarters, Allied Expeditionary Force, May 1944; https://history.army.mil/documents/cossac/Cossac.htm (accessed 22 January 2019).
12. US ABC-4/CS 1 December 1941. ARCADIA Conf Bk, quoted in G.A. Harrison, *US Army in World War II: European Theater of Operations: Cross-Channel Attack*, Whitman, 1951, p. 8 (emphasis added); http://www.ibiblio.org/hyperwar/USA/USA-E-XChannel/USA-E-XChannel-1.html (accessed 5 July 2017).
13. Hinsley, *British Intelligence in the Second World War*, Vol. 3, Part II, p. 11.
14. R. Bennett, *Ultra in the West: The Normandy Campaign 1944–45*, Hutchinson, 1979, p. 31.
15. 'Record of Western Front' (No. 1), 20 February 1943, BLEPK 0080.1.5.
16. '3M Order of Battle: France and the Low Countries', No. 12, 21 May 1944, TNA HW13/161.
17. 'Record of Western Front' (No. 1), 20 February 1943, BLEPK 0080.1.5, p. 5.
18. Hinsley, *British Intelligence in the Second World War*, Vol. 3, Part II, p. 19.
19. TNA WO208/4308, reproduced in Hinsley, *British Intelligence in the Second World War*, Vol. 3, Part II, Appendix IV.
20. TNA WO208/4308 and 3573, quoted in Hinsley, *British Intelligence in the Second World War*, Vol. 3, Part II, p. 25.
21. 'Record of Western Front' (No. 5), 17 April 1943, BLEPK 0080.1.11, p. 2.
22. 'Record of Western Front' (No. 3), 20 March 1943, BLEPK 0080.1.8, p. 25a.
23. Ken Ford and Steven J. Zaloga, *Overlord: The D-Day Landings*, Oxford: Osprey Publishing, 2009, pp. 218–19; 203–4.
24. 'Record of Western Front' (No. 8), 5 June 1943, BLEPK 0080.1.15, p. 8.
25. 'Record of Western Front' (No. 17, 16 October 1943, BLEPK 0080.1.26, p. 4.
26. COS(43)416(0), 30 July 1943, quoted in Hinsley, *British Intelligence in the Second World War*, Vol. 3, Part II, p. 7.
27. Quoted in Ibid., Vol. 3, Part II, p. 8.
28. 'Record of Western Front' (No. 10), 3 July 1943, BLEPK 0080.1.18, p. 7.
29. 'Record of Western Front' (No. 12), 7 August 1943, BLEPK 0080.1.21, p. 6.
30. Hinsley, *British Intelligence in the Second World War*, Vol. 3, Part II, pp. 26, 29.
31. Ibid. p. 15.
32. Ibid., Vol. 2 (1981), Appendix 4.
33. 'Record of Western Front' (No. 3), 20 March 1943, BLEPK 0080.1.8, p. 5.
34. Hinsley, *British Intelligence in the Second World War*, Vol. 3, Part II, p. 28n.
35. 'The History of Hut Three', Vol. I, TNA HW3/119, p. 76.
36. https://en.wikipedia.org/wiki/Luftwaffe_Field_Division (accessed 6 July 2017).
37. TNA WO208/4308 and 4309, quoted in Hinsley, *British Intelligence in the Second World War*, Vol. 3, Part II, p. 26.
38. 'Record of Western Front' (No. 6), 8 May 1943, BLEPK 0080.1.12, p. 2.
39. 'Record of Western Front' (No. 7), 20 May 1943, BLEPK 0080.1.14, p. 2.
40. 'Record of Western Front' (No. 8), 5 June 1943, BLEPK 0080.1.15, p. 3.
41. 'Record of Western Front' (No. 10), 3 July 1943, BLEPK 0080.1.18, pp. 8–9.
42. 'Record of Western Front' (No. 7), 22 May 1943, BLEPK 0080.1.14, p. 1.
43. Hinsley, *British Intelligence in the Second World War*, Vol. 3, Part II, p. 29.
44. 'Record of Western Front' (No. 17), 16 October 1943, BLEPK 0080.1.26, p. 9 (my emphasis).
45. Führer Directive No. 51, 3 November 1943, quoted in Harrison, *US Army in World War II*, Appendix D.
46. Hinsley, *British Intelligence in the Second World War*, Vol. 3, Part II, p. 18.

47. Ibid., 32 and fn.
48. Bennett, *Ultra in the West*, p. 49.
49. 'Record of Western Front' (No. 20), 4 December 1943, BLEPK 0080.1.30, p. 7.
50. Hinsley, *British Intelligence in the Second World War*, Vol. 3, Part II, p. 33.
51. Hut 3 Headlines 7854, 15:36 hrs 19/11/1943, BLEPK 0043.27.248.
52. 'Record of Western Front' (No. 21), 18 December 1943, BLEPK 0080.1.31, p. 4.
53. 'Record of Western Front' (No. 20), 1 December 1943, BLEPK 0080.1.30, Appendix.
54. Boyd, 'Significance of MAGIC and the Japanese Ambassador to Berlin: (V)', p. 475.
55. Henry F. Graff, interviewed by Carl Boyd, 11 May 1988, quoted in ibid., p. 463.
56. Boyd, 'Significance of MAGIC and the Japanese Ambassador to Berlin: (V)', p. 464.
57. 'MI14 Report on the Visit of the Japanese Ambassador in Berlin to the German Defences in France', TNA WO208/4311, reproduced in full in Hinsley, *British Intelligence in the Second World War*, Vol. 3, Part II, Appendix 5.
58. Boyd, 'Significance of MAGIC and the Japanese Ambassador to Berlin: (V)', p. 474.
59. R. Doerries, *Hitler's Last Chief of Foreign Intelligence: Allied interrogations of Walter Schellenberg*, Routledge, 2004, p. 204.
60. Hinsley, *British Intelligence in the Second World War*, Vol. 3, Part II, p. 18.
61. Ibid., 18n.
62. Ibid., 46.
63. 'Record of Western Front' (No. 21), 18 December 1943, BLEPK 0080.1.31, p. 4, emphasis added.

5 INVASION PLANNING IN 1944

1. This quotation, along with most of the content of this section, is drawn from D. Michie, 'Codebreaking and Colossus', in Copeland, *Colossus*, pp. 223–48.
2. Bennett, *Ultra in the West*, p. 41.
3. TNA DEFE3/133 Message VL4792; see also Bennett, *Ultra in the West*, p. 41.
4. 'Theatre Intelligence Section Report (Martian)', No.77, 5 January 1944, TNA WO219/1938, p. 1.
5. 'Record of Western Front' (No. 23), 22 January 1944, BLEPK 0080.1.33, p. 5.
6. 'MI14 Weekly Intelligence Appreciation', 12 February 1944, TNA WO208/4312, p. 2.
7. 'Western Front Committee, Minutes of Meeting Held on 3rd March 1944', BLEPK 0080.1.36, p. 1.
8. 'The History of Hut Three', Vol. I, TNA HW3/119, p. 87.
9. Ibid., p. 106.
10. Ibid., p. 90.
11. 'Western Front Committee, Minutes of Meeting Held on 10th March 1944', BLEPK 0080.2.2, p. 1.
12. 'Record of Western Front' (No. 27), 10 March 1944, BLEPK 0080.2.2, p. 11.
13. Bletchley Park Roll of Honour; https://www.bletchleypark.org.uk/roll-of-honour/5904 (accessed 18 January 2018).
14. 'History of Hut 6', Vol. I, TNA HW43/70, p. 243.
15. 'Record of Western Front' (No. 28), 17 March 1944, BLEPK 0080.2.3, p. 6.
16. 'Record of Western Front' (No. 33), 21 April 1944, BLEPK 0080.2.7, pp. 2–3.
17. 'Record of Western Front', Nos 30 (BLEPK 0080.2.4), 31 (BLEPK 0080.2.5), 32 (BLEPK 0080.2.6) and 34 (BLEPK 0080.2.8).
18. 'Record of Western Front' (No. 27), 10 March 1944, BLEPK 0080.2.2, p. 6.
19. 'Record of Western Front' (No. 28), 17 March 1944, BLEPK 0080.2.3, p. 4.
20. 'Record of Western Front' (No. 34), 28 April 1944, BLEPK 0080.2.9, p. 4.
21. 'Record of Western Front' (No. 38), Supplement 4, 26 May 1944, BLEPK 0080.2.14.001.
22. 'History of Hut 6', Vol. II, TNA HW43/71, p. 150.
23. 'Record of Western Front' (No. 27), 10 March 1944, BLEPK 0080.2.2, p. 5.
24. http://www.axishistory.com/axis-nations/148-germany-heer/heer-armeen/2717-panzergruppe-west (accessed 19 July 2017).

25. 'Record of Western Front' (No. 28), 17 March 1944, BLEPK 0080.2.3, pp. 5–6.

26. https://en.wikipedia.org/wiki/2nd_Parachute_Corps_(Germany) (accessed 19 July 2017).

27. 'Record of Western Front' (No. 32), 14 April 1944, BLEPK 0080.2.7, p. 3.

28. 'Record of Western Front' (No. 36), 12 May 1944, BLEPK 0080.2.11, p. 3.

29. 'Record of Western Front' (No. 31), 7 April 1944, BLEPK 0080.2.6, p. 2.

30. Alexander, 'Cryptographic History', p. 87.

31. ULTRA Message KV 325, TNA DEFE3/35.

32. 'Record of Western Front' (No. 28), 17 March 1944, BLEPK 0080.2.3, p. 5, paragraph 7.

33. 'Record of Western Front' (No. 33), 22 April 1944, BLEPK 0080.2.8, p. 3, paragraph 8.

34. Message VL8188 of 11 March 1944, TNA DEFE3/146.

35. Hinsley, *British Intelligence in the Second World War,* Vol. 3, Part II, p. 66.

36. 'Record of Western Front' (No. 27), 10 March 1944, BLEPK 0080.2.2, p. 5, paragraph 7.

37. 'Record of Western Front' (No. 35), 5 May 1944, BLEPK 0080.2.10, p. 5, paragraph 1.

38. 'Record of Western Front' (No. 36), 12 May 1944, BLEPK 0080.2.11, p. 3, paragraph 3.

39. 'Record of Western Front' (No. 32), 14 April 1944, BLEPK 0080.2.7, p. 2, paragraph 1.

40. ULTRA Message KV2624, 2 May 1944, TNA DEFE3/45.

41. 'Record of Western Front' (No. 35), 5 May 1944, BLEPK 0080.2.10, p. 5, paragraph 1.

42. ULTRA Message KV3763, 14 May 1944, TNA DEFE3/155.

43. Hinsley, *British Intelligence in the Second World War,* Vol. 3, Part II, p. 799.

44. 'The History of Hut Three', Vol. I, TNA HW3/119, p. 113.

45. ULTRA Messages KV2002 and KV2234, 25 April 1944, TNA DEFE 3/43.

46. ULTRA Message KV2272, 28 April 1944, TNA DEFE 3/44.

47. ULTRA Message KV2295, 20 April 1944, TNA DEFE 3/44.

48. ULTRA Messages KV5097 and KV5129, 25 May 1944, TNA DEFE 3/160.

49. ULTRA Message KV7584, 11 June 1944, TNA DEFE 3/170.

50. ULTRA Message KV6705, 7 June 1944, TNA DEFE 3/166.

51. ULTRA Message KV7853, 13 June 1944, TNA DEFE 3/171.

52. Hinsley, *British Intelligence in the Second World War,* Vol. 3, Part II, p. 50.

53. BAY/KV 97, 103, 123, 8–13 May 1944, reproduced as Appendix 7 in Hinsley, *British Intelligence in the Second World War,* Vol. 3, Part II, pp. 768–92.

54. Naval Section ULTRA/ZIP/SJA/140, 5 May 1944, TNA HW1/2768, Para 6.

55. '3M Order of Battle', No. 10.

56. '3M Order of Battle', No. 12.

57. Bennett, *Ultra in the West*, p. 53.

58. Ibid., p. 55.

59. Hinsley, *British Intelligence in the Second World War,* Vol. 3, Part II, p. 69.

6 UNDERSTANDING GERMAN EXPECTATIONS

1. L. Ellis, *Victory in the West,* Vol. I: *The Battle of Normandy*, HMSO, 1962 (Naval and Military Press facsimile, 2004), p. 15.

2. Ibid., p. 16.

3. Ibid., p. 36.

4. Hinsley, *British Intelligence in the Second World War,* Vol. 3, Part II, p. 41.

5. A. Burne, *The Battlefields of England*, Methuen, 1950.

6. A. Conan Doyle, *The Sign of the Four*, 1890, Chapter 6.

7. R. Bennett, 'Fortitude, Ultra and the "Need to Know"', *Intelligence and National Security*, 4:3 (1989), p. 483.

8. M. Howard, *British Intelligence in the Second World War*, Vol. 5: *Strategic Deception*, HMSO, 1990, p. 104.

9. Hinsley, *British Intelligence in the Second World War,* Vol. 3, Part II, p. 45.

10. Ibid., p. 47.

11. Howard, *British Intelligence in the Second World War,* Vol. 5, p. 109.

12. J. Reymond, *D-Day Fortitude South: Kent's Wartime Deception*, Kent Arts and Libraries, 1994, pp. 37ff.
13. Hinsley, *British Intelligence in the Second World War*, Vol. 3, Part II, p. 43n.
14. Howard, *British Intelligence in the Second World War*, Vol. 5, p. 51.
15. Hinsley, *British Intelligence in the Second World War*, Vol. 3, Part II, p. 42.
16. D. Kahn, *Hitler's Spies: The extraordinary story of German military Intelligence*, Arrow, 1980 (first published 1978), p. 402.
17. Ibid., p. 405.
18. B. Macintyre, *Operation Mincemeat: The true spy story that changed the course of World War II*, Bloomsbury, 2010, p. 235.
19. Kahn, *Hitler's Spies*, p. 407.
20. For example, B. Macintyre, *Double Cross: The true story of the D-Day spies*, Broadway, 2012, p. 289.
21. Kahn, *Hitler's Spies*, p. 477.
22. Howard, *British Intelligence in the Second World War*, Vol. 5, p. 51.
23. M. Barbier, *D-Day Deception: Operation Fortitude and the Normandy Invasion*, Stackpole, 2009 (first published 2007), p. 158.
24. Howard, *British Intelligence in the Second World War*, Vol. 5, p. 46.
25. F. Hinsley and C. Simkins, *British Intelligence in the Second World War*, Vol. 4: *Security and Counter-Intelligence*, HMSO, 1990, p. 13.
26. Birch, 'A History of British Sigint 1914–1945', Vol. III, p. 843.
27. GCHQ, 'Key Personalities', p. 145.
28. P. Twinn, 'The Abwehr Enigma', in Hinsley and Stripp, *Codebreakers*, pp. 123–31.
29. Birch, 'A History of British Sigint 1914–1945', Vol. II, p. 518.
30. 'Use of ISOS by Section V During the War', typescript, 1946, TNA HW19/321, p. 10.
31. Ibid., p. 15.
32. Ibid., p. 19.
33. For example, Smith, *The Secrets of Station X*, pp. 255–6.
34. Bennett, 'Fortitude, Ultra, and the "Need to Know"', pp. 482–502, specifically 485, 492 and 494 n.4; Hinsley, *British Intelligence in the Second World War*, Vol. 3, Part II, p. 45; R. Hesketh, *Fortitude: The D-Day deception campaign*, Overlook Press, 2000.
35. 'Use of ISOS by Section V during the War', p. 20.
36. The author acknowledges the help of Michael Smith in bringing this material to his attention.
37. J. Masterman, *The Double Cross System in the War of 1939 to 1945*, printed privately 1946, p. ix.
38. Howard, *British Intelligence in the Second World War*, Vol. 5, p. 49.
39. Ibid., p. 50.
40. Masterman, *The Double Cross System*, p. xviii.
41. 'Record of Western Front' (No. 21), 18 December 1943, BLEPK 0080.1.031, p. 9.
42. Abwehr Message Milan–Lyons, quoted in 'Record of Western Front' (No. 23), 22 January 1944, BLEPK 0080.1.033, p. 2.
43. 'Record of Western Front' (No. 25), 19 February 1944, BLEPK 0080.1.035, p. 2.
44. 'Record of Western Front' (No. 24), 5 February 1944, BLEPK 0080.1.034, p. 2.
45. 'Record of Western Front' (No. 29), 26 March 1944, BLEPK 0080.2.4, p. 2.
46. 'Record of Western Front' (No. 30), 1 April 1944, BLEPK 0080.2.5, p. 2.
47. 'Record of Western Front' (No. 28), 19 March 1944, BLEPK 0080.2.3, p. 2.
48. 'Record of Western Front' (No. 34), 30 April 1944, BLEPK 0080.2.9, p. 3.
49. Hinsley and Simkins, *British Intelligence in the Second World War*, Vol. 4, p. 302.
50. Masterman, *The Double Cross System*, p. xxi.
51. Message CX/MSS/T50/43, quoted in Hinsley, *British Intelligence in the Second World War*, Vol. 3, Part II, p. 46.
52. Ibid., p. 47.

53. C-in-C West Appreciation, 21 March 1944, Intercept CX/MSS T146/19, KV 353, TNA HW5/463.
54. Message KV733, decrypted 12 April, quoted in Bennett, *Ultra in the West*, p. 50.
55. Message from C-in-C Navy to all ranks, 17 April 1944, ZTPG/232340, TNA DEFE 3/408.
56. Hinsley, *British Intelligence in the Second World War*, Vol. 3, Part II, p. 56.
57. C-in-C West Appreciation, 8 May 1944, KV3763, 14 May 1944, TNA DEFE 3/155.
58. Message from Luftflotte Three, 9 May 1944, KV3243, TNA DEFE3/147.
59. C-in-C West Appreciation, 8 May 1944, KV3763, 14 May 1944, TNA DEFE 3/155.
60. Message VL 4834, 26 January 1944, TNA DEFE3/133.
61. Message VL 9732, 29 March 1944, TNA DEFE3/157.
62. Message KV 773, 20 March 1944, TNA DEFE3/38.
63. BAY/KV 179, 30 May 1944, quoted in Boyd, 'Significance of MAGIC and the Japanese Ambassador to Berlin: (V)', p. 477.
64. CAB 121/394 JIC (44) 232(0), 3 June 1944, quoted in Hinsley, *British Intelligence in the Second World War*, Vol. 3, Part II, p. 63.
65. Howard, *British Intelligence in the Second World War*, Vol. 5, pp. 115–18.
66. OKM Message VL 9126, 8 March 1944, decrypted 22 March 1944, TNA DEFE3/157.
67. Howard, *British Intelligence in the Second World War*, Vol. 5, pp. 115–18.
68. Ibid., p. 129.
69. Ibid., p. 122.
70. Ibid., p. 122.
71. 'Record of Western Front' (No. 34), 30 April 1944, BLEPK 0080.2.9, p. 3.
72. R. Bennett, *Behind the Battle: Intelligence in the war with Germany 1939–45*, Sinclair-Stevenson, 1994, pp. 251–52.
73. F. Ruge, 'Naval Operations: Special report', unpublished typescript, 21 May 1946; https://www.history.navy.mil/research/library/online-reading-room/title-list-alphabetically/r/rommel-atlantic-wall.html (accessed 25 May 2018).
74. Hinsley, *British Intelligence in the Second World War*, Vol. 3, Part II, p. 67.
75. Ibid., p. 65.
76. Telegram from Japanese Military Attaché, Vichy, 17 February 1944, TNA HW1/2686.
77. 'Record of Western Front', No. 28, 17 March 1944, BLEPK 0080.2.3, p. 6.
78. Enigma messages VL8188, 11 March 1944, TNA DEFE3/146; VL8758, 8846, 18 and 19 March 1944, TNA DEFE3/149; and VL9037, 21 March 1944, TNA DEFE3/150, quoted in Hinsley, *British Intelligence in the Second World War*, Vol. 3, Part II, p. 66.
79. Message from Naval Attaché Berlin, 4 May 1944, ULTRA/ZIP/SJA/139, TNA HW1/2768.
80. Ruge, 'Naval Operations: Special report'.
81. Hinsley, *British Intelligence in the Second World War*, Vol. 3, Part II, p. 66.

7 GETTING ASHORE

1. M. Arthur, *Lost Voices of the Royal Navy*, Hodder & Stoughton, 2005, p. 490.
2. German *Torpedoboote* were larger than their British equivalents and were classified by the Allies as equivalent to small destroyers.
3. http://forum.axishistory.com/viewtopic.php?t=186069 (accessed 18 July 2016).
4. Two of these guns, one from HMS *Ramillies* and the other from HMS *Roberts* are preserved outside the Imperial War Museum in Lambeth.
5. R. Kershaw, *D-Day: Piercing the Atlantic Wall*, Ian Allan, 2008 (first published 1993), pp. 178–80.
6. Message ZIP/ZTPG/248717, 6 June 1944, in 'ZTPG 24800-248999, 3/6/44–6/6/44', TNA DEFE 3/424, p. 761.
7. Message listed in Hinsley, *British Intelligence in the Second World War*, Vol. 3, Part II, p. 836.
8. Message ZIP/ZTPG/248767, 6 June 1944, in 'ZTPG 24800-248999, 3/6/44–6/6/44', TNA DEFE 3/424, p. 813.

9. Hinsley, *British Intelligence in the Second World War*, Vol. 3, Part II, p. 91.
10. Ibid., p. 93.
11. Beesly, *Very Special Intelligence*, p. 231.
12. Ibid., p. 238.
13. Hinsley, *British Intelligence in the Second World War*, Vol. 3, Part II, p. 97.
14. Ibid., p. 159.
15. Ibid., p. 162.
16. Ibid., p. 163.
17. S. Zaloga, *The Atlantic Wall (1): France*, Osprey, 2007, p. 5.
18. Ibid., pp. 24–5.
19. M. Zambra, 'A History of British SIGINT, 1914–1945', Vol. III, Appendices, p. 816. (Monica Zambra completed the work after the death of Frank Birch.)
20. GCHQ, 'Key Personalities', p. 50.
21. Fortunately for historians, a good deal of the paperwork associated with this project has been preserved in the National Archives, and so it is possible to tell the story of Dugmore's interception project in a fair amount of detail. 'Y' Unit in Hut 18 at Bletchley Park. Lt Dugmore's organisation of a wireless interception station at Bletchley Park to provide an immediate service of German naval messages for Hut 8 (ENIGMA machine processing) during the early days of OVERLORD (the invasion of Europe June 1944). TNA HW8/86.
22. E. Dugmore, 'Report on Proposal to Employ Receivers on Intercept Work at B.P. During Emergency Period', 4 April 1944, TNA HW8/86.
23. Memorandum from F.H. Hinsley to D.H.N.S. (E. Jackson), 7 May 1944, TNA HW8/86.
24. Notes on a meeting held on 28 May 1944 between NS II, Hut 8 and NS V respecting coverage programme of NS V, TNA HW8/86.
25. Message copies contained in TNA ADM223/195.
26. Message ZIP/ZTPG/248611, 5 June 1944, in 'ZTPG 24800-248999, 3/6/44–6/6/44', TNA DEFE 3/424, p. 648.
27. J. Mallmann Showell, *Hitler's Navy: A reference guide to the Kriegsmarine 1935–1945*, Seaforth, 2009, p. 99.
28. These further messages are preserved in 'ZTPG 24800-248999, 3/6/44-6/6/44', TNA DEFE 3/424.
29. http://www.uss-corry-dd463.com/d-day_u-boat_photos/marcouf_rpts_translated.htm (accessed 4 June 2018).
30. Hinsley, *British Intelligence in the Second World War*, Vol. 3, Part II, p. 126.
31. '3M Order of Battle', No. 10.
32. Messages KV5081 and KV5158, 24 May 1944, TNA DEFE3/160, and KV5416, 27 May 1944, TNA DEFE3/161.
33. 'Record of Western Front' (No. 38), 26 May 1944, BLEPK 0080.2.13, p. 6.
34. Ford and Zaloga, *Overlord*, p. 120.
35. Ibid., p. 128.
36. Unit locations from http://www.6juin1944.com/assaut/allemagne/en_index.php?id=716 (accessed 29 May 2018).
37. Bennett, *Ultra in the West*, p. 55.
38. '3M Order of Battle', No. 10.
39. '3M Order of Battle', No. 12.
40. Ford and Zaloga, *Overlord*, p. 60.
41. M. Hastings, *Overlord: D-Day and the Battle for Normandy 1944*, Pan, 1999 (first published 1993), p. 115.
42. Ford and Zaloga, *Overlord*, p. 61.
43. Hastings, *Overlord*, p. 115.
44. Ford and Zaloga, *Overlord*, p. 62.
45. Unit locations from http://www.6juin1944.com/assaut/allemagne/en_index.php?id=352 (accessed 29 May 2018).

46. Ford and Zaloga, *Overlord*, p. 62.
47. Ibid., p. 45.
48. '3M Order of Battle', No. 10.
49. '3M Order of Battle', No.12.
50. 'Record of Western Front' (No. 34), 30 April 1944, BLEPK 0080.2.9, p. 6.
51. 'Record of Western Front' (No. 38), 25 May 1944, BLEPK 0080.2.13, p. 8.
52. 21 AG Assessment, 14 May 1944, WO205/532, quoted in Hinsley, *British Intelligence in the Second World War*, Vol. 3, Part II, p. 842.
53. Ibid.
54. Harrison, *US Army in World War II*, p. 319n.
55. Ford and Zaloga, *Overlord*, pp. 47–48.
56. Kershaw, *D-Day*, p. 117.
57. 'Record of Western Front' (No. 32), 22 April 1944, BLEPK 0080.2.7, p. 4.
58. ULTRA Message KV2624, 2 May 1944, TNA DEFE3/45.
59. 'Record of Western Front' (No. 37), 20 May 1944, BLEPK 0080.2.12, p. 7.
60. Hinsley, *British Intelligence in the Second World War*, Vol. 3, Part II, p. 840.
61. H. von Luck, *Panzer Commander*, Cassell, 2002 (first published 1989), p. 173.
62. Unit locations from http://www.6juin1944.com/assaut/allemagne/en_index.php?id=352 (accessed 29 May 2018).
63. Hinsley, *British Intelligence in the Second World War*, Vol. 3, Part II, p. 137.
64. J. Ferris, 'Intelligence before Overlord: Knowledge and assumption in allied planning for the invasion of Normandy, June 1943–June 1944', 2013; http://www.nids.mod.go.jp/publication/senshi/pdf/201403/10.pdf (accessed 25 September 2018), p. 148.
65. Ibid., p. 156.

8 STAYING ASHORE

1. This section is based on Wilf Neal's own testimony, recorded in Pidgeon, *Secret Wireless War*, pp. 203–9.
2. Hinsley, *British Intelligence in the Second World War*, Vol. 3, Part II, p. 131.
3. R. Neillands, *The Battle of Normandy 1944*, Cassell, 2002, p. 40.
4. Hinsley has already provided an admirable account of this. See Hinsley, *British Intelligence in the Second World War*, Vol. 3, Part II, Chapters 46, 47 and 48.
5. 'History of Hut 6', Vol. I TNA HW43/70, p. 238.
6. Ibid., p. 236.
7. Hinsley, *British Intelligence in the Second World War*, Vol. 3, Part II, p. 846.
8. 'History of Hut 6', Vol. I. TNA HW43/70, p. 245.
9. 'History of the Fish Subsection'.
10. 'The History of Hut Three', Vol. II, TNA HW3/120, p. 328, emphasis added.
11. H. Skillen, *Spies of the Airwaves: A history of Y sections during the Second World War*, Hugh Skillen, 1989, p. 395.
12. J. Gilbert and J. Finnegan (eds), *US Army Signals intelligence in World War II: A documentary history*, Center of Military History, 1993, p. 196.
13. Skillen, *Spies of the Airwaves*, p. 398.
14. Williams, 'The Use of ULTRA by the army', p. 8.
15. Ibid., p. 2.
16. Ibid.
17. Ibid.
18. COS minute to Prime Minister, 23 May 1944, TNA CAB121/394, reproduced in Hinsley, *British Intelligence in the Second World War*, Vol. 3, Part II, Appendix 10.
19. Hinsley, *British Intelligence in the Second World War*, Vol. 3, Part II, p. 67.
20. Ibid., p. 128.
21. Skillen, *Spies of the Airwaves*, p. 399.

22. Hinsley, *British Intelligence in the Second World War*, Vol. 3, Part II, p. 146.
23. ULTRA message KV6893, 07.50hrs, 8 June 1944, TNA DEFE3/167.
24. ULTRA message KV6705, 7 June 1944, TNA DEFE 3/166.
25. ULTRA message KV7035, 02.30hrs, 9 June 1944, TNA DEFE3/168.
26. ULTRA message KV7225, 04.39hrs, 10 June 1944, TNA DEFE3/168.
27. ULTRA message KV7681, 14.33hrs, 12 June 1944, TNA DEFE3/170.
28. T. Copp, *Fields of Fire: The Canadians in Normandy*, University of Toronto Press, 2004, p. 84.
29. ULTRA message KV7450, 10.40hrs, 11 June 1944, TNA DEFE3/169.
30. Bennett, *Ultra in the West*, p. 75.
31. ULTRA message KV6958, 15.44hrs, 8 June 1944, TNA DEFE3/167.
32. ULTRA message KV7002, 21.27hrs, 8 June 1944, TNA DEFE3/168.
33. ULTRA message KV7311, 16.02hrs, 10 June 1944, TNA DEFE3/169.
34. ULTRA message KV7591, 00.08hrs, 12 June 1944, TNA DEFE3/170.
35. ULTRA message KV7662, 11.01hrs, 12 June 1944, TNA DEFE3/170.
36. ULTRA message KV7671, 13.16hrs, 12 June 1944, TNA DEFE3/170.
37. ULTRA message KV7693, 15.04hrs, 12 June 1944, TNA DEFE3/170.
38. ULTRA message KV7738, 21.59hrs, 12 June 1944, TNA DEFE3/170.
39. Harrison, *US Army in World War II*, pp. 364–5.
40. Hinsley, *British Intelligence in the Second World War*, Vol. 3, Part II, p. 184.
41. Ellis, *Victory in the West*, Vol. I, p. 237.
42. ULTRA message KV6933, 13.13hrs, 8 June 1944, TNA DEFE3/167.
43. Hinsley, *British Intelligence in the Second World War*, Vol. 3, Part II, pp. 178–80.
44. Ibid., p. 182.
45. Ellis, *Victory in the West*, Vol. I, p. 260.
46. ULTRA message KV7415, 05.12hrs, 11 June 1944, TNA DEFE3/169.
47. ULTRA message KV7638, 06.51hrs, 12 June 1944, TNA DEFE3/170.
48. ULTRA message KV7645, 07.14hrs, 12 June 1944, TNA DEFE3/169.
49. http://www.oradour.info/ (accessed 15 June 2018).
50. ULTRA message KV7798, 05.47hrs, 13 June 1944, TNA DEFE3/171.
51. ULTRA message KV7978, 04.18hrs, 14 June 1944, TNA DEFE3/171.
52. ULTRA message KV8707, 21.57hrs, 18 June 1944, TNA DEFE3/171.
53. ULTRA message KV9009, 08.24hrs, 21 June 1944, TNA DEFE3/176.
54. P. O'Brien, *How the War Was Won: Air-sea power and allied victory in World War II*, Cambridge University Press, 2015, p. 371.
55. ULTRA message KV6635, 18.50hrs, 6 June 1944, TNA DEFE3/166.
56. ULTRA message KV7305, 15.34hrs, 10 June 1944, TNA DEFE3/169.
57. Hinsley, *British Intelligence in the Second World War*, Vol. 3, Part II, p. 182.
58. ULTRA message KV7986, 05.24hrs, 14 June 1944, TNA DEFE3/171.
59. Hesketh, *Fortitude*, p. 210.
60. Ibid.
61. Hastings, *Overlord*, p. 203.
62. R. Lewin, *Ultra Goes to War: The secret story*, Hutchinson, 1978, p. 32.
63. Calvocoressi, *Top Secret Ultra*, p. 118.
64. TNA HW19/178 and HW19/179.
65. Masterman, *The Double Cross System*, p. 78.
66. Hinsley, *British Intelligence in the Second World War*, Vol. 3, Part II, p. 178n.
67. Ibid., p. 176.
68. ULTRA message KV6088, 22.21hrs, 14 June 1944, TNA DEFE3/172.
69. Hinsley, *British Intelligence in the Second World War*, Vol. 3, Part II, p. 175.
70. ULTRA message KV8251, 02.09hrs, 16 June 1944, TNA DEFE3/173.
71. C-in-C West Appreciation, 26 June 1944, CX/MSS/T232/41, 7 July 1941, TNA HW5/518.
72. Hinsley, *British Intelligence in the Second World War*, Vol. 3, Part II, p. 177.

73. ULTRA message KV8484, 12.01hrs, 17 June 1944, TNA DEFE3/173.
74. ULTRA message KV8881, 05.17hrs, 20 June 1944, TNA DEFE3/175.
75. Hinsley, *British Intelligence in the Second World War*, Vol. 3, Part II, p. 216.
76. ULTRA message KV9364, 06.05hrs, 24 June 1944, TNA DEFE3/177.
77. Ellis, *Victory in the West*, Vol. I, p. 253.
78. Neillands, *The Battle of Normandy 1944*, p. 191.
79. Bennett, *Ultra in the West*, p. 100.
80. ULTRA message XL1649, 18.49hrs, 11 July 1944, TNA DEFE3/54.
81. ULTRA message XL792, 03.10hrs, 13 July 1944, TNA DEFE3/177.
82. Hinsley, *British Intelligence in the Second World War*, Vol. 3, Part II, p. 200.
83. ULTRA message XL1589, 10.30hrs, 11 July 1944, TNA DEFE3/54.
84. Ellis, *Victory in the West*, Vol. I, p. 294.
85. Hinsley, *British Intelligence in the Second World War*, Vol. 3, Part II, p. 236.
86. Neillands, *The Battle of Normandy 1944*, p. 336.
87. Hinsley, *British Intelligence in the Second World War*, Vol. 3, Part II, p. 238.
88. ULTRA messages XL4682, 15.36hrs, and XL4685, 16.17hrs, 4 August 1944, TNA DEFE3/112.
89. ULTRA message XL4744, 00.22hrs, 5 August 1944, TNA DEFE3/112.
90. ULTRA message XL4997, 19.48hrs, 6 August 1944, TNA DEFE3/113.
91. ULTRA message XL4999, 20.01hrs, 6 August 1944, TNA DEFE3/113.
92. Neillands, *The Battle of Normandy 1944*, pp. 338–42.
93. ULTRA message XL5125, 19.18hrs, 7 August 1944, TNA DEFE3/114.
94. Bennett, *Ultra in the West*, p. 116.
95. ULTRA message XL5461, 03.49hrs, 10 August 1944, TNA DEFE3/115.
96. Hinsley, *British Intelligence in the Second World War*, Vol. 3, Part II, p. 254.
97. Bennett, *Ultra in the West*, p. 120.
98. Ibid., p. 122.

9 THE IMPORTANCE OF BLETCHLEY PARK TO OVERLORD

1. Birch, 'A History of British Sigint 1914–1945', Vol. III, p. 809.
2. Williams, 'The Use of ULTRA by the army', p. 10.
3. http://www.ticomarchive.com/home (accessed 9 July 2018).
4. Rifleman J.S. 'Les' Wagar, C Coy, Queen's Own Rifles of Canada (Juno Beach), quoted in R. Neillands and R. De Normann, *D-Day 1944: Voices from Normandy*, Cassell, 2001 (first published 1993).
5. 'Use of ULTRA by M.I.14', unpublished typescript, 21 December 1945, TNA HW3/173, Para 6.
6. Ibid., Para. 11.
7. 'The History of Hut Three', Vol. I, TNA HW3/119, p. 46.
8. Eisenhower's statement in event that the D-Day landings failed, 5 June 1944. Dwight D. Eisenhower Library, National Archives Identifier 186470, quoted in S. Tucker, *D-Day: The essential reference guide*, ABC-CLIO, 2017, p. 229.
9. F.H. Hinsley, 'The Counterfactual History of No Ultra', *Cryptologia*, 20:4 (1996), pp. 308–24.
10. Winterbotham, *The Ultra Secret*, p. 191.
11. Williams, 'The use of ULTRA by the army'.

A NOTE ON SOURCES AND FURTHER READING

1. Obituary: Ralph Bennett, *Daily Telegraph*, 23 August 2002: http://www.telegraph.co.uk/news/obituaries/1405119/Ralph-Bennett.html (accessed 21 January 2019).
2. GCHQ, 'Key Personalities', p. 13.
3. Bennett, *Ultra in the West*, p. 13.
4. Ibid., p. 15.

5. 'History of Hut 6', Vol. II, TNA HW43/71, pp. 28ff.
6. Bennett, *Ultra in the West*, p. 49.
7. Gannon, *Colossus*, pp. 516ff.
8. Ibid., p. 517.
9. Obituary: Professor Harry Hinsley, *Independent*, 19 February 1998: http://www.independent.co.uk/news/obituaries/obituary-professor-sir-harry-hinsley-1145675.html (accessed 21 January 2019).
10. GCHQ, 'Key Personalities', p. 76.
11. Hinsley, *British Intelligence in the Second World War*, Vol. 1, p. vii.
12. Ibid., p. viii.
13. Ibid., p. ix.
14. Ibid., p. x
15. Now in TNA Series HW14.

ACKNOWLEDGEMENTS

The wartime site of the Government Code and Cipher School at Bletchley Park holds a significant place in the history of the Second World War. Fortunately, having narrowly survived demolition in the early 1990s, the site is now preserved and is open to the public as a historic visitor attraction. This book came about as a result of the decision to create a new exhibition in the recently restored Teleprinter Building at Bletchley Park, telling the story of the impact of signals intelligence (SIGINT) on the Normandy invasion of 1944. Much of the story told for visitors to Bletchley Park in existing exhibitions has concentrated on the internal processes of the site and the remarkable achievements of the codebreakers who inhabited it. However, little has been made of why this mattered – what effect it had on the outcome of the Second World War. The D-Day exhibition is an attempt to redress this balance by examining directly the battlefield effects on that particular campaign of intelligence created at Bletchley Park.

As the research historian at Bletchley Park it was my privilege (and indeed my day job) to carry out the necessary research to support the new exhibition. It rapidly became apparent that not only had this particular story not been told in print for over thirty years, but that the declassification of previously secret wartime documents allowed for a new interpretation of the story, strikingly different in some respects from that which had previously been described. It was therefore a relatively obvious decision to turn the exhibition research into a full-length book on the subject.

I was fortunate that when I first proposed the idea of a book to the management and trustees of Bletchley Park, they were immediately supportive, granting me the time and facilities to produce this account. This has been aided by access not only to the archives of GC&CS held by the National Archives in London, but also to the collection of materials held here at Bletchley Park by the Bletchley Park Trust, and I am grateful for the support of the archivists at both institutions. A full list of the sources consulted is included in chapter notes.

I would also like to acknowledge the generous help and support received from the historian and curator of the museum at GCHQ in Cheltenham. Numerous other friends and colleagues either read portions of the manuscript or provided comment and support in other ways, and to them I am also grateful.

Particular thanks go to my colleagues at Bletchley Park for their practical and moral support on this project; to Iain Standen and Rebecca Foy for allowing me the time out to write within my working day; to Peronel Craddock, for protecting my peace and quiet in what is otherwise a very busy department; and to the rest of the Collections and Exhibitions team for alternately observing and then ignoring the signs on my office door saying I was busy!

Finally, I would like to thank my wife, Elizabeth, who as an historian working on her own book at the same time, provided an atmosphere of healthy competition throughout the writing of this one.

INDEX

INDEX OF MILITARY UNITS

GENERAL INDEX